HORSESTORY

VOLUME III:
MORE THAN A MACHINE

by

Vicki Watson

Riding a horse is not a gentle hobby, to be picked up and
laid down like a game of solitaire. It is a grand passion. It
seizes a person whole and once it has done so, he/she will
have to accept that his life will be radically changed.
                                        —Ralph Waldo Emerson

Table of Contents

Introduction

In the past, a horse was viewed as a piece of equipment needed to get a job done. Beginning in the early 1900s, machinery took over much of the work that had been performed by equines. A machine could do the work cheaper and faster. Although "progress" was perhaps inevitable, we lost something valuable when we replaced living beings with inanimate, unfeeling objects. A horse is more than a machine.

Horses can perform duties a machine cannot, while at the same time, maintaining a warm relationship with their owner or handler. Few horses demonstrate that better than Reckless, a mare who served faithfully with a Marine unit in the Korean War.

> *Reckless was a very special horse and undoubtedly bonded through a spiritual connection of love with her Marines. The noise and waves of concussion can't be described, but she endured it all. I believe an angel had to be riding Reckless, since she was alone and without a Marine to lead her. I have always cherished my horses. But after watching and learning more about that little mare of the Reckless Rifles, mine are even more special because I know they have the same Creator.*

> *—Sgt. Harold E. Wadley, USMC*

In 2023, there were an estimated 6.65 million horses in the United States, owned by 1.5 million people[1]. Although some of those animals still serve in old-time roles such as farming, the more common use of horses today is for recreation and entertainment.

This final volume of the Horsestory series highlights the roles horses continue to play in modern times. When available, the stories of specific animals are recounted. A book could be written about each of these chapters—and many have. If you're intrigued by these topics, dig in, and research more about them.

> *I call my horses "divine mirrors"—they reflect back the emotions you put in. If you put in love and respect and kindness and curiosity, the horse will return that.*

> *—Allan Hamilton*

Vicki Watson

---

[1] *horsecouncil.org/economic-impact-study*

1

Equine Bookmobiles

Over the years, horses have delivered a variety of things. A surprising one is books. The first mobile library, called a "perambulating library" began in 1857. It circulated between eight villages in northwest England. In that case, a man walked the route, pushing a wheelbarrow-like cart filled with a modest selection of books.

That concept was improved upon with a horse-drawn book wagon which could carry more books. The first horse-drawn bookmobile in the United States was the idea of Maryland librarian Mary L. Titcomb. In 1905, she managed the delivery of books from Washington County's public library to Maryland's rural areas by horse-drawn cart.

The horses, Dandy and Black Beauty, driven by the library janitor, Joshua Thomas, pulled Titcomb's wagon, which contained 200 books. Mrs. Titcomb instructed Thomas that there should be "no hurrying from house to house, but each family must be allowed ample time for selections."

During its first six months, the book horses covered their route thirty-one times, averaging thirty miles each trip. Joshua Thomas, Dandy, and Black Beauty served their patrons for over five years. However, in August 1910, the book deliveries came to an abrupt end when a freight train collided with the wagon at a crossing. Thomas and the horses survived, but the book wagon was destroyed. In 1912, the service resumed, using an International Harvester truck rather than the horses and wagon.

Other parts of the country also used horse-drawn book wagons, particularly during the Depression, due to gas rationing and travel limitations. In the early 1900s, Berea College started taking books to Kentucky's isolated mountain communities by wagon. Horses from the Berea College farm pulled wagons packed with hundreds of books. Berea's bookmobile service continued until 1943.

Horses weren't the only equines to bring books to people. Another early mobile library was a mule-drawn wagon carrying wooden boxes full of books. Created in 1904, the mules served rural Chester County, South Carolina.

In 1943, librarians in Nutley, New Jersey, remodeled a former milk wagon to carry 300 books. The librarians hired a driver for $5 per trip. A boy rang a bell ahead of the wagon to alert people that Teddy the Library Horse was approaching.

With the end of World War II and the country's economic recovery, motorized vehicles replaced the horse-drawn bookmobiles.

2

Gypsy Queen

The poet Ralph Waldo Emerson said, "Dare to live the life you have dreamed for yourself. Go forward and make your dreams come true."

Sergeant Frank Melvin Heath's dream was to ride a single horse across the country—"to hit some part of every state in the United States and return to Washington, riding the same horse, the horse traveling all the way upon his own feet."

In order to make that dream come true, Frank had to find a horse who could stand up to such a grueling journey.

> *A racehorse was not what I wanted. He is too fiery for one thing, and he has not the "bread basket" to carry feed to do him for long distances.*[1]

Heath contacted the Morgan Horse Farm in Vermont, but found their horses too expensive. A lengthy search led him to a horse he thought might work. Lacking other options, Frank purchased the black, six-year-old mare for $100. Two men approached him as he rode the horse home. His eyes were drawn to a fiery, bay mare one of the men rode. "There's my horse!" Heath immediately traded the black mare and an additional ten dollars for the bay.

> *My new mount was coming ten that spring (February 1925). She stood so proud and queenly that, on a sudden impulse, I renamed her Gypsy Queen.*[2]

Gypsy Queen nearly ended Frank's journey before it began. On their way home, they encountered a steam shovel. As they started to pass it, the machine let out a sudden, loud bang. Queen grabbed the bit in her teeth and took off at a dead run on the slick pavement.

© Frank M. Heath - Cissel Saxon Post No. 41 American Legion - Silver Spring, Md.

---

[1] *Forty Million Hoofbeats, Frank M. Heath, 17*
[2] *Heath, 19*

Frank pulled hard on the left rein, hoping to stop her by throwing her off balance. Queen nearly fell, but managed to regain her footing and remain upright. Frank turned the frightened horse to face the steam monster. Once convinced it was harmless, the mare continued at a calm walk.

She had received her ABCs in learning that when I patted her on the neck, assuring her that something was "all right," she could depend on it.[1]

Heath and the mare began their two-year journey on March 31, 1925, riding ten miles from Silver Spring, Maryland to Washington, D.C. Frank was fifty-six years old; Gypsy Queen, ten.

Although unregistered, Queen was reportedly a Kentucky Morgan. The mare performed a variety of gaits, including a smooth foxtrot, a jog, and a faster trot. She did not like to canter, preferring a gallop instead. Of course, galloping was not suited to a journey of thousands of miles. Most of the time, the pair simply walked.

She had two distinct walks—a quick, snappy one, which she assumed "in society," being very proud, and a long, strong stride she took automatically on the open road.[2]

Frank was an expert horseman, having served as a cavalryman during the First World War. On their journey, he regularly exchanged his expertise for food and shelter for himself and Gypsy Queen. "If you happen to have a lame horse and nobody seems to understand what's wrong with him—if there's anything I could suggest to help the horse, I'll be pleased to do so."

One example was a horse in Michigan who had been lame in his right front leg for eight months. The horse's condition had "baffled all examiners." It's unclear what Heath did for the animal, but he "put the horse back on his axis," and it walked off at once, much improved.

The long journey caused significant wear and tear on Queen's hooves and legs. At the start, Frank fitted the mare with rubber pads, covering the soles of her front hooves. Throughout the trip, one of

<hr>

[1] *Heath, 20*
[2] *Heath, 19*

his greatest challenges was keeping her sound by adjusting the pads and trying various shoes and shoeing techniques.

In larger cities, cars outnumbered horses. Finding a stable and food for Queen was often challenging. Frank relied on those who helped him to recommend suitable lodging for their next stop.

To the proud automobile drivers who mocked him for traveling the old-fashioned way, Frank's response was, "I never have tire trouble, or run out of gas and oil. I'll travel just as far on one horsepower as they will on many—and get a lot more satisfaction out of the trip."[1]

Not fully trusting Frank, Queen continued to fear traffic. To avoid the vehicles, she sometimes jumped over the stone wall separating a homeowner's property from the road.

I knew this would not do. For one thing, the opposite side of the stone wall was not always a safe place to light. … As it once happened, she landed right in the middle of a flower garden. The lady, who was working there with a rake, was not expecting us. We did not seem to be altogether welcome. We jumped back.[2]

To ensure their safety, Frank decided he had to train Queen to obey him. He resorted to using the end of the reins to swat her on the left side of her head when she appeared ready to make a leap.

In August 1925, in Oklahoma, Frank exhibited Queen at a carnival. He advertised her as "Gypsy Queen, Toughest Horse in the World. $1,000 to Prove that She is Not. See her Alive Today." Apparently, no one earned the $1,000, and the Queen had a well-deserved rest.

For some time, Frank had searched for a horse to use as a pack animal to ease the burden on Queen. In June 1926, in Montana, he purchased Cheyenne Belle, a seven-year-old, brown mare considered an "Indian bronco." Frank was a little worried about the look of her eyes and her facial expression.

At times (in fact, generally) the expression is kind—and generally she is gentle. But on occasion there comes an expression, not of fire, like in Queen's eyes, but of dumbness, like an alligator half asleep.[3]

Frank's concerns were well-founded. A month later, on July 29, they arrived in Yellowstone Park. In the midst of the summer heat, a swarm of flies tormented both horses. When Frank attempted to kill a horsefly on Belle, the frantic mare kicked him on his knee. He hobbled around and mounted Queen by moving the horse into a ditch.

X-rays taken two days later at the Helena Veteran's Hospital showed Frank's kneecap was broken.

---

[1] Heath, 99
[2] Heath, 49
[3] Heath, 230

Although the hospital stay put him behind schedule, Frank was determined to continue his journey as soon as he was released. He worried that Queen, pastured during his hospitalization, would become soft.

Frank realized Belle wasn't suitable for the trip, and he sold her. He left the hospital on October 9, picked up Queen, and resumed traveling on the twelfth. It would be just Frank and Queen for the rest of the journey. Frank's goal had been to complete their trip in July 1927. But, his two-month hospital stay, along with other delays, including floods, inspections, and quarantines, resulted in the pair reaching Washington, D.C. in November.

Gypsy Queen weighed 950 pounds at the start of their journey and 1,025 pounds on their return—a tribute to the mare's strong constitution and Frank's excellent care. During their journey of two years, seven months, and four days, Frank and Queen had grown inseparable. The pair covered 11,356 miles, both arriving home in excellent health. Their adventure together only strengthened Frank's high opinion of horses.

I love a horse because, next to man—or to what man is capable of being—he is God's most noble creature. It is foolish to presume that a horse is a creature of the past. His days of drudgery are about over, thank Heaven. Man, tardily, has harnessed steam and electricity to do the heavy work and gasoline for the speed fiend. But he has not made and cannot make a car that sees, hears and thinks. Do you believe I could make a chum, a buddy, of steel?[1]

Despite all the wonderful places he'd visited, Frank decided there was no place he'd rather call home than his small farm in Silver Spring, Maryland. "Gypsy Queen is going to have an easy time the rest of her life."

At fourteen, Gypsy Queen had a filly, sired by Kinster, a Standardbred. Gypsy Princess proved to be as strong and capable as her dam.

Queen enjoyed her retirement for nine years. In 1936, at twenty-one, her health failed, and Frank made the difficult decision to have his faithful companion put down.

Her skeleton was donated to the College of Agriculture at the University of Maryland, and the rest of her remains buried at the Rosa Bonheur Memorial Park pet cemetery in Elkridge, Maryland. A bronze plaque in Gypsy Queen's memory describes her as "A Faithful and Loyal Companion."

Frank Heath kept a journal of his trip, published in 1941 as the book *Forty Million Hoofbeats*. He died in 1945 and was buried near his family in Spokane, Washington.

---

[1] *Heath, 135*

3

Frontier Nursing

A son was born to Mary Breckinridge's mother when they lived in Russia; Mary was fourteen at the time. Although doctors were present, a Russian midwife was Mrs. Breckinridge's main caregiver. Mary never forgot that first encounter with a midwife.

How did a Tennessee girl, born in 1881, find herself in Russia? Mary was from a prominent Southern family. Her grandfather, John C. Breckinridge, served as vice president under James Buchanan. Her father was a congressman and the U.S. Minister to Russia. Mary lived in several countries as she grew up.

Although the male Breckinridges served important roles in the United States, Mary was never encouraged to pursue higher education. At twenty-three, she married Henry Ruffner Morrison. When her husband passed away less than a year later, Mary entered the three-year program at St. Luke's Hospital of Nursing in New York. In 1910, she graduated as a registered nurse.

She married her second husband, Richard Ryan Thompson, in 1912. The couple had a son, Clifton, called "Breckie," in 1914 and a daughter, Polly, in 1916. Their daughter, born prematurely, lived only six hours. In her grief, Mary poured herself into raising Breckie. But her son passed away shortly after his fourth birthday.

After the loss of their children, Richard and Mary divorced. Those tragic experiences spurred Mary to find a way to improve healthcare for children and mothers. During the summer of 1923, she rode horseback over 650 miles to study the state of healthcare in rural Kentucky.

That summer I rode thirteen different horses and three mules. Among them was every variety of sore, ringbone, kidney disorder, and other equine complaint. Only two were even fairly good saddlers. The bridles were often pieced with rope and the girths tied on with wire or string. The blanket was often a meal sack.[1]

---

[1] *Wide Neighborhoods: A Story of the Frontier Nursing Service, Mary Breckinridge, 116*

Later that year, Mary completed midwifery school in England, becoming a certified midwife. In 1925, she created the Frontier Nursing Service to aid the people in the eastern Kentucky mountains. The inaccessibility of the area was a factor in Mary's choice.

> *I felt that if the work I had in mind could be done there, it could be duplicated anywhere else in the United States with less effort.*[1]

Breckinridge had to recruit her nurses from England, since there were no schools for midwives in the U.S. One of the biggest challenges for the FNS was transportation in an area where there were virtually no roads or bridges.

> *There wasn't a motor road within sixty miles when our work began, so that horses and mule teams provided all the transport we had.*[2]

To reach their patients in Appalachia, the midwives rode horses, earning the nickname "Angels on Horseback." Their uniforms consisted of blue-gray coats, breeches, white shirts, ties, caps, and knee-high boots. It was difficult to find safe, gentle horses who could handle the rough terrain. Mary was happy when she located one for herself.

> *My chief woe during the summer was the lack of a decent horse. With the help of my cousin William Preston, I had bought a magnificent horse, Teddy Bear, who was to become one of my closest friends in the years ahead.*[3]

Teddy Bear injured his leg on a protruding nail in a barn before he even made it to Mary's home. She rode an old mule until Teddy recovered.

> *It was good to have my own horse at last and I needed him because I lived in the saddle in those days.*[4]

During their first year of operation, Mary purchased seven saddles, seven bridles, four halters, three curry combs, four brushes, and eight blankets for a total cost of $123.66. She found a local man who made saddlebags by hand from high-quality leather for $13 a pair. Each nurse rode with two saddlebags—one for midwifery supplies and the second for general medical equipment. Since the nurses never went anywhere without the bags, mountain children were sometimes told the young women brought their mothers' babies in the saddlebags.

---

[1] *Breckinridge, 158*
[2] *Breckinridge, 167*
[3] *Breckinridge, 164*
[4] *Breckinridge, 177*

In 1925, construction began on a log cabin, Wendover, known as "The Big House." This served as Mary's home as well as the FNS headquarters. From 1925 to 1931, the Frontier Nursing Service built six clinics, and in 1928, the Hyden Hospital. Two midwives lived at each clinic with their horses and a milk cow. The goal was for a nurse to be able to reach any patient in her five-mile region within an hour by horseback.

The midwives claimed, "If he can get to me, I will get to her." Meaning if a husband could reach the midwife's clinic (there were no telephones in the area at the time), she would somehow make it to their cabin on horseback.

Mary, a great communicator, was quite successful at getting cash contributions and other donations. Local cows were often too lean to produce much milk. When people heard of the need, a Holstein, October, was donated. October produced six gallons of milk each day for the infants at Hyden Hospital. Later, a second Holstein, November, was added.

In addition to assisting with home births, the FNS provided general medical care. Martha Lewis, Mary's first patient, suffered a severed artery in her hand. Martha and her husband rode their mule to Wendover to seek her help. In addition to the typical childhood illnesses, the FNS nurses saw a lot of burn victims. The long skirts of young girls sometimes caught fire from the open fireplaces used to heat the cabins.

The FNS accepted volunteer couriers; single women over eighteen, serving six to eight weeks. Many were privileged young women with riding skills who craved a bit of adventure. They groomed, saddled, and bridled horses; ran errands for supplies, mail, and medicine; and accompanied nurses on their rounds. By the early 1930s, there was a long waiting list for the courier positions.

During the Prohibition years, the production and sale of alcohol was illegal. Moonshiners and bootleggers[2] operated in the mountains to avoid detection. One bootlegger stole an FNS mare, Diana, and used the horse to pack liquor from his stills to a truck on the highway. When he no longer had a need for her, the man abandoned Diana. Someone found the horse and returned her to the FNS, but she was never quite the same after that hard work and the neglectful care of her kidnappers.

Having completed her rounds on Teddy Bear one day, Mary turned the horse loose in his pasture. While frolicking about, the horse fell over the edge of a ravine. Though Mary hoped for a recovery, Teddy's injuries proved fatal.

I could not help but grieve. Teddy Bear had been my sole companion over thousands of miles of lonely trails. I remembered the time when my girth broke on the edge of a precipice, my saddle turned and I fell under him, and how he stopped stock still to look down at me until I picked myself and the saddle up. ... Recollections of all his endearing ways came back to me, like his

---

[1] *Breckinridge, 176*
[2] *Moonshiners made the illegal alcohol and bootleggers smuggled it out for sale.*

nuzzling at my uniform pockets for apples. Several horses have I loved in my lifetime but none had ever come so close to me as Teddy Bear and none, I knew, ever would again.[1]

Losing Teddy Bear was not only sad, it proved to be nearly fatal for Mary. In Teddy's place, she rode a horse they had received on trial—Traveller.

He was so nervous an animal, with such a tender mouth, that I used a light bit on him. Everything in the mountains appalled him. He had a way of springing and starting into a run at the sight of a pig wallowing, at the sound of dried cucumber tree leaves rustling. He forded the rivers in a series of bounds.[2]

On a drizzly day in November 1931, Mary rode Traveller on a steep mountain trail, accompanied by two other women. Part of the nurses' attire for inclement weather was a billowy cape that served as a raincoat. When a gust of wind puffed the cape out, Traveller must have believed the terrifying thing might eat him. The horse bolted. Mary stuck to the saddle, but after several miles, she realized she couldn't hold on much longer.

I had plenty of time in which to decide how to take the fall. I had no intention of being thrown over his head, and I didn't want to go off to the left and roll down the precipice. When I lost all sensation in my knees, I threw myself forward on Traveller's neck, dropped the reins, cleared the stirrups, and rolled over to the right. We were going at such terrific speed that I hit the rocky ground with force.[3]

Mary's friends rushed her to the hospital where X-rays revealed she had broken her back. After a seventeen-month recovery, she resumed her rounds, riding a calm, gentle mare, Carminettie. Patient training convinced Traveller that the rain capes were not out to get him, and experienced riders were able to ride him on their rounds.

From 1925 until post-WWII, when Jeeps took over, horses were the FNS's

means of transporting nurses to Kentucky families. At its peak, the Frontier Nursing Service owned over sixty horses. Without those reliable, sure-footed equines, the FNS could not have functioned.

Although we have photos, and even some video of the animals, most of their names, breeds, and personalities have been lost to time. A few mentioned in Breckinridge's autobiography include Babbette, Dixie, Lady Ellen, Lassie, Nellie Gray, Puck, Rick, Remus, and Tramp.

Mary Breckinridge served as the director of the FNS until her death on May 16, 1965. By that time, FNS had treated nearly 60,000 patients and delivered over 14,000 babies. The Frontier Nursing University in Versailles, Kentucky was founded in 1939 as the Frontier Graduate School of Midwifery and is still in operation today.

---

[1] *Breckinridge, 266*

[2] *Breckinridge, 283*

[3] *Breckinridge, 284*

4

Tschiffely's Ride

Many considered the idea ridiculous and impossible, but thirty-year-old Aimé Félix Tschiffely, A.F., was determined to ride horseback 9,600 miles from Buenos Aires, Argentina, to Washington D.C. Undeterred by the naysayers, he planned to start as soon as he found the right equine partners.

Tschiffely located two Criollo horses—Mancha (The Spotted One) and Gato (The Cat) to join him on his adventure. The Criollos, known for their intelligence and endurance, are descendants of Arabian and Barb horses brought to Argentina by the conquistadors in the 1500s. Tschiffely was not a native Argentinian. He was born in Switzerland and had moved to Buenos Aires to teach school. One goal of his ride was to show the world that Criollos were one of the hardiest horse breeds.

Until recently, the two horses had lived in the wilds of the Argentine pampas.[1] Tschiffely described the pair as "the wildest of the wild." Mancha, a red and white pinto, was eighteen when their journey began. Never entirely tamed, he often kicked at people who came near him. Once

---
[1] *South American low grasslands*

during his training, he sent Tschiffely sailing over a fence. Eventually, Tschiffely gained a level of control over the animal.

Gato, a sixteen-year-old buckskin, was less temperamental and tamed down more quickly than Mancha. These ages seem unusual for horses setting out on such an arduous journey, but Criollo horses are known for their longevity and are considered at their peak between the ages of ten and twenty.

Neither horse had excellent conformation, a point even Tschiffely admitted.

> *Their sturdy legs, short thick necks and Roman noses are as far removed from the points of a first-class English hunter as the North Pole from the South. Handsome is as handsome does, however, and I am willing to state my opinion boldly that no other breed in the world has the capacity of the Criollo for continuous hard work.[1]*

Having spent their lives in the wild, nearly everything in the civilized world frightened the horses—streets, houses, stables, and especially cars. But after a period of acclimatization, the trio left Buenos Aires on April 23, 1925. A Belgian police dog started out with them, but after being kicked by Mancha on the first day, the dog was sent back.

Tschiffely traded off riding one horse while the other carried a pack. Initially, a lead rope was attached to the pack horse, but soon, the horses stuck together, and no rope was necessary. The horses became so bonded to Tschiffely that he rarely had to tie them. He turned the pair loose at night and always found them waiting for him the next morning.

The journey was fraught with danger on many fronts. They encountered treacherous mountain passes, sweltering deserts, sandstorms, hail, mosquitoes, malaria, vampire bats that bit the horses' backs, crocodiles, and poisonous snakes.

Tschiffely described crossing a four-foot-wide, 450-foot-long, wobbly, swinging bridge, suspended high above a raging river. Mancha walked ahead of him, led by an Indian guide.

> *As we approached the deep sag in the middle, the bridge began to sway horribly, and for a moment I was afraid the horse would try to turn back, which would have been the end of him; but no, he had merely stopped to wait until the*

---

[1] *Tschiffely's Ride, Aimé Tschiffely, xviii*

12

Tschiffely's route led them across the Panama Canal, through Central America, into Mexico, then across Texas, Oklahoma, the Ozarks, Missouri, Mississippi, Indiana, Ohio, and across the Blue Ridge Mountains. While riding through the Blue Ridge, Tschiffely's journey almost came to a tragic end. Pedestrians are supposed to walk on the left side, facing oncoming traffic. However, since Mancha shied when he saw vehicles speeding toward him, Tschiffely preferred to ride on the right with traffic coming behind him. One day, a man intentionally swerved his car to the right, striking Mancha.

Before I could do anything the car hit my horse violently, knocking him down, and opening a gash in his flank and left hind leg. The driver did not stop, and before he disappeared around the curve he honked the horn and waved his hand at me. ...

After the first shock Mancha rose, and although he bled profusely, I found that no bones were broken. I washed him down at a stream, and at a farm house I obtained iodine, with which I disinfected the wounds.[2]

Although Tschiffely reported the incident to the police, they never caught the man.

---

[1] *Tschiffely, 139*
[2] *Tschiffely, 431*

In September 1928, Tschiffely reached Washington, D.C. where President Calvin Coolidge invited him to the White House. Tschiffely shipped the horses on to New York, where he received the New York City medal. The three then returned home to Argentina by ship.

Tschiffely wrote two books about his journey. The first, *Tschiffely's Ride*, describes the ride in great detail. In the second, *The Tale of Two Horses*, Mancha and Gato narrate the story for young readers.

After their journey, Tschiffely left Mancha and Gato to enjoy retirement on a friend's El Cardal Ranch in Argentina. By then, the two horses were inseparable. Gato died in 1944 at thirty-five. Mancha followed in 1947, dying on Christmas Day, at forty. Mancha and Gato are buried side by side at the ranch.

Shortly before Christmas 1953, Aimé Tschiffely checked into a hospital in London for a minor operation. He died unexpectedly on January 5, due to complications from the surgery. His ashes were spread near the memorial for his horses on the El Cardal Ranch.[1]

---

[1] *Tschiffely had earlier stated younger ages for the two horses, but later corrected them in the 1952 edition of his book, Tschiffely's Ride.*

5

Mustang Defenders

Phillip Chappel amassed a fortune by capturing Mustangs and selling them as war horses. Britain purchased more than 100,000 from him during the First World War. When the war ended and motorized vehicles became increasingly popular, the demand for horses dried up. With his lucrative income gone, Chappel needed another way to make money.

He launched Ken-L-Ration in 1923, the first company to sell canned dog food made from horse meat. Those same Mustang herds that had provided a supply of war horses became the source of meat for his pet food. By 1925, Chappel's Rockford, Illinois plant processed 200 horses daily.

To ensure a steady supply of Mustangs for the plant, he owned and leased 1.6 million acres in Montana, Wyoming and the Dakotas. Draft horse stallions were introduced into the herds to increase the Mustang's size, resulting in more meat from each horse.

Ken-L-Ration's advertisements focused on their premise that horses were the optimal meat source for dogs. They used a cartoon strip featuring two dogs, Angus and Buddy, who learned about the supposed evolution of the horse and the equine's destiny as canine food. Chappel Brothers also highlighted the fact that they raised horses specifically for slaughter.

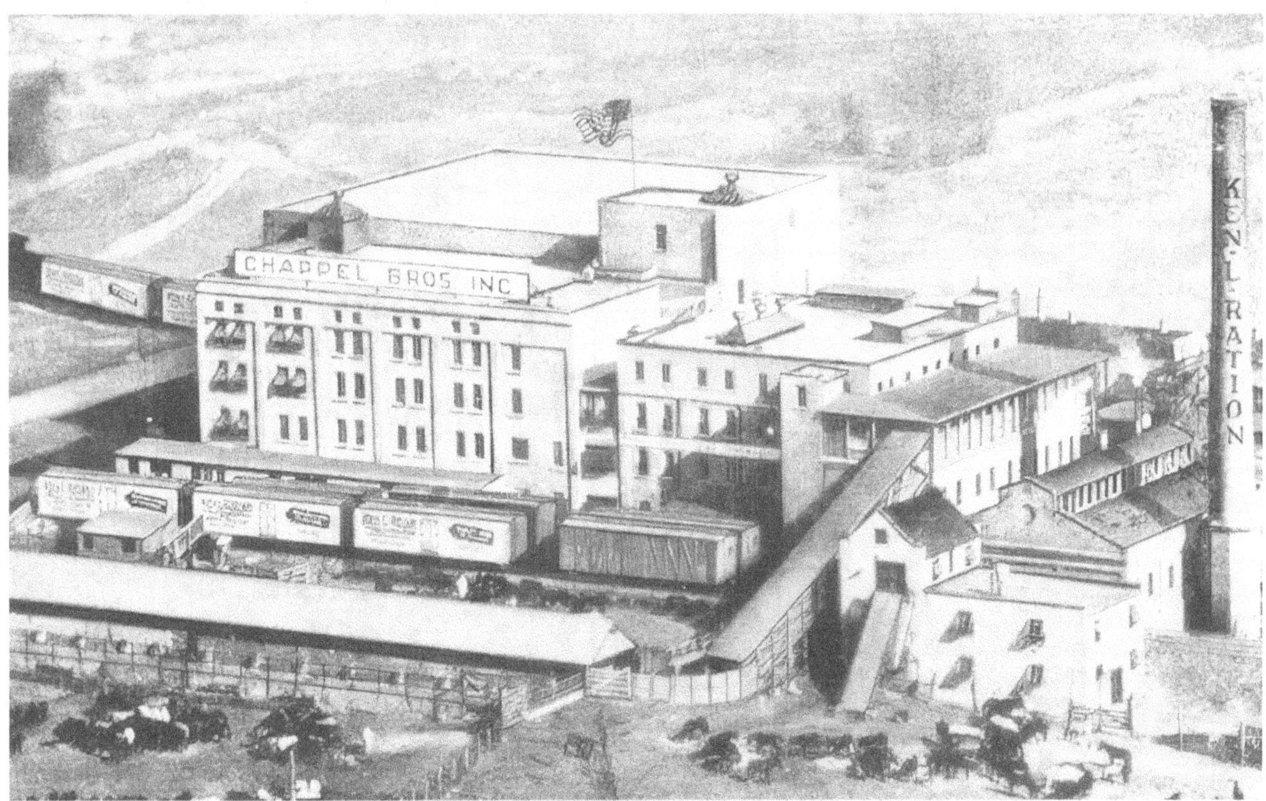

Out in the Western Range States where the dawn horse roamed 55,000,000 years ago, Chappel Bros. Inc. have brought together the descendants of the two bands of horses that separated in Siberia almost a million years ago.

Out there on the vast Chappel ranches, *meat horses* are raised for Ken-L-Ration by breeding imported Belgian, Shire and Percheron stallions to the Western range mares.

These Chappel horses are the healthiest meat animals in the world. For fifty million years the meat of the horse has been the *natural* and *best* food for dogs and today science has proved positively that—

> "In canine nutrition, the meat of the horse has a higher nutritive (biological) value than the best quality meat generally used."
> Mariner & Hoskins, Inc.

Mariner & Hoskins Biologic Laboratory, one of the oldest and most reliable research institutions in the world, made the statement quoted above after eighteen months of research and actual feeding experiments.

Your quality dealer sells Ken-L-Ration because he knows that it is better to make a smaller profit on a product that brings you back, than to make a larger profit on the single sale of a cheap, unsatisfactory product, with price as the only thing to recommend it.

Give Your Dog a Ken-L-Locket

Change of address can be made easily on the handy blank securely enclosed in the Ken-L-Locket. This special offer for a limited time only. Send 1 Ken-L-Ration label and 5 cents NOW

CHAPPEL BROS. INC.
161 Peoples Avenue, Rockford, Ill.
I am enclosing one Ken-L-Ration label and 5 cents—in stamps or coin. Please send one Ken-L-Locket to

Name ___________________________
Street and number ___________________________
City ___________________ State ___________

My dealer's name is ___________________________

Chappel Bros. maintain the world's largest herd of meat horses to provide the best meat for Ken-L-Ration. … 1,600,000 acres of America's richest range country—as large as the state of Delaware - make up this mighty kingdom.

In October 1925, a small fire occurred at the Rockford plant. When three more fires broke out in the following weeks, Chappel knew they could not be accidental. He had a ten-foot fence built around the four-story building and hired armed guards to patrol the perimeter.

In December, the guards surprised a man lurking about in the dark. When the intruder ran, the guards fired at him. Upon investigating the area where they'd seen the stranger, the guards discovered a suitcase filled with 150 sticks of dynamite.

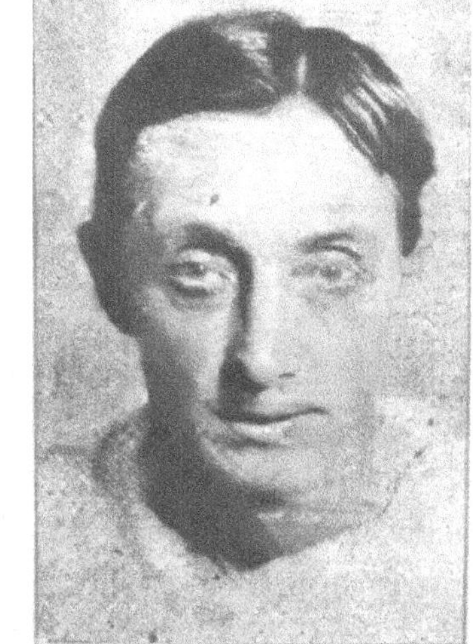
Frank Litts

The following day, they found the intruder, Francis Litts, lying in a field. He had been shot in the back but was still alive. Litts could only whisper, "I did it for the horses."

Litts, forty-one, had grown up in Montana and Idaho and loved horses. When he learned Mustangs were being rounded up and sold to Chappel's plant, he resolved to put a stop to it.

Litts hoped his trial would be publicized so others would learn what was happening to the Mustangs. However, that kind of publicity was the last thing Chappel wanted. Whether Chappel had some influence over the court is unclear, but the judge ruled Litts was insane, thereby avoiding a public trial.

In 1926, Litts was sent to an asylum. He escaped from the facility after seven days. A year and a half later, Frank Litts was back in Rockford with another supply of dynamite, determined to finish his mission—destroying Chappel's plant. Unfortunately for Litts, a woman spotted him in a hotel lobby. She had worked at the jail where Litts had been held during his first arrest. The woman notified the police. Frank was arrested and returned to prison where he died at fifty.

Through most of the 1920s, the Rockford plant made half a million dollars a year. The Ken-L-Ration brand expanded to produce cat and other pet foods. Quaker Oats purchased the company in 1942. Quaker continued the slaughter of the Mustangs until the end of World War II.

In 1946, the Bureau of Land Management (BLM) was created. The BLM initially sided with the ranchers and worked to remove wild horses from the grazing lands or at least ignored the ranchers' efforts to eliminate them. By the 1950s, the Mustang population had dropped to approximately 25,000 due to cruel techniques such as plane roundups and poisoning the horses' watering holes.

Few are aware of Frank Litts' effort to save the Mustangs. More know about the work of Velma Bronn Johnston, better known by her nickname, "Wild Horse Annie." Mrs. Johnston was as passionate about protecting the Mustangs as Litts; however, she chose to fight for them by legal means.

Velma Bronn was born on March 5, 1912, in Nevada. At eleven, she came down with a fever, then aches in her joints and muscles. The mysterious illness progressed until she could not walk. Her parents took her to Children's Hospital in San Francisco, which accepted children from poor families who couldn't otherwise afford treatment.

Velma had polio. Doctors put her in a body cast from her head to below her hips to prevent the disease from twisting her back. Her parents returned home while Velma remained in the hospital for six months. When the cast was removed, Velma's body was disfigured anyway. Her left eye drooped, her teeth no longer aligned, one shoulder was higher than the other, and her back bulged. But unlike other polio victims, she could walk.

Although Velma had missed much of her sixth-grade year, She passed a test that allowed her to advance to the next grade with her class. She had been shy before, but became even more so after her hospitalization, when her classmates teased her about her appearance. Perhaps those difficult school years gave Velma a heart for the Mustangs.

After high school, she became a secretary in Reno, Nevada, where she met her future husband. After Charlie and Velma's wedding, they purchased sixteen acres, which they named the Double Lazy Heart Ranch. While driving to work one day, Velma saw blood dripping from a stock trailer ahead of her. She followed it, thinking one of the cows in the trailer was injured. When the truck pulled into a stockyard, Velma was horrified to discover the trailer wasn't hauling cattle; it was packed with captured Mustangs.

That moment changed the course of Velma's life. Although she didn't act immediately, she couldn't erase the picture of those suffering Mustangs from her mind. She decided to talk to someone at the Bureau of Land Management (BLM), naively thinking they would be concerned about the welfare of the horses. The man assumed she was a rancher's wife who had come to complain about the Mustangs grazing on their property. The agent assured her the BLM was doing all it could to get rid of the horses. Velma was awakened to the fact that the BLM was not on the side of the Mustangs.

Velma and Charlie began working behind the scenes to sabotage Mustang roundups, releasing horses they found penned in unattended corrals. At meetings, they spoke out against the cruel roundup techniques. Velma worked with Nevada State Senator James Slattery to propose a state ban on mechanized horse roundups.

Her actions made Velma unpopular with ranchers in the area. When she received threatening phone calls, she began carrying a gun. The BLM director intended to insult her by calling her Wild Horse Annie, but Velma proudly adopted the name.

The Nevada state bill passed in 1955, but the BLM had inserted a clause specifying that the law only applied to horses on private land. Because most Nevada horses grazed on public lands, the new law had little impact.

In 1959, with the help of U.S. Congressman Walter Baring, HR2725 passed, banning aerial roundups on public land. This became known as the Wild Horse Annie Act. The BLM did very little to enforce the act, so the roundups continued.

In April 1971, Velma traveled to Washington, D.C. to testify before the House Committee on Public Lands. As a result, the Wild and Free-Roaming Horses and Burros Act passed in December of that year and was signed by President Nixon. The law made it a crime to hunt the horses by aircraft or motorized vehicles. Polluting watering holes for the purpose of trapping or killing animals was also banned. The BLM was required to implement management programs to maintain a sustainable number of horses on federal land.

In 1976, an amendment to the Wild and Free-Roaming Horses Act allowed the departments of the Interior and Agriculture to again use helicopters and motorized vehicles to round up the horses. This reversal removed much of the power of the 1971 act. But there was no longer anyone to fight for the horses. Velma Johnston had cancer and would die the following year.

6

BLM Mustangs

A s of 2013, the BLM had 179 herd management areas (HMAs). These are areas of federal land where feral horses are protected and permitted to live, currently covering 31.6 million acres. Over half of the Mustangs today are in Nevada. Others are found in Montana, Idaho, Wyoming, Utah, Oregon, California, Arizona, North Dakota, and New Mexico. Freeze brands on the left side of a Mustang's neck show its year of birth and registration number.

The BLM created an adoption program to help maintain the number of horses in the wild. However, most people don't have facilities suitable for keeping a wild horse safely, let alone the experience to train one.

The first nation-wide Mustang adoptions occurred in 1976. Ironically, horses were rounded up by helicopters for these sales. Most horses are adopted for a fee of $125. Kiger Mustangs, from the south-

eastern part of Oregon, are only rounded up once every three or four years. They have the purest Spanish bloodlines and usually sell for higher prices at the adoptions, sometimes as high as $7,000 or more.

The BLM protects adopted Mustangs for a year. After that time, the adopter receives title to the horse. This was done to prevent kill-buyers from purchasing horses for slaughter. However, it isn't completely effective, as the horses may be sold to anyone after the one-year period ends. No horse slaughter plants operate in the United States—the last closed in 2007[1]. Now, horses destined for slaughter are shipped to Canada or Mexico.

Although the adoption program has seen some success, there are nowhere near enough adoptions to regulate the population of the herds. Of the 10,000 foals born in 2017, only 2,500 were adopted. Horses that are captured but not adopted are kept in long-term holding pens at a cost to taxpayers of $50,000 per horse over the horse's lifetime. A cheaper alternative is ranches used as eco-sanctuaries, where the government pays the rancher to allow Mustangs to graze on their pastures.

One attempt to create interest in Mustang ownership is an event called the Extreme Mustang Makeover. One hundred trainers are given a hundred days to gentle and train a Mustang. The horses and trainers then compete for cash prizes at a multi-day show. At the end of the event, the trained Mustangs are sold at auction.

---

[1] *Although half a dozen states ban equine slaughter, there is no federal law which prohibits it. The SAFE Act (Save America's Forgotten Equines) is currently in committee pending further action by the House and Senate.*

Mustangs are versatile horses and are used in a variety of disciplines. Years ago, they were ridden extensively in the more challenging parts of the Pony Express route. A name that often comes up is a famous pinto Mustang, Hidalgo, owned by Frank Hopkins.

Hopkins, half-Lakota, claimed to have won 400 endurance races across the U.S. as well as the 3,000-mile Ocean of Fire race in Arabia in 1891. He was supposed to have worked with Buffalo Bill Cody in his Wild West Show. Disney produced the movie Hidalgo about the horse and rider's adventures. However, no one has ever found evidence to support Hopkins' claims. In fact, most of the races he said he won, including the one in Arabia, probably never existed.

Another idea is the use of prison inmates to train Mustangs. One example is a program at the Northern Nevada Correctional Center. Inmates apply to be part of the Mustang program. Although most of the inmates have little to no previous experience with horses, they learn to train a wild horse for riding or as a pack animal. Mustangs trained through this program have been used by Nevada Fish and Game Wardens, the Forestry Service, and the Sheriff's Department. A few of these Mustangs have even found their way to the New York Police Department. The program has been life-changing for the inmates and the horses.

Andrew "Andy" was born in the Winnemucca area of Nevada. The tall, black colt was part of a BLM helicopter roundup in 1985. After being separated from his mother, he spent a winter at the National Wild Horse and Burro Center at Palomino Valley. That spring, he was considered too young to train, so he was sent to Muleshoe, Texas, to a BLM holding facility. In 1987, the colt was 16 hands tall and towered over the other two-year-olds.

Andy was shipped to the Wild
Horse Inmate Program at the Colorado
State Prison for training. From there,
Ginger Scott, a part-Cherokee horse-
woman, adopted him. Andy grew
another three inches, topping out at
16.3 hands. Andy wasn't a typical
Mustang suited for western-style
riding. His talents leaned toward a
discipline that was unfamiliar to
Ginger—dressage.

A young rider at the stable, Kelly
O'Leary, began working with Andy on
preliminary dressage exercises. The
Mustang enjoyed the work and made
steady progress. Soon, he was ready for entry-level shows. Ginger felt a dressage horse needed a
fancier name, so she called him JB Andrew. The "JB" stood for "jailbird," reflecting his time at the
prison where he was trained.

In addition to learning dressage, JB Andrew learned to love people. He'd always been obedient
and respectful, but as a young horse, he was distant and aloof. As the years passed, he bonded with
Ginger and Kelly.

Kelly and JB Andrew showed together until 2001, rising to progressively higher levels in the
dressage world. When his joints began to bother him, Andy was retired. He had reached the highest
dressage level of any Mustang. Breyer made a model of JB Andrew in 1996.

7

Woman Bronc Rider

Barrel racing has long been an all-female rodeo event. But in rodeo's early years, some brave women competed alongside men in events like bronc riding. A devastating accident suffered by one of those cowgirls, Bonnie McCarroll, resulted in limiting women's rodeo participation.

Bonnie was born Mary Ellen Treadwell, on a cattle ranch in Idaho in 1897. She rode her first horse at ten. At fourteen, she rode her first bronc. Bonnie described the experience.

I mounted, the boys let go, and the broncho began to behave like a wild cat. I held for about five seconds and then all at once I seemed to grow wings. Up I soared, and turned a sumersault, and the earth seemed about ten miles below. Then I went to sleep and woke in bed.

It's unclear why such an experience would cause anyone to want to continue riding broncs, but Bonnie did. However, not everyone approved of women competing in such events as evidenced by this quote from the New York Times.

Any woman who thirsts to wear trousers and ride broncos is victim of a curious mental disorder.[1]

At a Boise rodeo in 1913, Bonnie met cowboy Frank McCarroll, an accomplished bulldogger, roper, and bronc rider. The two married in 1915 and traveled the rodeo circuit together for the next fourteen years.

Bonnie was a crowd favorite. In 1922, she won the bronc riding championship at Madison Square Garden and Cheyenne Frontier Days in the same year. She also performed as a trick rider in Wild West shows, sometimes jumping her horse over a car.

A photo from the 1915 Pendleton Round-Up caught Bonnie falling upside down from the bronc "Silver." The widely published image brought the cowgirl nationwide attention.

In that same Pendleton arena, on September 19, 1929, thirty-four-year-old Bonnie rode her last bronc. She and Frank planned to retire after the Round-Up. She'd drawn the horse Black Cat.

---

[1] *New York Times, May 27, 1876*

That year, cowgirls were required to ride hobbled. That meant a rope connected the stirrups together under the horse's abdomen, reducing their movement.

Black Cat was more agitated than usual that day. After exploding from the chute, the horse flipped over backward. Bonnie was hopelessly connected to the bronc. The hobble kept the stirrups from moving freely, making it difficult for Bonnie to kick her feet out of them. Black Cat somersaulted forward, then rose and continued bucking across the arena. A rodeo pickup rider tried to free her, but it wasn't until Bonnie's boot came loose, that she fell from the horse. Frank raced to her side. She was rushed to the hospital, but Bonnie died ten days later.

Her tragic accident meant the end of women's bronc riding. Officials banned females from rough stock events, considering them too dangerous. The Cowboy Turtles Association (CTA), formed in 1936, cited McCarroll's death as the rationale for excluding women's events. In 1948, female competitors formed their own group, the Girls' Rodeo Association (GRA) which later became the Women's Professional Rodeo Association (WPRA).

The era of tough cowgirls like Fannie Sperry Steele, Tad Lucas, Mabel Strickland, Lorena Trickey, and Vera McGinnis came to an end. Those women were all inducted into both the Cowgirl Hall of Fame and the National Rodeo Hall of Fame.

8

Elmer Gantry

Eleanor Getzendaner first saw the bay Thoroughbred in 1924 on a Nebraska ranch. She wanted to buy the yearling colt, but his price exceeded her pocketbook. Two years later, she came across the horse again; however, this time, he was emaciated after a winter on sparse pasture. His poor condition resulted in a significant price drop. Getzendaner purchased the bay for $150. She named him Elmer Gantry, after a hypocritical evangelist in a Sinclair Lewis novel.

Next, she began training Gantry. Getzendaner was no stranger to horses. Born on an 1,800-acre ranch near Champion, Nebraska, at four, she rode her Shetland pony unaccompanied. Later, Eleanor and a sister, Lois, started their own training business. They worked with some rough stock and earned every bit of their fee—five dollars per horse.

In 1927, twenty-year-old Eleanor's main equine project was Aviator, a bay Mustang. He had demonstrated his superior jumping skills by clearing the farm's pasture fences. Eleanor had never entered a horse show, but she believed Aviator would do well in an upcoming Chicago jumper event. The only obstacle was getting the horse there from her Nebraska farm. Finding no other option, Eleanor and Lois hitched an open trailer to their Ford touring car and hauled Aviator there themselves.

A month before the show was to open, they began the journey, taking turns at the wheel, and feeding Aviator cane stalks through the rear window. While one drove, the other seized a nap in the back seat. They started on a Thursday morning and reached Chicago at noon the following Sunday. On the 950-mile trip, they had stopped for only one night's sleep. They reached Chicago in a daze and got lost six

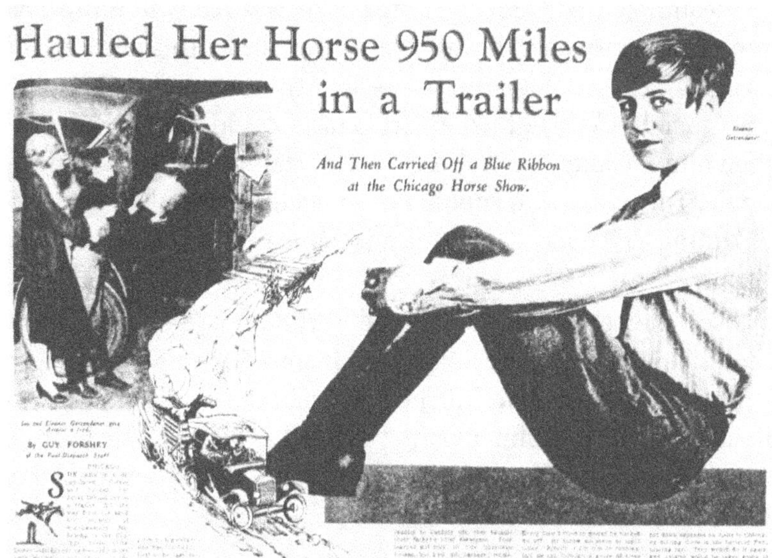

times between the city limits and Parkview Riding Academy, where they found quarters for Aviator and put him to bed in fresh straw.[1]

---

[1] *St. Louis Post-Dispatch, Missouri, Dec. 25, 1927*

The sisters found short-term jobs to earn money while they waited for the show's opening day. Aviator performed as well as Eleanor had believed he would.

> *Inspired—or maybe he was scared—by the blazing lights, the gaudy bunting and the cheering crowds, Aviator aviated as he had never done before. He soared and made nonstop flights all over the place. Although he was just a green hick from the short grass who had never seen a tanbark arena, who had never laid eyes on a brush fence or a stone wall barrier, and who had never performed under any lights save the Nebraska sun and moon, he jumped everything but the stockyards arch and at the proper time he trotted out with a blue ribbon.[1]*

Though Aviator was a success at that show, Elmer Gantry was the one who was destined for nationwide fame. Under Eleanor's training, the intelligent and athletic Gantry became a jumper, show horse, cow pony, and generally amazing all-around equine. For several years, the two performed at a variety of shows and exhibitions.

At eleven, Gantry experienced a bout of periodic ophthalmia (equine recurrent uveitis or moon blindness). The attacks recurred, and by 1935, cataracts covered both of Elmer's eyes. The horse would never see again.

Getzendaner retired him to pasture, but each time the other horses left him, Gantry panicked. Some advised Eleanor to put him down. Her bond with Gantry was so strong, she refused. Eleanor couldn't stand to see her once-great horse spending his days alone and depressed. To better understand what he was experiencing, she blindfolded herself and attempted to walk around.

Determined to retrain him, she began working with Gantry on a fairly level stretch of ground. They started at a slow walk as she taught him to respond to voice commands. When they approached a change in the ground level, she told him, "Careful up," and "Careful down." She used her voice or the clapping of her hands to direct Gantry to come to her. When he gained confidence with these exercises at a walk, she increased the speed to a trot. Eventually, she could ride him at a canter and even a gallop.

Eleanor sensed Gantry telling her he was ready to jump again. At first, she walked him up to a jump until he touched it with a leg or his chest. This allowed the horse to judge its height. Gantry learned a new set of commands—"Ready," "Gather," and "Up high" or "Up low," depending on the jump's height. As a sighted horse, Gantry could clear five-foot jumps. He never regained that level when blind. Gantry's retraining took a year and a half. What the pair accomplished together amazed people. The horse who couldn't even see the jumps was able to jump three feet eight inches. According to Eleanor, "It is not miserable to be blind; it is miserable not to be able to endure blindness."

Word spread about the incredible blind horse—all the way to Hollywood. During the Great Depression, people were hungry for inspiration and encouragement. Elmer Gantry's life made the perfect feel-good movie. The horse signed the contract himself with an inked hoof mark. And, best of all, fifteen-year-old Elmer Gantry starred as himself. Eleanor insisted his contract provide an unlimited supply of carrots to reward him after he performed each jump, and he was to be applauded after every stunt.

The original title *Gantry the Great* was later changed to *Pride of the Bluegrass*. The storyline strayed from the facts of Gantry's life. The movie Gantry goes blind during the Kentucky Derby. After he was retrained, he competed in the Grand National Steeplechase at Aintree, England. There was no

---

[1] *St. Louis Post-Dispatch, Missouri, Dec. 25, 1927*

need to depart so wildly from the truth of Gantry's story. His real accomplishments were amazing enough.

During filming, a veterinarian, who was an eye specialist, examined Gantry to see whether his sight might be restored. When the vet reported the bleak chances of an operation's success, Getzendaner decided not to risk surgery.

Warner Brothers released *Pride of the Bluegrass* on October 7, 1939. The movie's trailer described it as "the most thrillingly different motion picture you have ever seen!" It was considered a B-movie due to its low budget, quick filming, and lack of top actors. Although it wasn't a blockbuster, the film often played as the second feature at matinees. Getzendaner exhibited her movie star horse around the country until Gantry was well into his twenties.

9

Early Equine Movie Stars

Advertised as the smartest horse in the movies, Trigger was also one of the most beautiful. The intelligent horse knew over a hundred tricks, including walking on his hind legs, bowing, sitting in a chair, signing "X" with a pencil, lying down, and covering himself with a blanket.

Trigger was even housebroken. This allowed his owner, Roy Rogers, to take the horse for personal appearances in a variety of places as well as visiting sick children in hospitals.

Actor Roy Rogers was known as "The King of the Cowboys." Born Leonard Franklin Slye, in Ohio in 1911, he later adopted his stage name. The actor credited much of his fame to his horse. If not for Trigger, there would have been no Roy Rogers.

Roy purchased the palomino, Golden Cloud, for $2,500. The horse also received a stage name. Trigger seemed to better convey his role in the Westerns he would become famous for, as in "quick on the trigger."

During his twenty-year career, Trigger appeared in eighty films and a hundred episodes of the *Roy Rogers Show* on television. He also had his own comic book series.

In 1942, Rogers purchased his trademark Bohlin black saddle, extensively ornamented in silver, with a matching breast collar, bridle, and tapaderos. The saddle was used in many of Rogers' films and television episodes. It later sold for $386,500.

Dale Evans, born Frances Octavia Smith, first appeared in a film with Roy Rogers in 1944, *The Cowboy and the Senorita*. At the time, Dale could not ride; she learned on the movie set.

Roy proposed to Dale on horseback at a rodeo, and they were married in 1947. Dale wrote the couple's theme song "Happy Trails" and several inspirational Christian books. In order to star in films together, Dale needed a horse that would complement, but not outshine, Trigger. They located Soda, a buckskin Quarter Horse in Wyoming. As a young colt, he had been abused by a horse trader. A cattle rancher rescued Soda when the horse was being hauled to a slaughterhouse. Through kind and consistent care, the rancher regained the horse's trust.

Dale renamed Soda "Buttermilk Sky" or simply "Buttermilk." Roy wasn't pleased that the Quarter Horse could outrun Trigger. During filming, Dale was required to hold him back so Trigger was always in the lead.

Trigger retired in 1957 and died in 1964 at thirty-three. Rogers had the horse stuffed and put on display at the Roy Rogers and Dale Evans Museum. The museum, originally located in California, later moved to Branson, Missouri. Buttermilk passed away in 1972 at thirty-one and joined Trigger at the museum. When the museum closed in 2009, RFDTV in Omaha, Nebraska, purchased the mounted Trigger for $266,500. Buttermilk sold for $25,000.

Although Trigger and Buttermilk are the most recognized equine stars, many horses appeared in movies before them, going back to the silent film era of the early 1900s. Silent films ended when the first talking movies began appearing in 1927.

One of those early stars was a pinto horse, Fritz, who appeared with actor William Hart. Fritz performed in at least eight silent films, the first of which was *Pinto Ben* in 1915. Hart and Fritz nearly died when they were caught in a whirlpool while filming *The Toll Gate* in 1920.

Once an animal got into it, he could neither swim out nor climb out. There was no bottom for his hind legs to reach, and he could only get his front hoofs on the ledge which was six feet under water. How Fritz did try. He struggled. He screamed. He looked at me with the eyes of a human being. He actually climbed the arched side walls until he turned himself over backwards.

Twice, we went down in those cold whirling depths, and twice we fought our way to the surface again. I knew the next time would be the last. Fritz spoke to me. I know he did. I heard him, and I spoke to him. I said, "God, help us, Fritz!" And God did help us. My little friend could not struggle any more. His eyes were glazed with coming death, and as we were going down for the last time, the strong current we had been fighting carried us over the ledge back toward the way we came in. As we sank, we touched the bottom and regained our feet.[1]

Tom Mix, born in 1880, was another early Western film star. His first movie was *The Cowboy Millionaire* in 1909. Mix appeared in over 300 films over his career, from 1909 to 1935, all but nine of which were silent.

Mix's popularity was due in part to his horse Tony. Tony, possibly a Morgan, was a sorrel with a blaze, snip, and two hind stockings. He was the first horse to be given equal billing with his human co-star. His name appeared in three movie titles: *Just Tony* (1922), *Oh You Tony* (1924), and *Tony Runs Wild* (1926). The horse appeared in thirty-four films between 1922 and 1932.

They billed Tony as "The Wonder Horse" because of his extensive repertoire of stunts, including untying Mix's hands, opening gates, jumping high fences, untangling himself from ropes, loosening his reins, and jumping from one cliff to another. Tony enjoyed stealing and running off with Tom's ten-gallon hat. He was also known to nudge Mix into the arms of the movie's female lead.

Mix and Tony jumped through a glass window in *The Great K. A. Train Robbery* (1926). In 1921's *Trailin'*, a collapsing bridge sent both plummeting into the river. An ill-timed dynamite blast injured

---

[1] *My Life East and West, William S Hart, 289*

them in another film. Mix performed nearly all the stunts himself and was injured more than eighty times. Tony was so famous that a fan letter to him addressed to "Just Tony Somewhere USA" was actually delivered to the horse at the Mix ranch.

Tom Mix was killed in a car crash in 1940 at the age of sixty. Due to ill health, Tony was euthanized two years later at thirty-two.

Although Rex, a 16 hand, black Morgan stallion, was vicious, he starred in a dozen films over fifteen years. Originally named Casey Jones, the colt was foaled in 1915. He was abused early on and ended up at the Colorado Detention Center in hopes that someone there could train him. One day, an inmate took him out for a ride and never returned. The man's body had been dragged beside a stream. No one knows exactly what happened to the rider. Perhaps he started to fall off and his foot became stuck in the stirrup. Regardless, Rex gained a reputation as a killer.

Filmmakers chose Rex as the perfect horse for his debut film, *King of the Wild Horses* (1924). Other films that suited his temperament included *Black Cyclone* (1925) and *The Devil Horse* (1926).

While filming *The Law of the Wild* (1934), Rex charged the camera, sending the cast and crew scrambling for cover. One actor, Ernie Adams, dove under a car. Rex dropped to his knees,

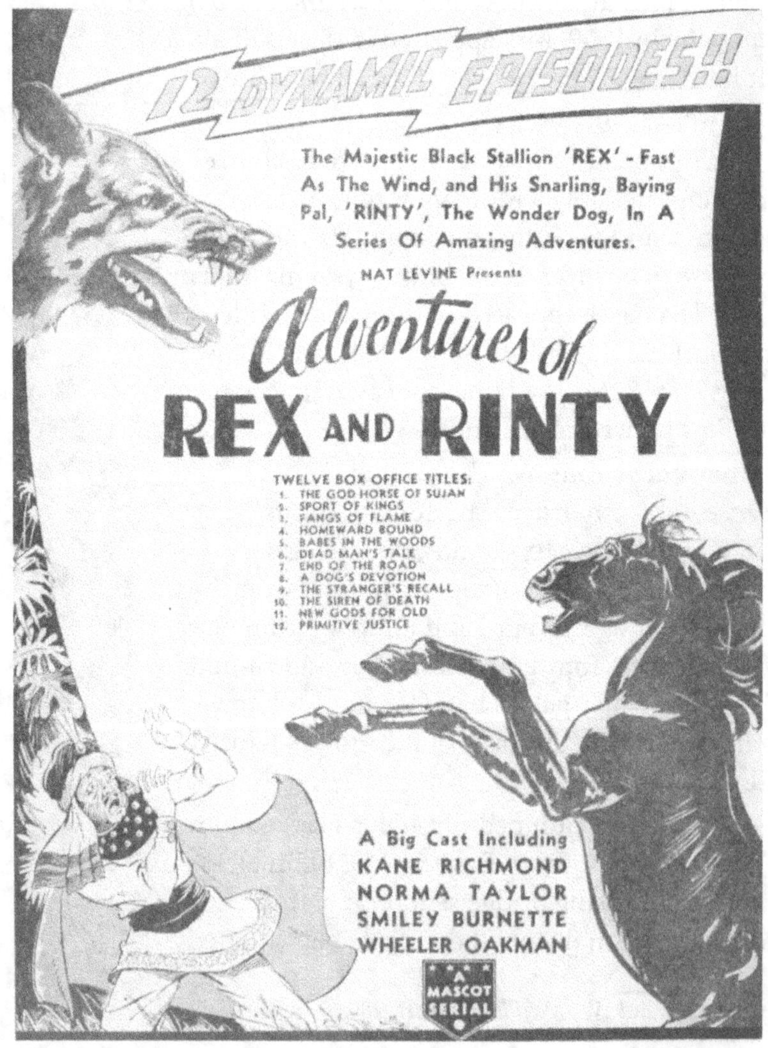

thrusting his head sideways under the vehicle in an attempt to bite the man. Understandably, few actors wanted to get close to the horse, so they used an equine double for closeup scenes. Another black named Missed-A-Shot was one of Rex's doubles.

At twenty, Rex starred with the German Shepherd Rin Tin Tin Jr. in a twelve-part series, *The Adventures of Rex and Rinty* (1935).

The dangerous stunts performed in early movies injured or killed many horses during filming. A popular stunt was a horse falling when he was "shot" by a gun or bow and arrow. The falls were sometimes achieved by having unsuspecting horses run into pits. Another technique was the use of a "Running W" rig. Wires from the cinch connected to the horse's front legs. Yanking on the wires pulled the animal's legs out from under him.

They subjected horses to another unspeakable horror—the tilt chute. A greased, slanted ramp was used to send a horse over the side of a cliff. Most did not survive such a fall. We will never know the exact number of equine deaths, but the following examples illustrate the low value movie producers placed on the lives of the horses in their films.

- *The Charge of the Light Brigade* (1936) — Twenty-five horses died during the filming of the charge scene.
- *Jesse James* (1939) — A horse wearing blinders died when a tilt chute forced him off a cliff over seventy feet into water where he drowned.
- *Stagecoach* (1939) — Several horses were tripped using the Running W device and died.
- *Ben-Hur* (1959) — Over a hundred horses died during the filming of the chariot race.
- *Heaven's Gate* (1980) — A horse injured by explosives had to be euthanized.

The American Humane Association began intervening in 1940 to protect horses and other animals in the film industry. However, in the 1960s, Hollywood backed away from those regulations.

In 1988, American Humane established Guidelines for Safe Use of Animals in Film Media. Today, films that AH believes have followed their guidelines for the safe participation of animals display the "No Animals were Harmed" message in the closing credits.

The modern use of CGI (computer-generated imagery) and animatronic animals has minimized the injury and death of horses, although they still occur. In the filming of *Flicka* (2006), two horses died in incidents the American Humane Association ultimately determined were unavoidable.

10

Phar Lap

Foaled on October 4, 1926, in New Zealand, Phar Lap was purchased at a bargain price, sight unseen, by David J. Davis, an American businessman living in Australia. Trainer, Harry Telford, had recommended the colt to Davis based solely on his pedigree.

When the colt arrived in Australia, both Davis and Telford were surprised by his thin, gangly appearance and awkward gait. Davis was furious and refused to put any money toward his training. Telford offered to train him for free in exchange for a three-year lease of the horse, with Davis to receive one-third of any winnings. Tommy Woodcock became Phar Lap's main groom and handler and called the horse Bobby.

The name, Phar Lap, seems to have come from the Thai word for "lightning." However, Phar Lap's racing career got off to a slower start than his name promised. He finished last in his first race as a two-year-old. He improved in his next three outings before finally winning the last race of his two-year-old season.

Phar Lap hit his stride as a three-year-old, winning thirteen races in 1929. He seemed to win effortlessly, often by several lengths. The horse had grown from a gangly yearling into a beautiful racehorse, larger than most at 17 hands. He was called "Big Red" or "The Red Terror."

Someone wanted to make sure Phar Lap did not win the Melbourne Cup, Australia's most prestigious race. On Saturday morning, November 1, 1930, Tommy Woodcock was riding a gray track horse, ponying Phar Lap back to his stable after a workout. Woodcock spotted a blue car sitting at a nearby crossroads. A man in the backseat appeared to be trying to hide behind a newspaper, and the car's license plate had been obscured. Woodcock was alarmed, but he continued on with Phar Lap.

> *Soon after, the car was started and drove up behind them. Woodcock turned sharply and pushed Phar Lap onto a footpath near a fence, placing himself and his horse between the oncoming car and Phar Lap. The driver honked the horn and attempted to swerve into Phar Lap. The horse reared and whirled around.*
>
> *Lucky for him he did so, as the back seat passenger, who had the lower part of his face covered with a handkerchief, poked out a double-barreled shotgun and fired point blank. The blast lodged pellets in the picket fence where Phar Lap had stood just seconds before.*
>
> *It was all over in a second. They didn't stop to fire a second shot.*[1]

Two police officers were assigned to guard Phar Lap. He won the Melbourne Stakes race that afternoon and the Melbourne Cup three days later. Although a reward was offered, the shooter was never found.

In 1932, owner David Davis decided to take Phar Lap out of Australia. Harry Telford, then part owner, could not make the trip, so Tommy Woodcock served as Phar Lap's trainer. The horse was so attached to Woodcock, that on the sea journey, he made a fuss if the man left his sight. Phar Lap

---

[1] *The Mercury, October 31, 1936, Phar Lap Memories*

stayed in a special stall built for him on the deck. He even had a sandpit to roll in. Woodcock ate his meals on deck where Phar Lap could see him. He even slept next to the horse's stall.

Their first stop was Tijuana, Mexico, for the Agua Caliente Handicap on March 20, the richest horse race at the time. Phar Lap defeated eleven opponents, setting a track record. It was his last win—and his last race.

From Mexico, Phar Lap was shipped to a ranch in Menlo Park, California to rest before his next race. Early on April 5, Woodcock went to the stable to check on the horse. His first clue that something was wrong was when Phar Lap refused the lump of sugar he offered him.

When he nosed up to me with his morning salute I felt his breath quite hot. I felt under his rug to find him steaming. In a few seconds I had Bill Neilsen, the Newcastle veterinary surgeon, who was a member of our party, running rule over Phar Lap.[1]

The vet treated Phar Lap for colic, but that afternoon, he collapsed and died in Woodcock's arms. An autopsy revealed the horse's stomach and intestines were inflamed. Race fans have debated his cause of death for decades. Was it simply colic? Some claim Mafia gangsters poisoned the horse. Others say he ingested poison while grazing on treated grass.

In 1936, Woodcock admitted Telford gave him tonics to administer to Phar Lap, but he claimed he never used them. "To please Telford I would take the bottle, but would pour a quantity down the drain each day so that he would think that I was carrying out his instructions."

Tests on Phar Lap's hair in 2006 found arsenic, supporting the poisoning theory. In 2008, Harry Telford's handwritten notebook was found, revealing recipes for "tonics" that may have been given to Phar Lap. The tonics included ingredients such as arsenic, strychnine, cocaine, and caffeine—all

---

[1] *The Courier-Mil Brisbane, September 19, 1936*

believed to boost the horse's performance. Telford's eighty-two-page notebook was sold at auction for $37,000.

With Tommy Woodcock as Phar Lap's constant companion, it's hard to believe anyone else could have gotten close enough to the horse to poison him. The mystery of Phar Lap's death may never be solved.

In his career, Phar Lap won thirty-seven of fifty-one races. He often won while carrying heavy weights, including 138 pounds in the Melbourne Cup.[1]

Phar Lap's mounted hide is on display at the Museum of Victoria in Melbourne. His skeleton is in the National Museum of New Zealand, and his unusually large heart (fourteen pounds) is at the Australian Institute of Anatomy.[2]

---

[1] *Racehorses usually carry 112 to 126 pounds, which includes the jockey's weight and about seven pounds of tack. The average male jockey is five feet two inches tall and weighs 108 to 118 pounds.*
[2] *An average horse's heart weighs eight to nine pounds.*

11

Seabiscuit

No one expected the knobby-kneed, solid bay colt to amount to much. Born on May 23, 1933, at Wheatley Stable in Kentucky, the groom present at his birth labeled him a runt. The colt's royal bloodlines weren't obvious from his appearance, but Seabiscuit was a grandson of the legendary Man o' War.

The foal's name continued the convention used for his father, Hard Tack. Both names refer to a biscuit or cracker eaten by sailors. Hard Tack was beautiful but so temperamental he was retired after a brief career on the track. Seabiscuit's mother, Swing On, also had an impressive pedigree, but she was too lazy and slow for racing.

The colt's owners hoped he had inherited the talent of his grandfather, but the most notable thing about Seabiscuit in his first year was his ability to sleep and eat. For his small size, the colt had a ravenous appetite. And while most horses doze standing up, Seabiscuit loved to lie down and stretch out for long naps.

The Wheatley's trainer, Sunny Jim Fitzsimmons, considered one of the best in the nation, had trained Hard Tack. He may have assumed Seabiscuit would be as difficult to work with as his father. Frustrated by the colt's laziness, Fitzsimmons instructed the rider to whip Seabiscuit as often as he could for a quarter mile. Frightened by the rough treatment, Seabiscuit ran faster than ever. That convinced the trainer that harsh treatment was the only way to get the horse to run.

Seabiscuit lost his first seventeen races as a two-year-old. He finished the 1935 season with five wins in a grueling schedule of thirty-five outings. Despite Seabiscuit's earnings of over $12,000, Fitzsimmons remained unimpressed. He'd entered Seabiscuit in several claiming races, hoping someone would take the colt off his hands. The trainer had other horses he'd rather focus on.

But no one was interested in Seabiscuit. That winter, he served as a training partner for Granville, one of Fitzsimmons' favorites. Seabiscuit became more irritable and unruly as he was held back in those practice sessions to let Granville "win."

The future appeared bleak for the short (15.2 hand), plain-looking colt. His prospects mirrored those of many Americans who felt hopeless during the Great Depression when one in four people were out of work. America's worst economic crisis began with the stock market crash of 1929. The Dust Bowl of the 1930s made matters even worse.

But with the help of an unlikely trio of men, the knobby-kneed colt overcame his poor start in life to become one of the most popular racehorses of all time. His rags-to-riches story inspired those who were struggling through the Depression.

The first of the three men was Charles Howard. As Seabiscuit was finishing his two-year-old season, Howard decided to enter the world of horse racing. When he was younger, he'd enjoyed horses and even served in the U.S. Cavalry. But then, he'd turned his attention to the latest invention.

In 1908, Howard pronounced, "The day of the horse is past, and the people in San Francisco want automobiles. I wouldn't give five dollars for the best horse in this country."

In 1919, Howard's automobile dealership was so successful that he purchased the 5,000-acre Ridgewood Ranch in Willits, California[1]. Automobiles made Charles a millionaire, but in 1926, one took the life of his son. When fifteen-year-old Frankie swerved his truck to miss a rock, he lost control, and the vehicle flipped into a canyon.

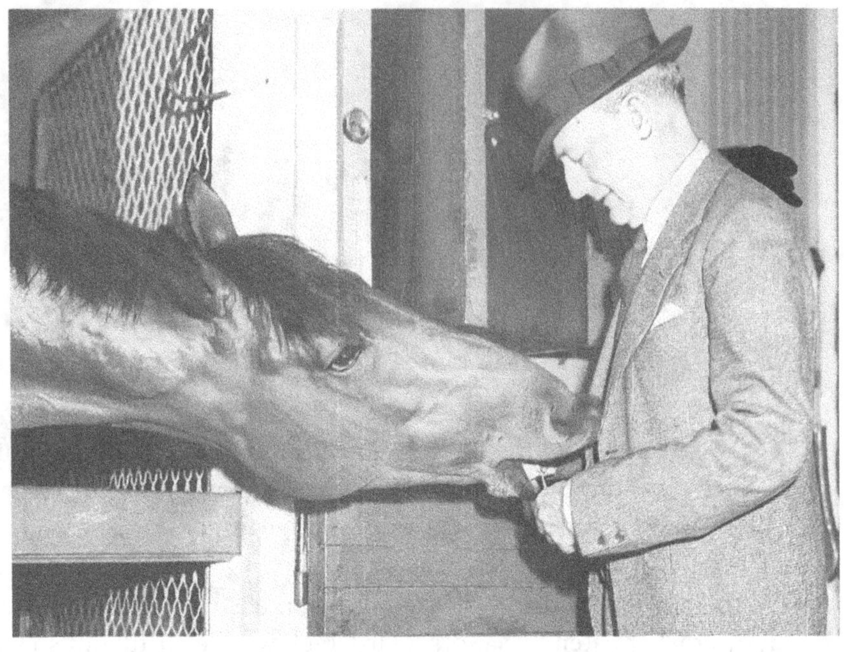

As a memorial to his son, Charles donated money to build a local hospital, the Frank R. Howard Memorial Hospital in Willits. Charles lost interest in his dealership and turned to horse racing. His second wife, Marcela, designed the Howard's crimson and white racing silks that featured an "H" inside a triangle. Next, Charles began looking for the best trainer. It didn't take long to find him.

In fact, Tom Smith, the second member of "Team Seabiscuit," was already on his way to California. Smith was the polar opposite of Charles Howard. Born in Georgia, Smith spent most of his early life in the West training horses for the Cavalry and working on cattle ranches. The man spoke so infrequently that some believed he was mute. But Tom was simply a man of few words, preferring the company of horses to people. Most recently, he had worked as a trainer for a Wild West show. When the tough days of the Depression brought the show to an end, Smith headed to the racetracks of California.

Nearly penniless, he lived in a horse stall as he searched for work. A friend recognized Smith's uncanny ability with horses and recommended him to Charles Howard. After a brief conversation, Charles hired the trainer on the spot.

The next step in developing Howard's racing stable was to locate a few fast horses.

In 1936, three-year-old Seabiscuit began his second racing season. One race took him to Suffolk Downs in Massachusetts where Tom Smith first saw

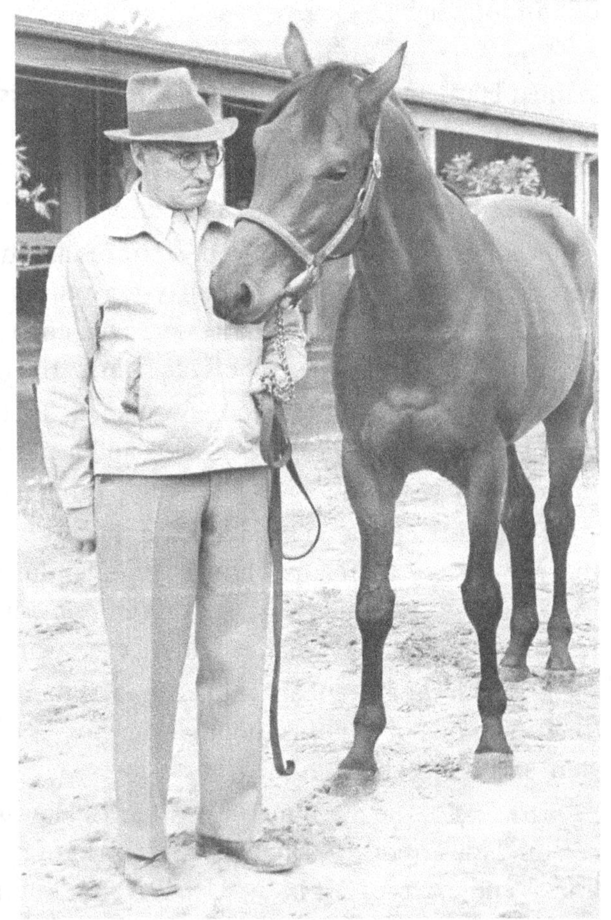

---

[1] *Some sources say Ridgewood Ranch was 5,000 acres; others say 16,000.*

Seabiscuit. As a groom led the colt down the track, the bay stopped and looked Smith directly in the eye. Tom stared back. He couldn't have said exactly what it was, but he saw something in Seabiscuit no one else had. "I'll see you again," he told the colt.

Two months later, at Saratoga in New York, Charles and Marcela Howard watched Seabiscuit win a race. They liked the horse, but didn't want to buy him without Smith's approval. When the trainer arrived at Fitzsimmons' barn to examine the prospect, he recognized the colt that had impressed him at Suffolk Downs. The normally reticent man nearly gushed his approval to the Howards. "Get me that horse. He has real stuff in him. I can improve him. I'm positive."

The Howards purchased Seabiscuit for $8,000 and moved him to the Detroit, Michigan fairgrounds. There, Tom Smith studied the angry colt, devising a plan to rehabilitate him. Seabiscuit was underweight and continually paced back and forth in his stall. He lunged at, and attempted to bite, anyone who passed too close to him.

Smith applied liniment to the horse's legs and wrapped them in thick, cotton bandages to ease his soreness. He brought in a goat to keep Seabiscuit company. The colt picked the poor goat up and tossed him out of the stall. Smith tried again; with a sturdier animal—Pumpkin, a palomino gelding. Seabiscuit liked the horse. Eventually, they shared a stall and became lifelong friends. Pocatell, a small dog with huge ears, and a monkey named Jo Jo joined Seabiscuit's menagerie.

It was time to add the third human member of Seabiscuit's team. This time, it seems Seabiscuit made the decision.

A few days after the horse arrived in Detroit, twenty-six-year-old Johnny (Red) Pollard walked into the barn, looking for work as a jockey. Tom Smith had run into Red out West and recognized him. When Red held out a sugar cube, the cantankerous Seabiscuit took it gently from his hand and nuzzled the young man's shoulder. The colt had selected his jockey.

Smith and Pollard agreed gentle techniques were the best way to gain Seabiscuit's trust. The first time they exercised the horse, he fought Red, doing the opposite of what the jockey asked. Smith suggested loosening the reins, not forcing the horse to do anything. With nothing to fight against, Seabiscuit relaxed.

Born in Canada in 1909, Red Pollard was one of seven children. The young man had been on his own since fifteen, when a family friend abandoned him at a racetrack in Montana. He'd struggled for a decade, trying to make a living racing horses. Pollard, at five-six, was tall for a jockey. He loved to read and often quoted Shakespeare to his fellow jockeys. He arrived in Detroit with a dismal six percent winning ratio, only six firsts in a hundred races. His previous racing had been at small tracks where there was little chance of riding a great horse. When he wasn't racing, Red tried unsuccessfully to pick up money by prize fighting.

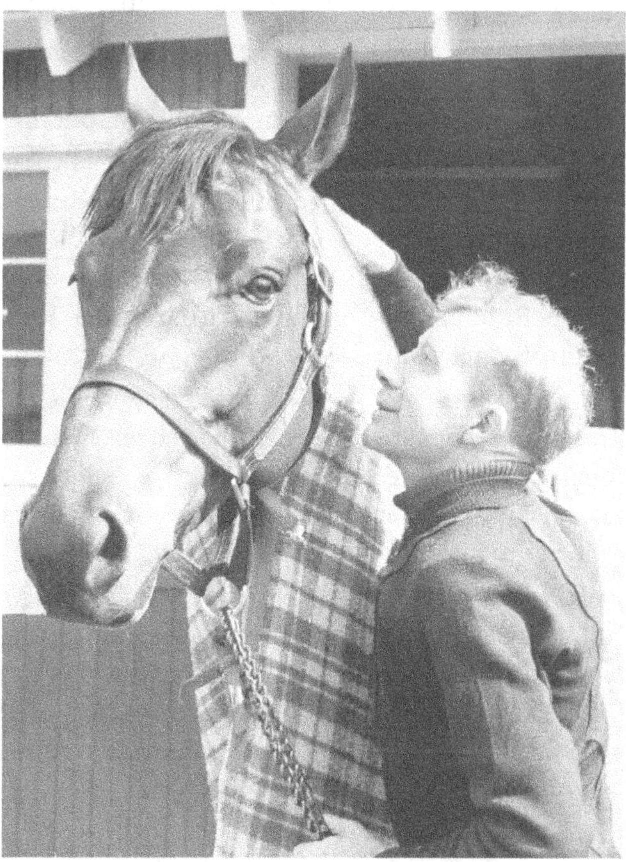

A few weeks after arriving in Detroit, Smith believed Seabiscuit was ready to compete again. In his first time back on the track, he finished fourth, followed by a second in the next race. Then, in August, Seabiscuit and Red had their first win.

At the end of the 1936 season, Charles Howard moved his staff and horses to Ridgewood Ranch for the winter. They worried about how Seabiscuit would hold up during the four-day trip by railcar from Michigan to California, but the horse had grown content with these people he loved and trusted. He walked calmly into the boxcar and lay down on the thick bed of straw. Other than occasional stops to stretch his legs, he slept most of the way.

To gain attention for the new Santa Anita track, built near Los Angeles in 1934, the 1937 Santa Anita Handicap offered a prize of $100,000. The race became known as the Hundred Grander. Over 60,000 people attended. Even more listened to it on the radio (in the days before television). Seabiscuit pulled ahead, and it seemed he would have an easy win. But inexplicably, toward the end of the race, Red Pollard slowed the horse, allowing Rosemont to come up on the outside to win by a nose.

Smith, Howard, and the media blamed the loss on Pollard. Red, threatened with losing his job as Seabiscuit's jockey, revealed something no one else knew. He was blind in one eye. He hadn't seen Rosemont coming up on his right until it was too late to speed Seabiscuit up again. In his early days as a jockey, a stone thrown up by another horse hit Pollard in the head, blinding him in his right eye. He'd told no one, knowing that if the track authorities found out, they would ban him from racing. Smith and Howard kept Pollard's secret and allowed him to continue as Seabiscuit's jockey.

Rather than diminishing Seabiscuit's fame, his loss made him more popular with racing fans across the country. They found it encouraging that the little horse with a big heart had almost beaten the larger, more expensive one.

Following the Santa Anita, Seabiscuit went on a streak, winning seven races in a row. By then, news reporters were hungry for information about the horse. But the tight-lipped Smith often refused to answer their questions. He exercised the popular horse at night so reporters couldn't monitor his progress. The Howards also owned Seabiscuit's brother, Grog. The two colts were almost identical. Smith worked Grog during the daytime to fool the reporters.

Seabiscuit's fans compared him to the 1937 Triple Crown winner, War Admiral. War Admiral, a son of Man o' War, was named Horse of the Year. Many claimed Seabiscuit was faster. The Triple Crown races were open only to three-year-olds. Since Seabiscuit was four, the two horses had never faced each other. Fans clamored for a match race between the favorites. Charles Howard agreed, but Samuel Riddle, War Admiral's owner, refused. He didn't consider Seabiscuit a worthy competitor of the great War Admiral.

In February 1938, Pollard suffered a terrible fall when riding another Howard horse, Fair Knightess. The mare clipped a horse's heels in a race and somersaulted over the jockey. Red broke his collarbone, shoulder, and several ribs, as well as suffering internal injuries. He hovered near death for several days but then began to recover. The mare recovered fully as well, and later that year, Pollard rode her to a win.

The 1938 Santa Anita race was coming up in March. Smith and Howard wanted to scratch Seabiscuit because of Pollard's injuries. In the time Howard had owned Seabiscuit, Pollard was the only one to ride the horse. Seabiscuit's trainer and owner both worried he would not run well for anyone else. But Red insisted his friend, George Woolf, a successful jockey, should ride in his place. From his hospital bed, Red filled Woolf in on how to ride Seabiscuit.

A horse bumped Seabiscuit early in the race, and the pack boxed him in. Despite his terrible start, Seabiscuit came on strong at the end, however, Stagehand edged him out by a nose in a photo finish. The close loss again increased his popularity.

Charles Howard was a wonderful promoter. Soon, all kinds of merchandise, such as Seabiscuit board games, wallets, and ladies' hats were sold. In 1938, the horse appeared on magazine covers and in newsreels. Seabiscuit was the subject of more newspaper articles than President Franklin Roosevelt.

By May, Red Pollard was back in the saddle. In June, at a track in Massachusetts, another trainer asked him to exercise a green two-year-old, Modern Youth. Thinking nothing of it and wanting to do a favor for a friend, Red hopped on the colt. When they were partway down the track, something spooked Modern Youth. He bolted toward the stable and slammed Pollard into the corner of a barn, shattering his lower leg. Doctors gave Pollard bad news—he would never walk again.

Meanwhile, Samuel Riddle had relented to the pressure for a match race. With Pollard injured, they turned again to George Woolf to ride Seabiscuit. Since War Admiral didn't like starting gates, Riddle requested a walk-up start instead. He believed that would give his horse an advantage. In preparation for the race, Tom Smith trained Seabiscuit to leap forward from a standstill upon hearing a bell.

The showdown between the two champions occurred on November 1, 1938, at Pimlico Track in Baltimore, Maryland. War Admiral's jockey was Charley Kurtsinger. When the officials couldn't find a bell to signal the start, trainer Smith offered his. Seabiscuit would start the race at the sound of the same bell he'd practiced with for weeks.

When the bell rang, Seabiscuit surprised everyone by jumping into the lead, where he remained for most of the race. Red had advised Woolf that midway through the race, he allow War Admiral to come close so Seabiscuit could get a good look at him. Pollard believed that looking into the other

horse's eyes gave Seabiscuit the fire to run faster. When War Admiral caught up with them, Woolf looked over at the other jockey and called out, "So long, Charley!" He loosened the reins and Seabiscuit shifted into a higher gear.

The little horse pulled ahead and beat the Triple Crown winner by four lengths. When reporters interviewed Woolf in the winner's circle, he stated that Seabiscuit was the best horse in the world, and he wished Red could have ridden him in the race. Seabiscuit was named the 1938 Horse of the Year.

In mid-November 1938, after months in the Massachusetts hospital, Pollard traveled to Ridgewood Ranch in California to recuperate. In his haste to prove he could not only walk but also ride, Red tossed his crutches aside. His foot came down wrong, and his leg snapped. Pollard was rushed to the Frank R. Howard Memorial Hospital. The surgeons determined the first doctors hadn't set the leg correctly. They broke the jockey's leg again and reset it.

In March 1939, Woolf was still riding Seabiscuit, this time in the Los Angeles Handicap. When the horse injured his left foreleg in the race, a veterinarian suggested putting Seabiscuit down. Smith and Howard wouldn't hear of it. They brought the horse back to Ridgewood, realizing he might never race again. When Seabiscuit joined Red at the ranch, the jockey joked that they only had four good legs between the two of them.

No one expected Red Pollard to ride again or Seabiscuit to race again, but by early 1940, Red convinced Smith and Howard that he and the horse were ready. Charles now viewed Pollard as a son and was reluctant to let the young man race. Another injury would likely ruin him.

But Howard also sensed the horse wanted to run. He had one more goal for Seabiscuit. The horse had lost the Santa Anita Handicap twice, each time by a nose. He wanted Seabiscuit to have one more chance to win that race. Although not fully healed, Red was certain he could ride. He created a stiff, leather leg brace he laced over the boot on his injured leg. When mounted, the brace relieved most of the pressure on his leg. Pollard and Seabiscuit ran three preliminary races before the Santa Anita, finishing third, fourth, and first.

In 1940, Seabiscuit was seven. In his third attempt at the Santa Anita, he faced horses half his age. The race drew a record crowd of 78,000. Mrs. Howard remained at the barn when Seabiscuit was led to the track. She couldn't bear the thought of seeing her horse or Red Pollard injured again.

Mrs. Howard needn't have worried; Seabiscuit finished his racing career in a blaze of glory. Not only did he win, he set a record and gave Red Pollard his biggest win.

Smith, still a man of few words, said, "Red, you put up a great ride today."

The jockey replied, "The greatest ride I ever got from the greatest horse that ever lived."

The people's horse retired from racing after the Santa Anita win, with a record of eighty-nine starts, thirty-three wins, fifteen seconds, and thirteen thirds. His total earnings were $437,730. During his first year of retirement, he sired seven foals—called the seven little biscuits. Both Seabiscuit and his grandfather, Man o' War, died in the same year, 1947. Man o' War was thirty; Seabiscuit was only fourteen. It's believed he died of a heart attack.

Christ's Church of the Golden Rule purchased Ridgewood Ranch in 1962. The church is working with the Seabiscuit Heritage Foundation to preserve Seabiscuit's bloodline.

12

Phantom Ranch

Phantom Ranch, located at the bottom of the Grand Canyon, is unique in that it can only be reached on foot, by mule or horse, or by rafting down the Colorado River. The Grand Canyon is known for its cliffs and sheer rock walls; however, Phantom Ranch consists of fourteen acres of mostly flat land.

Primitive camps were created in the area as early as 1906, but Phantom Ranch officially opened in 1922 with four cabins and a lodge that contained a kitchen and dining hall. Visitors stayed there at a rate of $6 per day. One of the few female architects in the U.S., Mary Colter, designed the buildings. Colter made use of local fieldstone and rough-hewn wood in the construction, creating a rustic look that harmonized with the natural beauty of the area. This style, known as National Park Service Rustic, served as a model for future buildings in the area and at other parks. The name Phantom Ranch is also credited to Colter.

President Franklin Roosevelt formed the Civilian Conservation Corps (CCC) in 1933 to provide work for young men during the Great Depression. Workers at Phantom Ranch's CCC Camp 818 earned $30 per month. Nearly 200 CCC employees worked at the ranch for three years, building and improving the trails and campgrounds, planting trees, upgrading sewage lines, building a swimming pool, and installing a phone line to the bottom of the canyon.

Construction materials, such as boards, window panes, and plywood were lashed to the backs of dozens of pack mules and carried to the bottom of the canyon. The wood beams were limited in length to eight to ten feet—the maximum a mule could carry. They were connected as needed during a building's construction. When creating the trails, mules carried 50,000 pounds of dynamite and over 30,000 drill bits. The mules also toted all the supplies for Phantom Ranch campers, employees, and residents. Each mule carried approximately 150 to 200 pounds.

In 1934, the most serious accident occurred at the CCC camp. While attempting to create a trail around a cliff, the ledge three young men stood on separated from the cliff wall. Ropes anchoring them snapped, and two CCC workers fell, along with tons of rock, down toward the river. Rescuers pulled them from the debris and placed them on stretchers.

Mules, who had carried all manner of equipment up and down the trail, handled these emergencies as well. The two-by-six-foot canvas stretcher was placed onto the packsaddle of a strong, steady mule—often Old Jim. The victim's head was positioned above the mule's ears and his feet over the tail, and all was secured with canvas straps. One man led the mule ambulance, while two others walked alongside to steady the stretcher. Although their injuries were serious, the two young men survived.

During the years the CCC worked in the Canyon, thirty-four injured men required transportation by Old Jim or other mules. The Canyon could be dangerous; however, nationwide more CCC workers died from truck accidents than any other cause.

Today, helicopters carry in the heaviest equipment, but a string of pack mules still daily hauls supplies to the ranch and carries out garbage. Phantom Ranch wasn't powered exclusively by mules. Bob was the last horse employed there. He was part of a team of four horses who pulled a coach on the South Rim for more than a decade.

> *Bob came up here from Colorado in 1917 when he was six years old. Uncle Henry broke him in for a stage horse to carry dudes along the rim of the Grand Canyon, and no one ever drove Bob after that but Uncle Henry. I have never seen a man so devoted to any animal and Bob knew it— he would follow him around like a dog. Bob was a beauty in those days—dapple gray coat, and plenty of pep, too. … Bob is the last of the stage horses used on the Rim drive. Bob was sent to Phantom Ranch in 1927. He is still there, enjoying his well-earned holiday and permitted to roam around at will and visit where he chooses.*
>
> *Now there is one thing Bob does object to—and that is being a saddle horse. The ranch gardener found that out one day when he hopped on his back. Old Bob would not buck with him—not Bob—he slowly reached around and took hold of the gardener's pants leg with his teeth and firmly pulled him off.*
>
> *Bob's only playmates now are the mules bringing dudes down to Phantom Ranch, and he always waits at the end of the trail, knowing when the mules are turned loose, they'll have a good play.*[1]

Bob enjoyed his retirement at Phantom Ranch and died there in 1940.

---

[1] *Anonymous article written during Bob's lifetime and later submitted to the Grand Canyon Pioneers Society Newsletter, March 1991*

13

Pack Horse Librarians

The difficult terrain and lack of roads in eastern Kentucky meant those homes were only accessible on foot or by horseback. Some hardy young women mounted horses and carried books to those remote homes and schools as part of the Pack Horse Library Project. The federal government funded the program as part of the Works Progress Administration (WPA) established by President Franklin D. Roosevelt to provide jobs during the Depression.

Although there was funding to pay the librarians, $28 per month, each community had to provide their own library building or book station to store the inventory. All the books came from donations. Pastor Benton Deaton in Leslie County donated a collection of books to get the first Pack Horse Library started in 1935. School PTA programs sponsored book drives. Libraries in other states donated old or discarded books. Boy Scout groups, Sunday schools, and other organizations also contributed books. By 1936, there were eight Pack Horse Libraries.

At the Pack Horse Library book station, a clerk processed donations and repaired frequently used books. Rotating books between locations ensured variety. Most were children's books. Magazines and

newspapers were popular with adults. The Bible was the most-often requested book. Four or five carriers delivered books from each station.

The Pack Horse librarians, almost always young women, were hired from the local communities in order to gain the trust of the remote families. Each carrier was assigned a route and rode her own horse or mule to deliver the books. Families could expect a pickup and delivery every two weeks.

A book woman rose at dawn and saddled up to ride to the book station which might contain up to eight hundred books. Based on the knowledge gained about the families on her route, the librarian selected as much reading material as she could fit into her saddlebags. Then, she set out on her journey—up the side of a mountain, along a narrow, rocky path, or through muddy creeks. If the terrain was too treacherous, she

dismounted and continued on foot, leading her equine partner. The librarians rode out three or four times each week, taking a different route each time. They covered eighteen to twenty miles a day to

places such as Troublesome, Hell-Fer Sartin Creek, and Cut Shin Creek. The latter is said to have been named when a logger cut his shin there with an ax.

One book woman, Grace Caudill Lucas, didn't own a horse, so she rented Bill, a gentle black gelding, for fifty cents a week. She also had to pay for the horse's feed. In the winter, her boots sometimes froze to the stirrups when water splashed up from the creeks they crossed. Once, during an all-night downpour, she had to spend the night with a family on her route.

Another librarian, Nan Milan, joked that the horse she rode, Sunny Jim, had shorter legs on one side than the other, so he wouldn't slide off the steep mountain trails.

Even though the books were loaned to the patrons rather than given away, the independent Kentuckians didn't want to accept charity. In exchange for the library books, they offered the librarians something—a hand-written recipe or sewing or quilting patterns. The librarians combined these items into scrapbooks to share with others on their routes. Families soon came to look forward to the next visit of the "book woman," "book lady," or "packsaddle librarian."

The librarians provided more than a delivery service. They sometimes read aloud to the children and to illiterate, sick, or injured adults. Some taught the children to read. Many families were just happy for the periodic visits that broke their isolation and loneliness.

Most of the families had never enjoyed books in their homes before the Pack Horse program. The supply of books introduced fresh problems. Some parents found their children weren't doing necessary chores because they wanted to read all the time. Others were spending more on lamp oil to allow for reading at night. As one father stated, "I can't get my gal [daughter] to do nothin' but read. My cornfield needs hoein' and settin' in a corner with her nose in a book ain't gonna get them weeds out!"

Miss Flossie Jones was one of five women working as a Pack Horse Librarian in Adams County, Ohio. She used an automobile in the summer, but when winter approached, she found Bob more reliable.

During the eight years of the program's operation (1935 to 1943), pack horse librarians in
Kentucky reached 100,000 people and 155 schools. The discontinuation of the WPA in 1943 ended
the Pack Horse Library Project due to the loss of funding. With the development of better roads in
the 1950s, motorized bookmobiles began to travel to the remote communities, providing the same
service as the book women, but certainly with a less personal touch.[1]

---

[1] *May Stafford operated a privately funded Pack Horse Library in Johnson County, Kentucky, in 1913 which served as a
prototype for the WPA program.*

14

Military Mascots

In 1893, a live goat, Bill, served as Navy's mascot during an Army-Navy football game. Navy beat Army by a score of 6 to 3. Was the goat instrumental in that win? Probably not, but regardless, the Army team decided they needed a mascot to counter Navy's goat.

In 1899, the team borrowed a large, white mule who pulled an ice wagon. They groomed the animal and outfitted it with a gray Army blanket, leggings, and black, gold, and gray streamers. The choice of the animal as the Army mascot was likely solidified when the mule "hoisted that astonished goat toward the Navy stands to the delight of the yelling, laughing crowd." Army won that game 17 to 5. Army returned the borrowed mule to his owner soon after the victory. Local mules appeared at their games from then on.

In 1936, they adopted the animal as the official mascot. Known for its strength, hardiness, and endurance, the mule was an appropriate choice. The animals have served faithfully in military operations over the years, hauling supplies, guns, and ammunition. Each year, one mule rider is chosen from the incoming class of West Point cadets, making a team of four that cares for the mules.

Fittingly, the first official mule mascot was a retired Army pack animal named Mr. Jackson. He arrived from the Front Royal Virginia Remount Station. Mr. Jackson served as the head mascot until

1948. In his retirement years, Jackson brayed loud protests when his replacement left the barn on game days. The retired mule had a home at West Point until his death in 1961 at thirty-five.

Pancho was the second mascot. Also known as Skippy, this smaller Ecuadorian mule's term (1939 to 1958) overlapped that of Mr. Jackson. The Ambassador of Ecuador, whose sons graduated from the Academy, donated the mule to West Point. For the 1942 Army-Navy game, Pancho appeared on the field disguised as a goat with horns.

The third mascot, Hannibal (originally named Bud), arrived in June 1947, after serving six years in the Army. He died on March 14, 1964, after being kicked by another mule.

During Hannibal's reign, two other mules also served as mascots—K.C. MO and Trotter. Both arrived in 1957. K.C. MO was difficult and occasionally threw his rider. He was retired to pasture in 1969. Before becoming a mascot, Trotter served with the 35th Quartermaster Pack Company at Fort Carson, Colorado. He was the only mule known to have performed four gaits—walk, trot, pace, and canter. Trotter could hold his gait for eight hours or about fifty miles. He retired in 1972.

In 1964, Buckshot, a gift from the U.S. Air Force Academy, became the first female mule mascot. Buckshot retired in 1986 at twenty-seven.

Additional mule mascots include:

- Hannibal II (originally Jack) 1964 to 1980
- Spartacus (called Frosty because of his white muzzle) 1973 to 1994
- Ranger I (his dam was a Percheron) 1978 to 1995
- Black Jack (died of cancer) 1985 to 1989
- Traveler (also Dan, one of the largest mascots at 16 hands) 1990 to 2002
- Trooper (also Ernie, loved donuts) 1990 to 2002
- Raider (also Joker, dam was a gaited mare) 1995 to 2011
- Ranger II (also George, dam was a Quarter Horse) 2002 to 2011
- General Scott (also Scotty, dam was a Clydesdale) 2002 to 2011
- Stryker (also Abe, half-brother of Ranger III) 2011

- Ranger III (also Apache or Rocky, half-brother of Stryker) 2011

- Paladin (also Jack, his dam was a Percheron) 2016

The rivalry between Army and Navy sometimes extended beyond the playing field. In 1990, several West Point cadets stole Bill the Goat XXVII from the Naval Academy. This particular goat was not serving as the Academy's mascot at the time. Bill was simply removed from his barn, located twenty miles from the Naval Academy, and hauled away in a pickup truck.

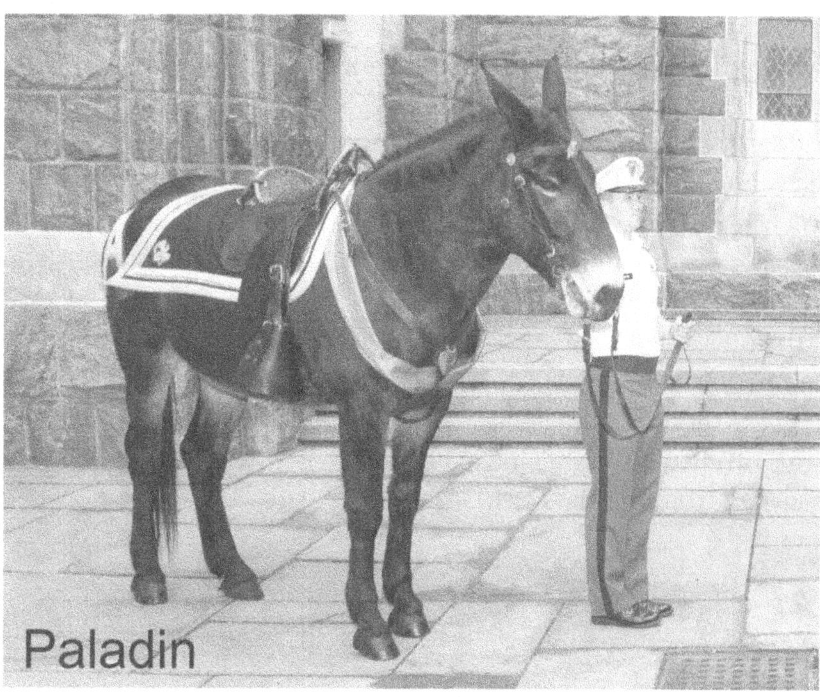

The midshipmen[1] at the Naval Academy did not take Bill's abduction lightly. They plotted revenge for a year, coming up with "Operation Missing Mascot." Their goal—kidnap the four West Point mascots—Spartacus, Trooper, Ranger, and Traveler.

Not wanting to harm the animals, they received help and advice from Weir "Tennessee" Denton, a sixty-seven-year-old Maryland mule farmer. Rather than retrieving the mules from a remote barn as had been the case with Bill, the midshipmen needed to remove the four large animals from the busy campus of the military academy. An initial attempt on November 29, 1991 failed, but the group tried again on December 5, two days before the football game between the rivals.

Seventeen midshipmen snuck onto the campus with a truck and livestock trailer. They disguised themselves as army men or military police. At 9:15 a.m., they arrived at the campus mule barn through an unguarded back gate and told cadets they were delivering mule feed. When some cadets realized what was happening, the midshipmen used plastic zip ties to restrain them. They cut the phone lines and locked the other employees in a room.

Within minutes, the mules were at the front barn door,

---

[1] *Midshipmen - students at the United States Naval Academy training to become officers.*

munching sweet feed. They loaded all four
without incident, and by 9:32, the trailer
pulled out the gate. The Army mules were
ridden by midshipmen at a pep rally at the
Naval Academy that evening.

The next day, Navy beat Army 24 to 3.
The mules were unharmed, and the Army
never pressed charges for "Operation
Missing Mascot."

In 2004, a statue of Hannibal, the
longest-serving Army mule (1947-1964)[1],
was unveiled at West Point, a 50th anniversary gift from the class of 1954.

---

[1] Some sources list Hannibals dates as 1948-1964.

15

The Quarter Horse

The Quarter Horse type began with a stallion called Steel Dust, who arrived in Texas as a yearling in 1844. His offspring were so skilled at driving Longhorns up the Texas trails, horses of his type were called Steeldusts.

Other influential horses in those early years were Shiloh, Billy, Sir Archy, Copper Bottom, Printer, and Tiger. Another important factor in the breed's development was the intermingling with the free-roaming Mustangs.

Founded in 1940, the American Quarter Horse Association (AQHA), in Amarillo, Texas, is the largest equine breed registry in the world. The origins of the breed trace back to the Spanish stock of colonial America, but much of the horses' cattle handling ability derived from those early Texas ranch horses.

Mounts with intelligence, stamina, and cow sense were vital to ranchers. Thoroughbreds and longer races dominated in the East, but in the Plains and Southwest, quarter-mile racing was popular. After a day's work, some of those hardy ranch horses competed on the race tracks.

One of the early ranches was the King Ranch, currently the largest ranch in the U.S. at 825,000 acres. The south Texas ranch, founded in 1853 by Richard King, is larger than the state of Rhode Island (776,960 acres). In 1869, the ranch registered its "Running W" brand, still in use today.

Old Sorrel, foaled in 1915, was the foundation sire of all King Ranch Quarter Horses. An Old Sorrel grandson, Wimpy, foaled on March 3, 1937[1], became the first registered AQHA horse when he won first place at the 1941 Fort Worth Exposition and Fat Stock Show.

---

[1] *Wimpy's birth year is variously reported as between 1935 and 1937.*

Wimpy P-1

Wimpy P-1[1] was a stocky, chestnut stallion with a star and a sock on his left hind leg. He stood 15 hands tall and weighed about 1200 pounds. Wimpy sired over a hundred and seventy foals. He died on August 14, 1959. A bronze statue of Wimpy stands in front of the AQHA Headquarters in Amarillo.

Two other King Ranch horses were among the earliest registered with the AQHA—Little Richard (P-17) and Tomate Laureles (P-19), both Old Sorrel sons.

---

[1] *The 'P' stands for Permanent registry.*

16

Across Canada

One day in May 1938, as twenty-four-year-old Mary Bosanquet bounced around in an overcrowded British bus, an idea came to her—"like a stone falling into a pond, the idea dropped into my mind."

Her unexpected brainstorm? To ride horseback across Canada. Part of her motivation was to escape the mounting gloom and apprehension in England as a seemingly inevitable war with Germany approached. She wanted to have a memorable adventure before the world self-destructed.

Mary realized she needed the support of her parents to pull off such an adventure. Surprisingly, when she presented the idea to her mother that evening, her response was, "I think it might be a very good idea."[1]

Her father, a foreign diplomat, was less enthusiastic. "Well, I should hate to do it myself, but if you want to, you'd better go ahead."[2]

Mary determined to embark on her journey the following spring.

One gift which I possess is the inability to worry beforehand about anything which I am to do, but the defect of this quality is an equal inability to make accurate plans.[3]

Her initial plan included sailing to Canada and then taking a train west across the country to Vancouver, British Columbia, where she believed she could purchase a quality horse cheaply. On March 31, 1939, Mary boarded the Duchess of Bedford with eighty pounds she'd saved for the journey. The ship headed across the Atlantic to Canada, landing in Halifax, Nova Scotia, on April 7.

When her train reached British Columbia, Mary stayed with the Lewis family in Kamloops, where she felt welcome by all—except the Lewis' parrot. Polly took an instant dislike to her and continually tried to bite her ankles.

Next, Mary began searching for her equine partner. After ten days of viewing a variety of horses, all of whom Mary rejected, she was taken to the Douglas Lake Ranch. There she found Timothy.

---

[1] *Canada Ride, Mary Bosanquet, 7*
[2] *Bosanquet, 7*
[3] *Bosanquet, 8*

Despite her initial impression, the cowboys at the ranch convinced Mary that Timothy would be a wonderful horse for her. The gelding performed a smooth, single-foot gait, which he could maintain for long periods of time at about six miles per hour.

Timothy and Mary made their way to Vancouver. Newspaper articles had reported her proposed ride, leading many in the area to discourage her from undertaking it. They reminded her that Vancouver to Montreal would be a journey of over three thousand miles. Mary was already aware of that and wasn't discouraged in the least.

Her supplies included an English saddle, sleeping bag, raincoat, ground sheet, saddlebags, clothing, writing material, toothbrush, comb, horse brush, hoof pick, string, a Bible, and the book *Travels with a Donkey*.

Mary set out on Timothy, traveling east through the Fraser Canyon into the Coast Mountains. She said, "Timothy's neck shone golden, and there were silver streaks in his mane." Later, she described the horse as red. It seems he may have been a dun or chestnut. Although on some days, Mary slept on the cold ground, her preference was to enjoy the hospitality of people along her route. She even received several marriage proposals from cowboys she encountered.

---

[1] *Bosanquet, 13*

give back to someone who needs it a little of this wealth of friendship which has been so freely given to me.[1]

When crossing the Rocky Mountains into Alberta, Timothy began experiencing lameness.

I am worrying a little about Timothy. He is in good heart and condition, but his legs are not perfect. He is straight in the shoulder and straight in the pastern, and jars the tendons as he walks. Today they are puffy and hot, after his climb over the mountain. I hope I may be able to keep him sound.[2]

When the pair reached Calgary, Mary had not been able to keep Timothy sound. She sold him there and bought another horse, a small, dark bay, Jonathan or Jonty. But Mary missed Timothy horribly and decided to buy him back.

This pony has a good front and is well sprung, with good bone and a short back. He is by a thoroughbred out of a range mare. He is lean and ewe-necked, not a beauty, but he has the Look. A horse either has it or he has not, and the pony has. So Timothy went to his new home, and I set out with the new horse into the prairies … In vain I petted the new horse and pointed out to myself what good paces he had.[3]

It was as I set out into the third prairie day that misery overcame me. My trouble was Timothy. The first day had been all right, but the further we travelled from Calgary the more passionately I longed for him. I remember our camps together, his beautiful muscles and the lights on his red-gold coat, our long days and the many mountain trails he had carried me, never going lame. On the morning of the fourth day I was in a bus, speeding back to Calgary. By the evening I had bought Timothy back again and was riding him out of the city.[4]

Jonty and Timothy became best friends. Mary used one horse as a pack animal while riding the other. Soon after repurchasing him, Timothy kicked her in the wrist. When she reached an area with a hospital, she learned her wrist was broken. Due to Timothy's lameness and the bad weather, Mary and the horses sat out the winter months in Dayton with the Skerten family, five hundred miles west of their Montreal destination. With time to contemplate as she rested, Mary thought about all her equine partners meant to her.

The horses had the depths of my love in those winter days. They have it now, though I may never see them again. Timothy is magnificent. His coat is red as the sunrise and smooth as satin all through the winter; the cascade of his splendid tail is silver and gold; he carries his head like a king and disdains humanity; he is power and beauty and pride. …

But Jonty is different. He has no particular splendour. He is little and dark, and his coat in the winter would do credit to a bear. There is no pride in his small face; it is simple and innocent and vivid. But Jonty is spirit for me. He is all I love and long for and have and have not. He is fire and flood and storm and laughter and loneliness. He is freedom and fearlessness and the will to do and the will to give, and passion and poetry and search. He is the secret of the wilderness and the sunlight of the plain; he is mountains and rivers and the moon in cloud-rack and the sun riding

---

[1] *Bosanquet, 51*
[2] *Bosanquet, 45*
[3] *Bosanquet, 63*
[4] *Bosanquet, 66*

into a storm; and all that is lost to cities, and all that is hidden from the wise; all I have found, all I am seeking, all I shall never find—little Jonathan, little dark Jonathan, so far away now.[1]

But, horses don't always live up to our romantic thoughts of them, and that January, Mary suffered an accident on a runaway Jonty.

We were making for the farm, and Jonty was frantic to go; he was pitching and throwing his head and bouncing me all over his smooth, naked back. At last, dexterously combining body and head action, he flipped me up onto his neck; then he seized the bit and away he went like the tail of a wind. There was no hope of stopping him, so I slid back into position and sat confidently enough, knowing that he meant to gallop up to the barn and stop. But I had not considered the speed at which he was going. He swung into the farm gate, but could not make the right-angled turn; instead he shot off the road and headed straight for a tree.

When he was almost breathing on the bark he swerved to the right, while I went straight on and hit the tree with the full force of our meteoric approach.

At first lying in the snow I could not breathe or move, but I found that my mind worked exactly as usual.[2]

Although stiff and sore for a long time, Mary suffered only a broken arm from the incident. After several weeks in a cast, she could ride again and help with the farm work.

That spring, Mary, who spoke German fluently, was surprised to learn of newspaper articles that accused her of being a German spy. The articles insinuated her ride wasn't an innocent adventure, but a scouting trip to prepare for a Nazi invasion of Canada. A Royal Canadian Mounted Police officer even interrogated her.

In May 1940, Germany invaded Belgium and the Netherlands. Then, in June, Paris fell. Mary went to Toronto and Montreal, desiring to help with the English children who had been evacuated to Canada, but no one would hire her.

Mary left Timothy with the Skerten family that August and departed on Jonty to complete her ride. Jonty and Mary both missed Timothy. They continued to Ottawa and Montreal, then turned south to visit New York City in November 1940. As she approached the city, Mary realized how much she would miss Jonty.

Whatever people say, a horse does not often become deeply attached to a person. But this has happened to Jonty. To part with a horse who will not miss one is bad, but to part with a horse who will miss one is bad indeed.[3]

It's unclear what became of Jonty, but almost certainly Mary found the horse a suitable home before returning to England.

In addition to her book detailing her experiences on the Canadian trip, *Canada Ride*, she also wrote *Journey Into a Picture* which covered her experience working with the YMCA in Italy during the later stages of the war. Mary became friends with Sabine Leibholz, Dietrich Bonhoeffer's twin sister. Through interviews with Sabine and Dietrich's friends, she wrote the first Bonhoeffer biography, *The Life and Death of Dietrich Bonhoeffer*, published in 1968.

---

[1] *Bosanquet, 128*
[2] *Bosanquet, 129*
[3] *Bosanquet, 189*

17

Amish Horses

The number of horses in the U.S. reached its peak at about twenty-five million in 1920.[1] The Amish are one of the few communities that have continued to use horses for both transportation and farming. The primary Amish groups that use horses are the Old Order and the Swartzentrubers.

Swartzentrubers are the most conservative, considering even the Old Order Amish too modern. Among other things, the Swartzentrubers allow no electricity, cars, tractors, bicycles, indoor plumbing, or photographs. They may use reflective tape on their buggies, but refuse to attach the triangular slow-moving vehicle signs, considering the bright orange color too flashy. Some have served jail sentences rather than add the triangles to their vehicles.

Lancaster County, Pennsylvania is home to the earliest and largest Amish settlement in the United States. Both the Amish and Mennonites, known as "plain people," come from an Anabaptist background.[2] Menno Simons, for whom the Mennonites are named, was a Catholic priest until he joined the Anabaptists in 1536. The fundamental disagreement at the time was over baptism—adult versus infant. Later, Jakob Ammann believed the Anabaptists weren't conservative enough in some areas. Views on shunning were a major issue. In the late 1600s, Ammann led a split, which became the Amish.

The Amish began coming to the United States in the 1700s. At that time, rural American families depended on horses for work and transportation, so the Amish lifestyle wasn't noticeably different. However, beginning in the early 1900s, the Amish refused to adopt modern inventions. First to be rejected was the telephone, followed by others such as radio, television, cars, trucks, and tractors.

Traveling by horse and buggy is an effective way to preserve community. Average speeds of five to eight miles per hour make it hard to stray too far from home. Most Amish limit their travel to a radius of twenty-miles or less.

Amish communities set rules regarding the shape and style of their buggies. The color is usually black,

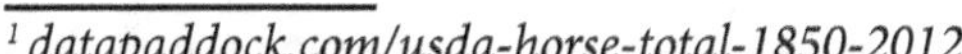

[1] *datapaddock.com/usda-horse-total-1850-2012*
[2] *Anabaptists are Christians who believe that only those who confess their faith in Christ should be baptized.*

brown, or gray, but some use white, and the Byler Amish of Pennsylvania have bright yellow ones. Other rules specify the permissible type of wheels, doors, and lighting, and whether or not it has a top and windshield. Lancaster Amish most often have gray-topped buggies. In Berne, Indiana, the Amish can not have a top on their buggies at all. They use heavy-duty umbrellas in bad weather. Buggies pulled by a single horse generally have room for about four adults. As with cars, buggies vary in price, ranging from $5,000 to $9,000 or more.

The Amish typically use Percherons and Belgians for farm work. For transportation, the most common breed is the Standardbred. They often buy harness-racing horses that weren't successful at the track but are plenty fast enough to pull a buggy. Some Amish teens have even been known to engage in a few buggy races.

Geldings are preferred, typically dark in color—bay, chestnut, or black. While the former racehorses have some training, they must adjust to pulling a buggy, which is larger and heavier than a racing sulky. They also need to get used to being driven in traffic. Other less-common buggy breeds are Saddlebreds, Morgans, and Dutch Harness Horses. Children may use a trustworthy pony and cart to travel to the local Amish school and back.

18

Equines in Modern War

With the introduction of tanks and machine guns in World War I (theoretically the war to end all wars), it became obvious that horses were no longer effective for modern warfare. However, millions were still used in World War II.

The Second World War started in Europe on September 1, 1939, but the United States did not become involved until December 7, 1941, after the Japanese attack on Pearl Harbor. The war continued until September 2, 1945.

In the late 1920s, the United States and England began mechanizing their fighting forces, replacing their cavalry units with motorized vehicles. During World War II, the last U.S. Army Cavalry charge occurred against the Japanese at Bataan in the Philippines on January 16, 1942. Lieutenant Ed Ramsey of the 26th Cavalry led the charge.

Ramsey received his military training at the Oklahoma Military Academy, where he also learned to play polo. Developing the skills for success at polo was considered helpful in preparing men for combat. Several of the cadets suffered broken bones during matches; two were killed. Ramsey's favorite polo pony, Bryn Awryn, accompanied him to the Philippines. The chestnut gelding stood 15.2 hands tall. Ramsey considered the horse clever, aggressive, and brave, and knew that he could turn on a dime.

With a force of only twenty-seven mounted men, most of whom were also polo players, Ramsey and Bryn Awryn led a successful charge and sent the larger Japanese force fleeing. Ramsey survived; however, due to lack of reinforcements, the horses and many of the other troops and civilians suffered a less favorable ending.

In contrast to the declining Army interest in horses, the demand for mules increased during the war. In 1943, the U.S. bought only four horses compared to

10,217 mules. Mules were preferred over horses because of their hardiness and sure-footedness. The animals were used primarily in the rugged mountains of Italy and the jungles of Burma, traveling over rough terrain where no roads existed.

> *It is an old cavalry axiom that a horse can go wherever a man can travel, and this is still not true of the tank, truck–or even the faithful jeep. This winter on the Russian front, horses have packed men, munitions, supplies and weapons over impossible and practically impassable terrain.*
>
> —*Stars and Stripes, March 26, 1944*

Surprisingly, the Coast Guard used the most U.S. horses during the war. Horses were used to patrol beaches on the East, West, and Gulf coasts, watching for enemy ships and submarines.

Although the number of equine deaths during the second world war was less than that of the first, it was still substantial.

- Civil War: one to three million
- World War I: eight million
- World War II: two to five million

Although the U.S. had shifted to motorized vehicles during WWII, Germany and the Soviet Union continued to rely heavily on horses. Together, they used over six million from 1939 to 1945. Germany had Panzer (armored tank) divisions, but they made up only twenty percent of the German military. Most of the Wehrmacht (Germany's armed forces), consisted of infantry (foot soldiers) and horses used to pull weapons and supplies.

Germany's reliance on horses was due to its low production of vehicles and limited access to both fuel and rubber for tires. It's estimated that at any time during the war,

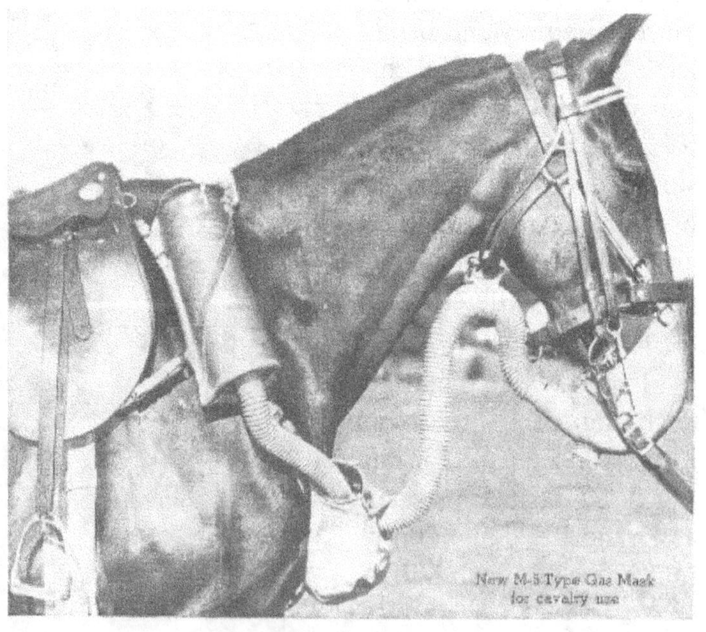

more than a million equines served in the German military. German farmers and horse breeders provided many of those animals—willingly or unwillingly. Other horses were confiscated from European countries occupied by Germany as the war progressed.

During Germany's bombing attacks on London (September 1940 to May 1941), the London Metropolitan Police force used horses to prevent looting, maintain order, and to help rescue victims.

On April 11, 1947, three police horses received the PDSA (People's Dispensary for Sick Animals) Dickin Medal. Although the following three horses were specifically honored, they represented the many police horses who served England during the war.

Olga was on duty when a bomb demolished four houses. A plate-glass window crashed in front of her. After bolting 100 yards, Olga returned to the scene of the incident and remained on duty with her rider, controlling traffic and assisting rescue operations.

While on patrol duty in Bethnal Green, a bomb exploded, showering both **Upstart** and his rider with broken glass and debris. Upstart was unperturbed and remained on duty, controlling traffic.

Regal twice found himself in stables set on fire by explosives. He received minor injuries and was covered by debris. Even when close to the flames, he did not panic.

Germany's invasion of Russia (Operation Barbarossa) from June to December 1941 was horrible for both men and horses. Although the Germans were initially successful, the Soviets stopped their advance with the help of a brutal winter in which temperatures reached forty degrees below zero.

> *Our poor horses are being pushed to the very limits and are suffering horribly. We can no longer offer them straw to lie on or hay to eat. They get ice-water to drink and have to nibble on small branches we gather from the forest. At night they have little shelter from the freezing cold, often having to lie with their bellies in the icy snow.*[1]

---

[1] *warfarehistorynetwork.com/article/horses-the-mechanized-myth-of-the-eastern-front*

As in other wars, many of the soldiers formed strong bonds with their horses. According to one German soldier:

In all the many months Siegfried has been my comrade, my protector; he has carried me out of trouble many times; he has listened for me and warned me of any danger. I had always relied upon him in a thousand and one situations. I had cried on his shoulder when I was in despair, and he had even made me laugh at some of his antics. He had never complained when I had nothing to give him, not even water. To me he had not been "just a horse," he had been my best friend, a friend in a thousand, full of warmth and understanding.[1]

[1] *warfarehistorynetwork.com/article/horses-the-mechanized-myth-of-the-eastern-front*

19

Sand Pounders

Operation Drumbeat, also known as The Second Happy Time (happy for the Germans, anyway), occurred in 1942 when German submarines (U-boats) attacked shipping and naval vessels along the east coast of the United States. During that time, the Germans sank hundreds of ships carrying oil and supplies for the Allied forces.

On June 13, 1942, the activity went beyond sinking ships. As Coast Guard seaman John Cullen walked along a deserted Long Island, New York beach, he encountered three men who claimed to be fishermen. However, a fourth man suddenly appeared, speaking to the others in German.

The men promised not to kill Cullen if he kept quiet. They released him, but Cullen did not keep quiet. He returned soon after with additional guardsmen. By then, the mysterious invaders were gone. The guardsmen discovered explosives that were left behind. It's believed the men had planned to attack factories that manufactured planes and other war products.

On the West Coast, the fear was an attack by the Japanese, who had bombed Pearl Harbor in 1941. The coastal fears prompted the formation of a Coast Guard Beach Patrol. The patrollers became known as "Sand Pounders." Initially, these were foot patrols; two men with rifles or sidearms and flare pistols. Each team patrolled two miles or less.

It was obvious horses could cover more territory. At first, beach patrol volunteers were required to provide their own mounts. That met with an overwhelmingly negative response, and the requirement of horse ownership was soon canceled.

Patrols were established on all three coasts. The Sand Pounders operated from 1942 to 1944. At a time when the Army was disbanding the Cavalry, the Coast Guard presented the largest demand for horses. In 1943, the Army Remount Centers supplied over 3,000 horses to the Coast Guard.

The Atlantic or East Coast patrols received horses from the Front Royal Remount Center in Virginia. Gulf Coast patrols received their equines from Fort Reno in Oklahoma. Fort Robinson in Nebraska provided horses for use on the Pacific or West Coast.

Applicants for the patrols included experienced horsemen, such as former cavalrymen, cowboys, rodeo riders, farmers, jockeys, horse trainers, and polo players. However, not every volunteer knew how to ride.

> *Many had never ridden anything but a hobby-horse. During training there were men so saddle sore they stood to eat their meals. Those horses from the U.S. Cavalry knew every trick in the book.[1]*

Tack was supplied by the Army. Other equipment, such as uniforms, radios, rifles, pistols, and flashlights were provided by the Coast Guard. Some Coast Guardsmen were trained in horseshoeing in Oklahoma, then sent to beach patrol stations where needed. The Coast Guard added dogs to the beach patrols to utilize their keen sense of smell and protective instincts. Canvas boots protected the dogs paws from rough shells.

---

[1] *Jack Hubbard, Cumberland County, recollection of training received at Hilton Head, SC*

Each district set up its patrol routes to deal with the complications of sand dunes, swamps, lengthy beaches, rocky cliffs, inlets, or rivers. Stabling for the horses and barracks for the men were built near existing Coast Guard stations or lighthouses. Lookout towers were often added.

At its peak, the patrols had about 24,000 men aged seventeen to seventy-three. The men worked in pairs, two to four hours per shift. The watches patrolled daily, regardless of weather. Thirty-five pound "portable" radios were considered state of the art communications equipment at the time. One rider in the pair carried the radio in a pack on his back. Beach patrols were not fighting units. Their duties were to watch for and report offshore enemy vessels and to prevent people on land from communicating with the enemy at sea.

Horses add an element of unpredictability to any endeavor. Undoubtedly, many mishaps occurred during the beach patrols. Once, a noisy Southern Pacific train engine passed by, startling a patrol horse. He threw his rider, along with the heavy radio, and galloped away into the night.

Another unfortunate incident was caused by a smaller creature—the mosquito. A North Carolina patrol rider fainted in the heat because of the extra clothing he'd worn to protect himself from the swarming insects. When his horse returned to the station without him, another guardsman searched for and found the man, unconscious. The rescuer, who had not worn protective gear, was attacked by mosquitoes and later came down with malaria.

As the tide of the war turned in favor of the Allies, and sonar became more effective at detecting U-boat activity, the need for the beach patrols decreased. The mounted patrols were disbanded on February 18, 1944. Some horses were returned to the Army, while others were sold at public auctions.

In Tillamook, Oregon, forty-nine patrol horses sold for an average of $117 each. The Coast Guard kept many of the dogs to use for sentry duty. Jarman *(right)*, who served on a beach patrol in California, was the last surviving equine Sand Pounder. He passed away at the ripe old age of forty in 1974.

It's impossible to say what the presence of the beach patrols prevented from happening. However, they were considered a success in that they calmed those who feared a coastal attack or infiltration. The Coast Guard has not used mounted patrols since World War II.

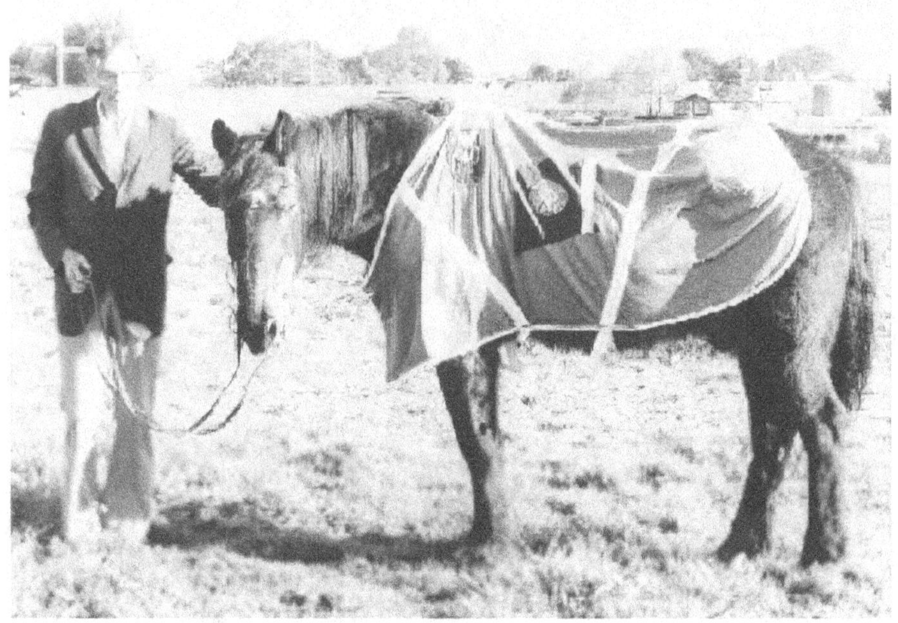

20

Heroic Mules

The hardy mules used as pack animals in the jungles of Asia and the mountains of Italy were loved by the soldiers who used and cared for them. Mules easily traversed the narrow, twisting trails that led to remote areas where much of the fighting occurred. They were also used to evacuate wounded personnel.

The Chindits (Burmese for lion) were a British special force, led by Colonel Orde Wingate. They fought the Japanese in several campaigns in Burma in 1943 and 1944. Thousands of mules transported weapons and supplies through areas the Japanese considered impenetrable. The hard-working mules were recognized as the heroes of the Chindit campaigns.

The Indian army supplied the first mules. Since the Indian animals were small, later operations imported larger, stronger mules from Argentina, South Africa, and the United States.

Someone decided the expedition would be safer if the mules were unable to make their distinctive mulish bray. The noise might give away the force's location. The animals were to be "de-voiced" or "de-brayed" before being transported to the war zone. Dr. A. J. Moffett, a British ear, nose, and throat surgeon, was asked to develop a technique for this.

A mule makes a loud braying noise that can be heard for two or three miles. The First Chindit Force—at that time a very hush hush operation—led by Colonel Orde Wingate used mules for transport. This braying of the mules alerted the

By experimenting on the larynx of a dead mule, Dr. Moffett established a procedure for cutting the vocal cords, so the animal could no longer make any sound at all. Then, he demonstrated the process to a veterinarian on three live mules.

Other veterinarians in the Royal Army Veterinary Corps continued to practice the de-voicing, with as many as two thousand mules being subjected to it. The first mules were given a general anesthetic and laid on their sides. Later veterinarians may have simply used a local anesthetic while the mules remained standing.

Although the de-voicing procedure helped conceal their location, Francis Turner believed there were undesirable consequences of the procedure. Turner was one of the men who transported the mules for the expedition. He believed the de-voicing "messed up" the mules, since they could no longer communicate with each other.

According to Turner, one of those effects was "a mule having to see before he would go as opposed to being able to talk before he went."

An example he cited was crossing a wide river. If the mules could have called to their companions who had already crossed, their communication would have encouraged them to keep swimming. But because they had no voice, the mules kept turning their heads back. Seeing other mules behind them on the shore, they fought to return, making river crossings a challenge.

____

[1] *pmc.ncbi.nlm.nih.gov/articles/PMC1550202/pdf/bmjcred00586-0046.pdf*

Pilots flew mules into Burma to support the Chindits and into other areas during the war. American WACO gliders[1] transported both horses and mules. Three mules were loaded into each glider. A soldier aboard the aircraft was instructed to shoot any mule that became violent before it could destroy the glider. The trip usually went smoothly, except for the quantity of manure produced by the nervous animals.

Even more amazing than mules flying in gliders were the mule paratroopers. During the Chindit's Operation, 1,300 mules were parachuted into Burma. An unsuccessful attempt was made by the US Army in 1942 to parachute mules. A dozen were taken up in an airplane. Six mules were pushed out the door, suspended in slings attached to parachutes. None of the six survived. The remaining mules, who wisely refused to budge, all lived.

Major Douglas Witherington and Lieutenant Colonel Ken Barlow, of the Royal Army Veterinary Corps, devised a safer way to parachute the animals. A sedated mule was secured by broad webbing straps in a partially inflated pontoon boat with additional padding placed around the animal.[2] The plane contained a specially designed track to ensure a smooth launch of the mule from a height of 600 feet. Each mule capsule was connected to six parachutes. After landing, the straps holding each mule

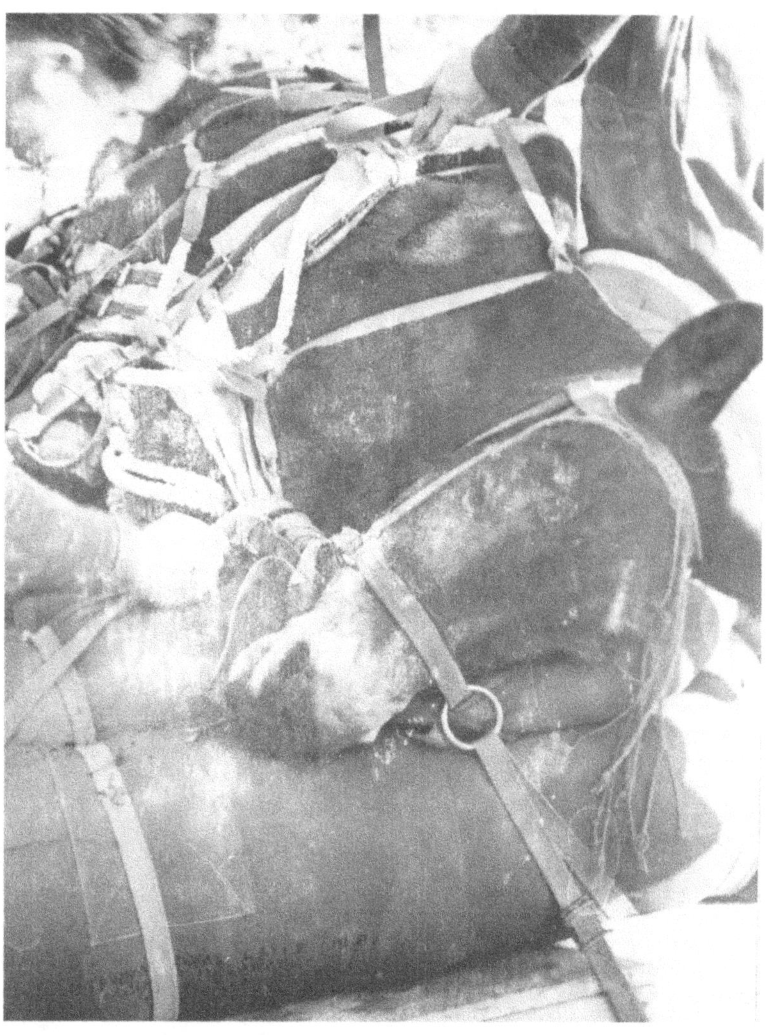

[1] *The military gliders had no engines and used no fuel. They were launched by being towed by a powered aircraft. The gliders were silent and able to fly low to avoid radar detection. They could land in tighter places than a typical aircraft.*

[2] *The mule to the right is NOT dead! He has landed and will soon recover from the sedation.*

were released. The sweaty mules showed signs of stiffness, but they recovered quickly and were soon able to assume their duties as pack animals.

Although considered heroes, only two mules were known to have made it back from the Chindit campaigns. Mabel and Yankee returned to India in 1943. Yankee had carried a wireless communication set for over 1,500 miles. Most of the mules who didn't die from exhaustion or disease were released to fend for themselves in the jungle. Lt. Dominic Neill, an Animal Transport Officer, recalled:

> *Our mules had become personalities and friends to my muleteers and we all suffered with them, as only a master can for his animal. One should not have favourites I suppose, but I did have one such mule; she was No. 850. She was a beautiful pale dun coloured, country-bred animal and larger than most of the Indian mules. I called her 'Blondie' and she carried the bedding for Column HQ and was led by Rifleman Harkabahadur Rai. She faired better than most during the operation, but in the end, just as we were about to re-cross the Irrawaddy we were ordered to let our mules and chargers go and drive them away from our ranks. This moment broke all of our hearts.[1]*

Despite suffering heavy losses, the Chindit campaigns were considered successful in their audacity to invade enemy territory and for disrupting Japanese communications and rail lines. The Chindits were disbanded in 1945.

---

[1] *chinditslongcloth1943.com/chindits-with-four-legs.html*

21

Chindit Minnie

Although most of the pack animals used during the Chindit special forces campaigns in Burma were mules, some horses were used. The native "horses" were small enough to be considered ponies. At White City, the Chindit's base camp in Burma, a pregnant pony mare[1] was inadvertently included with a group of pack animals.

The Lancashire Fusiliers, a unit in the Chindit force, controlled White City. One day, during a fierce Japanese attack, with mortar bombs exploding around them, the unnamed pony gave birth. The foal's arrival was a complete surprise to the brigade as no one had been aware of the mare's condition.

Surrounded by death and destruction, the men never knew whether they would live to see another day. They were captivated by this surprise gift of new life. During the bombing, Sergeant Lee saw to it that the mare and foal were protected. The men named her Minnie and stopped to visit her whenever they had a chance. The filly grew to love sugar and enjoyed drinking tea from a pot.

Having been born during a battle, Minnie had little fear of gunfire and bombs. However, one day an artillery shell landed in the pen where she and the other pack animals were kept. The explosion killed several mules. In the resulting panic, a mule kicked Minnie in the head. The filly suffered a deep gash above her right eye and was knocked unconscious.

The men feared Minnie would lose her sight if not her life. Periodic updates on her status were relayed throughout the camp. Sergeant Lee spent hours caring for the foal, and she fully recovered from the injury.

---

[1] *likely a Burmese Hill Pony, it's unclear what became of the mare*

When orders were received to evacuate White City in 1944, brigade members worried about their filly. Minnie was too small and fragile to travel far on foot. She had become a symbol of hope and survival to the soldiers. They refused to abandon her in the jungle.

The men arranged for a plane to transport Minnie, but first they had to attack a nearby runway to clear it of enemy forces. Then, the plane swooped in to pick up the filly, delivering her to the British base Dehra Dun in India. A few months later, Minnie was reunited with the returning soldiers. At Dehra Dun, she resumed her enjoyment of treats, sometimes even eating the tablecloths.

In 1947, Minnie traveled to England aboard the troopship, Georgic, dining on Spam and condensed milk during the voyage. Minnie became the official mascot of the Lancashire Fusiliers, leading the battalion in ceremonies and parades.

When her battalion left for service in the Middle East, Minnie went with them. She became ill and died of pneumonia in Egypt in 1951 at the young age of seven.

Minnie was buried at the military camp in Egypt. Two of her hooves were made into an inkwell and a paperweight and are on display at the Fusilier Museum in Manchester, England[1].

---

[1] *fusiliermuseum.com*

22

Kellogg Ranch

Kellogg is a familiar name to those who enjoy cereal. William Keith Kellogg (W.K.) and his brother John Harvey began selling Corn Flakes in 1906. W.K. was a lifelong horse lover. As a child, he owned a half-Arabian horse called "Old Spot" and grew to love the Arabian breed. In 1925, at sixty-five, W.K. constructed the Kellogg Ranch in Pomona, California, purchasing horses to stock it from the famous Crabbet Arabian Stud in England.

Eager to share his love of the breed, W.K. held shows each Sunday in the ranch courtyard to publicly display his Arabians. At the events, he handed out postcards depicting the horses as well as sharing samples of his breakfast cereals.

Some of his horses were used in Hollywood movies. The Kellogg Ranch became a popular destination for 1920s movie stars. Actor Rudolph Valentino borrowed the gray Kellogg stallion, Jadaan, for his 1926 movie, *Son of the Sheik*. A Kellogg employee, Carl Raswan, rode in some scenes as Valentino's stunt double.

As W.K. aged, he wanted to preserve the legacy of his farm and horses. In 1932, he donated the 750-acre ranch and eighty-seven of his Arabians to the University of California with the stipulation

that the property could only be used as long as the Arabian horse program remained, with a minimum of seventy-five horses. The school's College of Agriculture operated the farm for a decade.

In 1943, to support the United States in World War II, Kellogg convinced the University to turn the ranch over to the Army Remount Service. It became known as the Pomona Quartermaster Depot with Colonel F. W. Koester as its commanding officer.

Near the end of the war, American soldiers rescued twenty-one Polish Arabians, including the stallion Witez II. The horses were brought to the Pomona Depot in 1946, as well as seven part-Arabians, eight Lipizzaners, and one Anglo-Arab.

In 1947, the Army abandoned its horse-breeding program. The Pomona Depot was transferred to the Department of Agriculture, but it lacked the funds to continue the operation. They planned to sell the Kellogg Ranch and all the horses in 1948. News of the sale distressed the public as well as eighty-eight-year-old W.K. Kellogg. Arrangements were made for the ranch and its horses to become part of the California Polytechnic College in San Luis Obispo.

In 1974, the horses moved to a new facility, the W.K. Kellogg Arabian Horse Center, which is home to the Kellogg Arabians today. The facility has room for 150 horses and includes thirty-eight acres of pasture, three barns, a veterinary clinic, a farrier shop, four arenas, and covered grandstands for shows and exhibitions.

In 2000, the University began offering a bachelor's degree in animal science with an equine industry option. The Arabian breeding program has continued, as well as the shows, which present the horses to the public on the first Sunday of each month, from October through May.

Rudolph Valentino on Jadaan

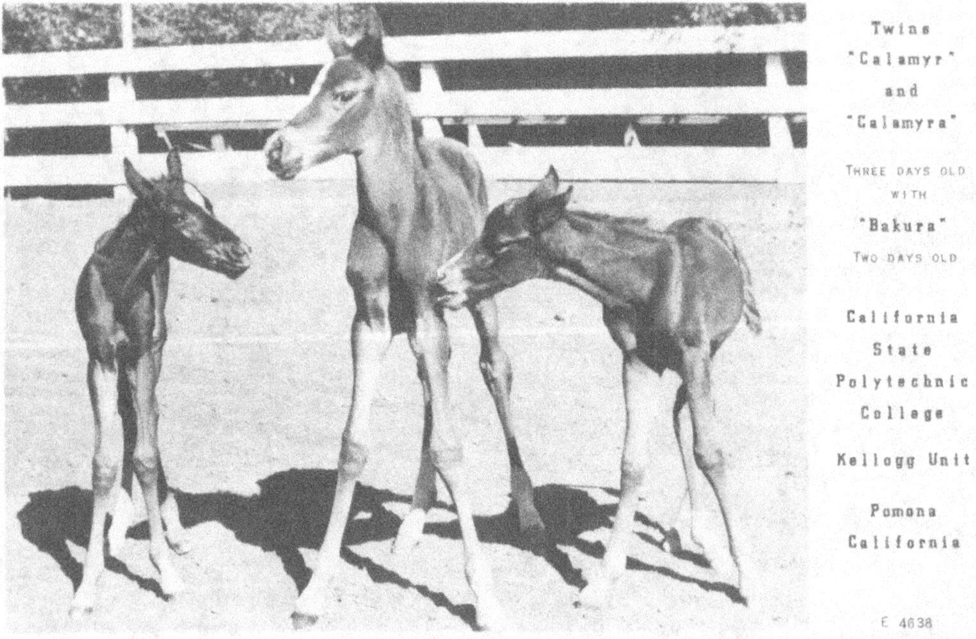

23

Operation Cowboy

In the middle of the deadliest war in history, a few dedicated horsemen did their best to protect the horses in their care. Janow Podlaski, Poland's most famous Arabian horse farm, lies near the eastern border of the country. The farm was home to Arabians such as the stallion Ofir and his sons Witez II, Witraz, and Wielki Szjlam.

In September 1939, Germany invaded Poland from the west, and Russia attacked from the east. Russia briefly occupied Janow Podlaski; however, they abandoned the farm in early October, taking most of the horses with them. When it came to their horses, the Poles feared the Russians more than the Germans. The Soviets were known to kill the animals for meat or force them into hard labor.

Gustav Rau, a German, temporarily managed Janow Podlaski following the Soviet withdrawal. Rau was an internationally known equestrian whose goal was to breed the perfect horse for Germany—for war, work, and sport. In addition to the Polish Arabians, Rau added Thoroughbreds and Lipizzaners to his stock.

Over the war years, the Germans confiscated Lipizzaners from Poland, Yugoslavia, Italy, and Austria and sent them to a farm in Hostau, Czechoslovakia. In 1942, the Lipizzaner mares from the Spanish Riding School in Vienna were also moved to Hostau for safekeeping.

Alois Podhajsky, director of the Riding School, wanted to keep his remaining horses safe from Allied bombs, which came ever closer to the school. In January 1945, he evacuated the Lipizzaner stallions from the school to St. Martin, Austria.

As U.S. General George Patton led his troops through Austria, he learned the Lipizzaner stallions were at St. Martin. Patton was a horse lover and an accomplished

steeplechase racer and polo player. Podhajsky arranged a special exhibition for the general and his men.

Podhajsky rode the stallion Neapolitano Africa during the performance. The Neapolitano bloodline was foundational to the Lipizzaner breed, dating back to 1790. Patton, impressed by the performance, placed the Spanish Riding School[1] and its horses under U.S. protection.

As the war neared its end, Allied forces approached Hostau

from the west while the Soviet or Red Army moved toward the farm from the east. Lieutenant Colonel Hubert Rudofsky, a German, was in charge of the farm. Although loyal to Hitler, the horses were his top priority. If the Russians arrived first, Rudofsky feared they would kill both the Hostau horses and the POWs housed there. For that reason, the German colonel surrendered the farm to the Americans.

U.S. Major Robert P. Andrews commanded the task force that arrived at Hostau. Once Andrews secured the farm, he had to figure out how to safely evacuate the horses. The animals outnumbered his men, and many of the hundreds of mares were pregnant or had young foals.

With the help of the Allied POWs, Russian Cossacks (who opposed Stalin), and even some German soldiers, Andrews defended Hostau against two Nazi attacks. On May 15, 1945, the Nazis retreated and "Operation Cowboy" began. The equine caravan's destination was thirty-five miles across the Czech border into Kotzting, Germany.

Soldiers rode some of the horses. They divided the rest into three groups and herded them. Military trucks, hastily modified to include loading ramps, transported the pregnant mares and those with young foals. Horse tack was packed into Jeeps and tanks. The horses rescued from Hostau included Lipizzaners, Arabians, Thoroughbreds, and Russian Kabarda and Dons.[2]

---

[1] *The Spanish Riding School, dating back to 1565, is located in Vienna, Austria. It was named for the heritage of its horses, from the Spanish Andalusians.*

[2] *The number of horses rescued varies widely between accounts. One listed the horses rescued from Hostau as 247 Lipizzaners, 64 Arabians, 144 Kabarda, 75 Don, and 59 Panje (a Polish breed). Other accounts say 375 Lipizzaners. It's unclear how many were Thoroughbreds.*

Alois Podhajsky met the Americans at Kotzting and sorted out which Lipizzaners belonged to the Spanish Riding School. Podhajsky set up temporary quarters for his horses at Reichersberg Airfield, converting the airplane hangars into stables. The Lipizzaner mares and foals returned to Piber, Austria in 1952, and in 1955, the stallions returned to the Spanish Riding School.

Hubert Rudofsky, the German commander of Hostau, spent eighteen months in a resettlement camp after the war. The authorities never charged him with any crime, and later he worked on an Arabian farm. It wasn't until 1986 that Rudofsky was recognized by the Spanish Riding School for his role in saving the Lipizzaner horses.

Gustav Rau remained an influential equestrian in Germany until his death in 1954. A street in Munich is named after him—Gustav Rau Strasse. The Rau Medal is the highest equestrian honor in Germany.

After Podhajsky recovered his Lipizzaners, the remaining Hostau horses were taken to Mansbach. General Patton visited there and selected 150 animals to be shipped to the United States as war prizes. The bay Arabian Witez II, the gray Arabian Lotnik, and others arrived at Newport News, Virginia, in late 1945. The horses spent the winter at the Front Royal Virginia Remount Station.

In early 1946, Witez and most of the Arabians were sent to the Army Remount at the Kellogg Ranch in Pomona, California. Many of the horses were sold at auction when the Remount service was disbanded. Witez remained at the Kellogg Ranch until 1948.

Earle and Frances Hurlbutt, of Calabasas, California, purchased Witez for $8,100 in 1949. The couple owned the stallion for the rest of his life. Witez was the 1951 Grand Champion at the All-Arabian show in Pomona, California. He sired 223 foals. The Arabian passed away in his sleep at the Hurlbutt Ranch in June 1965 at twenty-seven.

Lotnik was also auctioned. He eventually ended up on a ranch where he became a working horse for a time. In the 1960s, he lived at the Scottsdale Arabian Ranch, where he sired twenty-seven foals.

On December 9, 1945, General Patton was in an automobile accident in Germany. He died on December 21.

General Patton's wife died on September 30, 1953, after falling while riding her horse in a hunt in Massachusetts.

24

Striding Horses

Two of the most famous German horses during Hitler's reign weren't alive. Hitler commissioned sculptor Josef Thorak to create bronze statues of two larger-than-life stallions. Each statue was sixteen feet tall, thirty-three feet long, and weighed two tons. In 1939, they transported the Schreitende Pferde (Striding Horses) to the New Reich Chancellery in Berlin. The two stood guard at each side of the entrance to Hitler's headquarters.

When Berlin experienced repeated bombing raids in 1943, officials moved the statues outside the city for safekeeping. In the war's aftermath, many assumed the statues had been destroyed by Allied or Russian attacks.

The area of East Berlin where they were last seen became part of the communist German Democratic Republic (GDR), separated from the west by the Berlin Wall.

In reality, the two horses had survived the war and spent many years on an athletic field at a Soviet military base. In 1988, art historian Magdalena Busshart discovered the horses there and recognized them as Thorak's work. The following year, she published an article about the statues in a Frankfurt newspaper. A few weeks after her article was printed, the horses disappeared. It would be more than twenty-five years before they resurfaced.

In 2014, Arthur Brand, a Dutch art crime investigator, received a tip from someone who claimed to have seen the statues. Brand thought that whatever the person had seen must have been forgeries.

He believed the Russians had destroyed the horses during the capture of Berlin in 1945.

But back in 1989, Rainer Wolf of Bad Dürkheim, learned about the statues from Busshart's article. He made arrangements with Soviet authorities to purchase the bronze horses. Wolf smuggled them out of East Germany in pieces, disguised as scrap metal. He stored the statues for many years and in 2015, attempted to sell them for millions on the black market.

With investigator Brand's help, Berlin police found the statues in Wolf's warehouse. Although Wolf insisted he had legally purchased them, the German government claimed ownership.

In 2021, after a long legal battle, the Striding Horses officially became the property of the German government. They were restored and displayed at the Spandau Citadel. The public display of the horses has been controversial. Not all Germans believed Nazi art should be given such an honor.

25

King Ranch Thoroughbreds

The King Ranch in Texas is well known for raising Quarter Horses. However, in the 1930s, owner Robert Kleberg Jr. developed an interest in Thoroughbred horse racing. Although Kentucky was the home of most racehorses, Kleberg believed the rugged Texas environment would produce a tougher horse.

That proved true for two King Ranch Thoroughbreds—Stymie and Assault. Stymie, a chestnut great-grandson of Man o' War, was born on the King Ranch on April 4, 1941. King Ranch trainer Max Hirsch found it difficult to work with Stymie because of the colt's difficult disposition. On June 2, 1943, another trainer Hirsch Jacobs purchased Stymie in a claiming race for $1,500. At two and three, Stymie won just seven times in fifty-seven races.

On January 3, 1945, the federal government banned horse racing; however, it wasn't an official law. About two-thirds of the tracks cooperated with the request. This gave Stymie a needed rest. When racing picked back up that June, Stymie was like a new horse. He won again and again and became one of the top racehorses in the country.

In the Manhattan Handicap, on September 25, 1946, Stymie beat fellow King Ranch Thoroughbred, Assault (the Triple Crown winner). Assault finished third. This was the beginning of a rivalry between the two Texas Thoroughbreds.

Stymie raced into his eighth year, but in 1949, his career came to an abrupt end when he suffered a fractured sesamoid bone in his right foreleg in the Monmouth Handicap.

Out of 131 starts, Stymie won thirty-five times with career winnings of $918,485, making him the richest racehorse in the United States at the time.

Stymie died in 1962. He was inducted into the National Museum of Racing and Hall of Fame in 1975. Blood-Horse magazine ranked him #41 in their list of the Top 100 U.S. Thoroughbreds of the 20th Century.

Stymie's rival Assault had a similar background on the Texas ranch. In 1939, Robert Kleberg bought Bold Venture, winner of the 1936 Kentucky Derby and Preakness Stakes, for $40,000. Assault was one of Bold Venture's sons, foaled at the King Ranch

Stymie sketch by C.W. Anderson

on March 26, 1943. As a weanling, Assault stepped on a surveyor's stake, running it through the wall of his right front hoof. The injury was so serious, Kleberg considered euthanizing the colt.

Fortunately, a veterinarian decided to wait and see whether Assault would recover. He did, but his foot remained slightly misshapen. For the rest of his life, Assault walked with a limp that miraculously disappeared when he ran, earning him the nickname, the "Club-footed Comet."

Kleberg hired Max Hirsch, who had trained Bold Venture, to train Assault as well. Bill Hirsch, grandson of Max, said of the horse. "Assault was never meant to be a racehorse, you know he was more of an ugly duckling kind of horse than a real grand-looking horse."

Assault's exercise riders learned to pay attention. If the horse caught them daydreaming, he would leap sideways, sending them airborne, then he galloped around the track riderless. As a two-year-old in 1945, Assault's racing career got off to a disappointing start with a twelfth-place finish. He won twice that year in nine races. The following year is when Assault began to shine.

With jockey Warren Mehrtens aboard, he won the 1946 Kentucky Derby by a record-breaking eight lengths. A week later, he won the Preakness Stakes by a neck. Surprisingly, after those two victories, racing experts did not consider Assault the favorite for the Belmont Stakes. That honor went to a flashier horse, Lord Boswell, even though Assault had beaten him in both the Derby and the Preakness.

Assault stumbled at the start, then came from behind to win the Belmont by three lengths. The media favorite, Lord Boswell, finished fifth. Assault was one of the few Kentucky Derby winners not

born in Kentucky. He was the seventh Triple Crown winner and the first one born outside of Kentucky.

Assault's critics maintained he was only the best of a mediocre crop of 1943 colts, pointing out that the times in his winning races were nothing special. However, the horse's accomplishments were amazing considering that in addition to his injured hoof, Assault suffered from kidney, splint bone, ankle, knee, and bleeding problems.

Over his career, Assault raced forty-three times, finishing with eighteen firsts, six seconds, and eight thirds. His earnings of $675,470 made him one of the leading money earners of his time. Assault was inducted into the Racing Hall of Fame in 1964. He was ranked #33 on Blood-Horse magazine's ranking of the Top 100 Thoroughbred Racehorses of the 20th century. He died on September 2, 1971 at twenty-eight and is buried at the King Ranch.

26

Island Ponies

When children's author Margeurite Henry heard about a pony roundup and swim in Virginia, she visited Chincoteague Island in 1946 to experience the pony penning event for herself. While there, she met the Beebe family. The pony stars of the resulting book—Phantom, Misty, and the Pied Piper—were all real, but none of those ponies were wild. They were all owned by Clarence "Grandpa" Beebe.

On her visit, Mrs. Henry fell in love with the palomino pinto foal, Misty. She wanted to buy her to serve as the model for the main character in her book. Grandpa Beebe refused at first, but he finally agreed to sell her for $150, if Mrs. Henry would include his grandchildren, Paul and Maureen, in her story.

When Misty was weaned in November 1946, Grandpa Beebe shipped the filly from Chincoteague to Mrs. Henry's home, Mole Meadow, in Wayne, Illinois. By then, Misty had grown such a thick woolly coat, Mrs. Henry hardly recognized her. Her beautiful markings had disappeared. She wondered if Grandpa Beebe had sent the wrong foal.

Misty remained with Mrs. Henry for ten years, then she was sent back to the Beebe Farm in 1957 to raise several foals.

Mrs. Henry's book, *Misty of Chincoteague*, received the Newbery Honor award in 1948. She wrote three additional books in the Misty series—*Sea Star: Orphan of Chincoteague* (1949), *Stormy, Misty's Foal* (1963), and *Misty's Twilight* (1992).

The Chincoteague Pony has been an official registered breed since 1994. They average 12 to 13 hands tall. The ponies are called Chincoteague Ponies, although no "wild" ponies live on Chincoteague. The ponies live year-round on Assateague Island.[1]

Chincoteague Island and the southern part of Assateague are in Virginia. The northern part of Assateague Island is in Maryland. Maryland's herd is

---

[1] *None of the ponies are "wild." So-called wild horses are technically feral. Although they live in the wild, they are descended from domesticated animals.*

92

the smaller of the two, generally less than a hundred ponies. The National Park Service manages that herd. Virginia tries to maintain 150 adult ponies in its herd. The Maryland and Virginia ponies are separated by a fence at the state line. While people recognize such boundaries, ponies do not. Some Maryland-side ponies crossed over the line so repeatedly that they were donated to the Chincoteague herd. The ponies divide themselves into groups of two to twelve, called bands, each with its own territory.

Marguerite Henry brought attention to the pony roundup, but the event goes much further back—to the 1700s, when rounding up the feral ponies was a one-day, annual event on Assateague Island. It wasn't until 1925 that the ponies swam across the channel from Assateague to Chincoteague for the first official Pony Penning Day. Some of the ponies were auctioned to raise

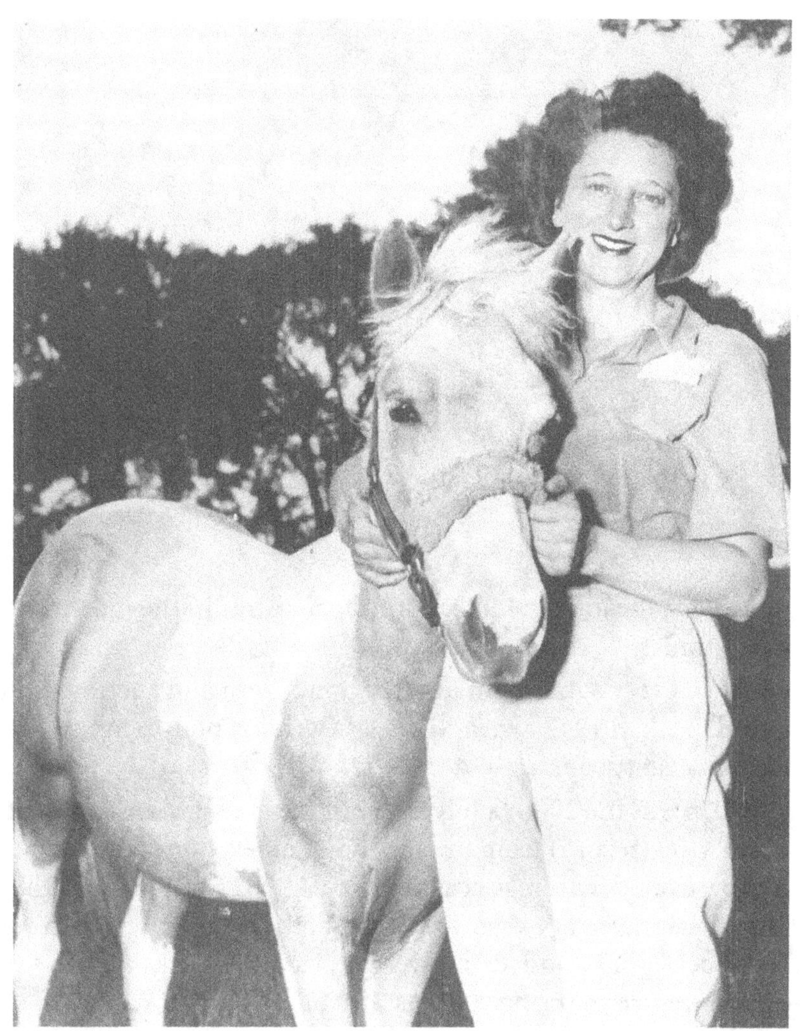

money for the local volunteer fire department. In the modern event, foals are auctioned rather than adult ponies.

Held every summer in July, the pony swim and auction draw 50,000 or more people to the small island. Back in 1947, when Misty was written, pony penning was completed in a couple of days. The current event spans a week.

2025 was the 100th anniversary of the pony swim. That year's auction set multiple records, raising $1,008,100 (record) from the auction of ninety-four foals at an average price of $10,724 (record). In comparison, the average cost of a pony in 2024 was $6,223. The prices may drop back to that level after the anniversary year. The highest buyback pony in 2025 was sold for $100,000 (another record). "Buyback" ponies inflate the average price. Buybacks are foals purchased by a group who are donated back to return to the herd on Assateague.

27

Additional Equine Stars

Old Westerns weren't the only films to utilize equine actors. Modern movies and television shows continue to feature equine stars.

The original *My Friend Flicka*, starring Roddy McDowell as young Ken McLaughlin, was filmed in 1943. A seven-month-old chestnut American Saddlebred filly, Country Delight, played Flicka. When she became entangled in barbed wire, the movie version used rubber bands with cork barbs to prevent injury. The sequel, *Thunderhead, Son of Flicka*, was made in 1945 with *Green Grass of Wyoming* following in 1948. Thunderhead was Flicka's white colt. Thirty-nine episodes of the *My Friend Flicka* TV series ran from 1955 to 1960. In the series, Flicka was a chestnut Arabian mare, Wahana.

1944 saw the release of the movie *National Velvet*, starring twelve-year-old Elizabeth Taylor as Velvet Brown. In the book of the same name, Velvet rides a horse called The Pie (for his piebald—black and white coloring). Inexplicably, in the movie version, the horse chosen to play the Pie, King Charles, was a seven-year-old chestnut with a blaze and four white stockings. Said to be a grandson of Man o' War, King Charles was born in 1937. The aggressive horse often tried to bite the movie's crew members. He would listen only to Elizabeth.

Although she had a stunt double, Taylor rode the horse in much of the movie. While filming one of the steeplechase scenes, she fell from King Charles, suffering injuries that led to lifelong back problems.

When filming of *National Velvet* was complete, Taylor received King Charles for her thirteenth birthday. Despite her fall, she loved the horse and kept him until he died twelve years later.

Fury was a popular television series, running from 1955 to 1960. Highland Dale, a Saddlebred stallion played

Fury. Broken Wheel Ranch owner Jim Newton adopted a city orphan named Joey, the only one Fury permitted to ride him. The horse often saved the day when anyone got into trouble on the ranch. The series was one of the few live-action shows that ran on Saturday mornings. In the introduction, the stallion raced inside the corral as the announcer read, "Fury! The story of a horse—and a boy who loves him."

Highland Dale also starred in the movies *Gypsy Colt* (1954), *Outlaw Stallion* (1955) and *Giant* (1956). The horse lived to be twenty-nine.

The television series *Bonanza* ran from 1959 to 1973. Each of the Cartwrights of the Ponderosa Ranch had his own horse. The father, Ben, rode Buck, a gentle buckskin. Lorne Greene (Ben) purchased Buck after the series ended and donated him to a therapeutic riding center. It's said that Buck lived to the unbelievable age of forty-five.

The oldest son, Adam, had Scout,[1] a chestnut Thoroughbred. Hoss's horse was Chub, a dark bay

Quarter Horse-Thoroughbred cross who weighed 1,250 pounds. The big horse carried the 6' 4" actor Dan Blocker, who weighed 300 pounds.

The youngest son, Little Joe, rode Cochise (real name Tomahawk), a black-and-white Paint. In 1964, someone broke into Fat Jones Stable in Hollywood, where the *Bonanza* horses were stabled. The intruder attacked Cochise with a knife and injured six other horses. Cochise and one of the other horses died. Although a reward was offered for information leading to his capture, the attacker was never found. Little Joe rode several other Paints with similar markings for the rest of the series.

Misty of Chincoteague (1961) was filmed on location in Chincoteague, Virginia. The main equine character from the book, Misty, was fourteen at the time—too old to play herself; however, she appeared as an extra in a few scenes. Three ponies played Misty at various ages—foal, weanling, and yearling. A dark brown foal, Emma, played the youngest Misty. The filly's coat had to be bleached to look like the palomino Misty.

---

[1] *Some sources list Adam Cartwright's horse as Sport.*

Actual Chincoteague ponies played the Phantom, the Pied Piper, Patches, the Black Comet, and others. Burton's Ranch provided most of the extra ponies.

Mr. Ed, the television series about a talking horse, ran from 1961 to 1966. The idea for the show came from short stories about a talking horse by Walter Brooks (author of the *Freddy the Pig* series of books). In the show, Ed, a palomino, only talked to one person, Wilbur Post.

Bamboo Harvester, previously a show and parade horse, played Ed. The gelding's sire was The Harvester, a Saddlebred. His dam, Zetna, was a half-Arabian.

To train Ed to "talk," the trainer ran a fine nylon filament down his halter and under his top lip. Tugging on the line made Ed wiggle his upper lip. The trainer held a crop against Ed's foreleg as the signal to stop talking. According to Alan Young (Wilbur Post), after the first season, the nylon

filament was no longer needed. Every time Wilbur stopped talking, Ed began moving his lips. They could hardly keep the horse from "talking!"

Alan Young stated Bamboo Harvester (1949–1970) died when he was given a tranquilizer by a caretaker who saw the horse having difficulty getting up onto his feet. The man mistakenly believed Harvester was having a seizure.

Mr. Ed's double was Pumpkin, a Quarter horse. You can tell when Pumpkin appeared in place of Bamboo Harvester because the double had a palomino-colored spot above his right eye, inside his blaze. Pumpkin appeared on *Green Acres* as Fred the talking horse. Pumpkin passed away in 1979.

Cass Ole was an Arabian stallion from Texas who played the title role in *The Black Stallion* (1979). Previously, he was a show horse, winning over fifty championships in his seven-year show career. After a nationwide search, Cass was selected for the film. His owners insisted Cass not be used in the running or swimming scenes or other stunts.

Fae Jur, an Arabian stallion from California, appeared in the shipwreck and beach scenes as well as when the Black defends Alec by stomping on a cobra. Junior and Star were additional horses used for the stunt scenes.

None of those horses liked to swim, so French Camargue horses were brought in for the underwater scenes. The horses live in the marshy areas of southern

France and are accustomed to water. Since Camargue horses are always gray, they had to be dyed black.

Cass' white star and socks were also dyed black for filming. They wove a wig into his mane to make it appear longer and fuller. He learned many new tricks for the role, including pinning his ears to show anger, rearing, stomping, nodding, and giving kisses. Cass returned to star in the sequel, *The Black Stallion Returns*. The Egyptian racehorse El Mokhtar appears with Cass in the sequel. Cass also appeared at President Ronald Reagan's inauguration. Cass Ole suffered a severe case of colic in 1993 and had to be euthanized.

Black Beauty, the 1877 Anna Sewell novel, has had at least six movie versions, the first in 1917. Many consider the 1994 Warner Brothers version the best.

A six-year-old Quarter Horse, Docs Keepin Time, was the primary equine actor. Doc was from a line of racing Quarter Horses. Four other horses had limited time as Beauty for specialized scenes such as in harness. Although Beauty was a male, the foal playing the newborn Black Beauty was a filly.

Doc was coated with a fire retardant gel to protect him from the flames in the movie's barn fire scene. Docs Keepin Time also played the part of the black stallion in the television series *The Adventures of the Black Stallion*, which ran from 1990 to 1993. In 1998, Doc played the role of Gulliver, the horse killed early in *The Horse Whisperer*.

Black Beauty's friend, the mare, Ginger, was played by a Quarter Horse gelding named Hightower. Hightower played Pilgrim in *The Horse Whisperer*.

A dapple gray Shetland/Welsh pony played Merrylegs. After filming, the pony was kept by the director Caroline Thompson and continued to be called Merrylegs.

The 2003 film *Seabiscuit* covers the life of the small Thoroughbred racehorse who became an unlikely champion and a symbol of hope during the Great Depression. A Thoroughbred gelding from Kentucky, Fighting Furrari, was cast as the equine star. For some of the race closeups, a custom Equicizer (mechanical horse) was used. Nine real horses served as Seabiscuit doubles—one was a

Quarter Horse, Triple Digit Cash (known as Biscuit), the rest were Thoroughbreds. Popcorn Deelites was a Thoroughbred used for race scenes. Gravy played the rearing, angry Seabiscuit. Muffin was the lazy Seabiscuit who liked to lie in his stall.

Jockey Chris McCarron served as a consultant on the film to keep the race scenes accurate. He was also cast as War Admiral's jockey in the match race against Seabiscuit. War Admiral, played by a black gelding Cobra Flight, was supposed to lose to Seabiscuit; however, McCarron couldn't hold him back. In early filming, he won instead. They replaced Cobra Flight with a more laid-back horse, Made to Space Jam, who was content to let Seabiscuit win.

Dreamer, released in 2005, is loosely based on the story of Mariah's Storm, a Thoroughbred filly who came back from a broken cannon bone to race again. In the movie, Sonador falls in a race and suffers a similar injury. An animatronic horse was used for the fall.

Harbor Mist, a former racehorse, plays Sonador when she hangs in her stall from a sling while her leg heals. Harbor Mist also carries Cale Crane's backpack. Cale likes to feed Sonador treats, including chocolate cake; however, none of the Thoroughbreds would eat it. Benny, a Quarter Horse, had to step in to fill that role. Benny is also the horse in the scene where Sonador gallops away with Cale. The racing scenes were covered by a gelding named Sacrifice. After filming was complete, Kurt Russell (Ben Crane) gave Dakota Fanning (Cale Crane) a palomino that she named Goldy.

In 2006, a new version of *Flicka* appeared. Sixteen-year-old Katy replaced the rancher's son, Ken. Alison Lohman, the actress who played Katy, had never ridden a horse before and had to learn fast. Ribbon, a six-year-old black gelding, possibly a Morgan plays Flicka. Pablo served as a Flicka double.

Sadly, two rodeo horses died during the making of the movie in April 2005. One broke his leg during a running scene. Another horse got loose from his handler and died after tripping on a trailing thirteen-foot lead rope, falling, and breaking his neck.

Although American Humane ruled that these were unforeseeable and unfortunate accidents, the "No

Animals Were Harmed" disclaimer wasn't given. The end credits read, "American Humane monitored the animal action."

Arguably the best racehorse of all time, the 2010 movie, *Secretariat*, covers the amazing Triple Crown victory of Big Red in 1973. Five horses played Secretariat. Copper was a Quarter Horse; the others were Thoroughbreds. Sky was actually a Secretariat descendant. Harbor Mist (who also had a main role in *Dreamer*) made an appearance.

Penny Chenery, Secretariat's owner in real life, selected Longshot Max and Trolley Boy as the horses who most closely resembled her horse. Those two appeared in close-up scenes.

Two of the three Triple Crown races were staged in the movie. The Preakness was depicted by showing Chenery's family watching the race on television, using actual footage of Secretariat's win.

War Horse (2011) displays the horrors of horses facing tanks, planes, machine guns, and poisonous gas in modern warfare (WWI). Eight million horses died in the First World War. Fortunately, they used an animatronic horse in the most dangerous scenes.

Fourteen actual horses portrayed the equine star Joey—two as a foal, four as a colt, and eight as an adult. Twelve-year-old Finder's Key, a Thoroughbred and reluctant racehorse, was the main horse playing the adult Joey. Finder was the only horse flown from America to England for the film. Forty-five minutes with the makeup crew were required to make all the Joey actors look identical—with four socks and a star. Finder also appeared as a double in *Seabiscuit* (2003).

Some Joey doubles included several Andalusians—Civilon, Sueno, Generoso, and Diego, as well as British Warmbloods—Abraham, Lincoln, and Sultan.

In an amusing twist, Finder, a gelding, was the horse used to play the mare who gave birth to the foal Joey. In a later scene, Finder jumped three and a half feet onto an approaching tank and then four feet down the other side.

More than 150 horses appeared in the movie. Some were specially trained "falling" or "lay down" horses that fell on cue onto a soft landing area. Scenes of dead horses consisted of fake animals along with some "lay down" horses.

28

Equine High Jumpers

The Thoroughbred Faithful might have had a successful racing career if he hadn't been so temperamental. But if that had been the case, the world would have never heard of him. The chestnut colt was born in Chile in 1933 and grew to 16.1 hands. In the early 1940s, Gaspar Lueje, a Chilean Army captain, bought the stallion, hoping to use him for dressage. Early in his training, the horse suffered an injury to his left hindquarter which took a considerable time to heal and left him with a slight limp.

Next, Lueje tried show jumping where the focus was not simply on clearing jumps but also on form, appearance, and behavior. Because of Faithful's high-spirited nature, that didn't go well either. One afternoon in 1947, a trainer was working on ground exercises with the horse, and Faithful bolted. When he realized he was free, the horse jumped the six-foot enclosure wall.

An army riding master, Rafael Montti Roa, witnessed Faithful's escape. Roa was so impressed by the jump, that he purchased Faithful and took him to the Quillota Cavalry Academy. There, the horse received a new name—Huaso—and a new trainer.

Captain Alberto Larraguibel was assigned to train the horse for high-jump competitions where all that mattered was a clean jump. The pair began a two-year training program. Alberto's goal was a lofty one—the Chilean and the world high jump records.

The culmination of their efforts occurred on February 5, 1949, at an officially sanctioned show in Viña del Mar, Chile. Huaso and another horse, Chileno, the two final contestants, advanced to a jumpoff. Each was given three attempts to clear an eight-foot-one-and-a-quarter-inch jump. Chileno crashed into the jump on his second attempt and dropped out of the competition.

Huaso refused the jump on his first try. On the second, his belly grazed the top rail. Alberto blamed those two failures on himself.

There was only the third and last attempt left. I recalculated again, and in the precise moment we flew … The most difficult moment was the apex of the jump. My eyes

The pair had done it! Considering that an average home's ceiling is eight feet high, Huaso's accomplishment seems impossible. Moreover, the horse was sixteen, and he'd been seriously injured in the past. Huaso was never ridden again after he set the record. He was permitted to roam freely around the Cavalry Academy. He died there twelve years later on August 24, 1961, at twenty-eight.

Although Huaso holds the official equine high jump record, several horses have had higher unofficial jumps.

Heatherbloom was a bay half-Thoroughbred foaled in Montreal, Canada, in 1895. Howard Willets of New York purchased him for $1,000 as a 16.1 hand, four-year-old and sent the horse to trainer Richard Donnelly.

Both his owner and trainer showed him, achieving success as a high jumper. His official record was seven feet ten and a half inches at Richmond,

Virginia, in 1905[1]. He had two higher, unofficial jumps. One was at the trainer's stable in 1902 when he cleared eight feet two inches. Harper's Weekly was there to do a feature article on the horse and recorded the jump in a photograph. The second jump was at Willets' Farm in White Plains, where he soared an inch higher, clearing eight feet three inches.

Willets had once refused an offer of $20,000 for Heatherbloom from the Barnum and Bailey Circus. In 1909, the horse injured himself jumping out of his corral at Willets' farm and had to be put down.

On June 8, 1923, Great Heart, owned by Francis S. Peabody and ridden by Fred Vesey, cleared an eight-foot-three-inch jump in Illinois at the South Shore Country Club's horse show. Great Heart was half Hackney horse and half Thoroughbred. Equine artist and author C. W. Anderson wrote a book, *Great Heart*, about the jumper in 1962.

In New York in the 1920s, Fred "Freddy" Wettach Jr. noticed a bald-faced Irish gelding in a group of horses his father had purchased as polo pony prospects. He thought one of the horses, King's Own, looked more like a jumper. He was proven right as the two experienced great success at many horse shows. Wettach's goal was to beat Heatherbloom's record.

One day in 1927, before a few witnesses and a photographer, Freddy set up a jump to the height of eight feet three and a half inches. He and King's Own cleared the jump with room to spare. Although impressive, the record was not official, since it was not part of a sanctioned competition.

Jumping such heights is considered too dangerous for horses now, so these records will likely remain unbeaten.

---

[1] *Some newspaper accounts have Heatherbloom's highest jump at eight feet six inches. His owner's name is spelled a variety of ways—Willitts, Willet, etc.*

The Guinness World Record for the longest horizontal jump by a horse over water is 8.40 m (27 feet 6.7 inches) at Johannesburg, South Africa, on April 25, 1975. The horse was Something, ridden by Andre Ferreira.

29

The Last Cavalry Horse

After years of herding cattle on a Nebraska ranch, becoming an army horse must have been a surprising change for Chief. The Army purchased the bay gelding, foaled in 1932, for $163. Initially, he was sent to Fort Robinson, Nebraska.

In April 1941, Chief joined the 10th Cavalry at Fort Riley, Kansas. He later moved to the 9th Cavalry. Although the U.S. entered World War II that year, Chief never left the country. The following year, he was transferred to the Cavalry School, where he remained until his retirement.

At the school, Chief rose to the rank of Advanced Cavalry Charger, helping train young men to become Cavalry officers. He was a favorite mount, since anyone could ride the gentle horse. Over the years, Chief safely carried many future officers on long cross-country rides over rough terrain, jumping fences and barricades, and swimming across rivers.

The last U.S. Cavalry charge on horseback occurred in 1942, during fighting against the Japanese in the Philippines. Mechanization meant jeeps, tanks, and trucks replaced the remaining Cavalry horses. In December 1949 and January 1950, all Cavalry horses sixteen and younger were sold at auction. The older ones would spend their retirement years at Fort Riley. A total of 222 horses were dispersed in about equal numbers in the two age groups. One of the older ones was Chief.

By the end of 1953, thirty retired horses remained at Fort Riley; the following year, just eleven. In 1955, five were left—Gambler, Joe Louis, Flicka, Strollalong, and Chief—all geldings except Flicka. By 1962, there was only Chief. Tourists visited the Riding Club to see the last living representative of the thousands of Cavalry horses who had once lived at the fort.

The Fort Riley veterinarian described the thirty-four-year-old Chief's condition as excellent. Every day, he exercised briefly in his private corral. After a short run, he would lie down and roll in the sand before grazing or dozing under a shady tree.

Chief died on May 24, 1968, at thirty-six. On June 1, he received a military funeral with full honors. Chief was buried standing upright in a marble casket at the foot of the Old Trooper Monument at Fort Riley.

Today, there are seven horse-mounted detachments in the 1st Cavalry Division. The units are used for drills, parades, rodeos, and other events to promote public relations. One of the most prominent is located at Fort Cavazos (Fort Hood) in Texas.

30

Reckless

Kim Huk Moon was a successful jockey and trainer in Seoul, South Korea. He had received a racehorse mare, Ah-Chim-Hai (Flame of the Morning) as payment for his work in a prisoner of war camp during World War II. In June 1948, Ah-Chim-Hai gave birth to a filly.

Kim gave the chestnut foal, with three stockings, the same name as her mother but called her Flame. Unfortunately, Ah-Chim-Hai died a week after the filly was born. Kim's friend, also a jockey, had a mare who had recently foaled. That mare became a foster mother to Flame, successfully raising both foals.

Although referred to as a Mongolian horse, Flame's exact breed is unknown. She was about 13 hands tall and not as stocky as a typical Mongolian. Some believe she may have been a Cheju (Jeju) pony, possibly with some Thoroughbred in her background. When she was almost two, Kim began training the filly for racing.

But on June 25, 1950, Communist North Korea invaded South Korea, initiating the Korean War. Although Flame showed promise as a racehorse, all racing in Korea was suspended. Flame's racing career ended before it even began. Instead, Flame, hooked to a rickety cart, took Kim, his mother, sister, niece, and nephew two hundred miles to safety in the southern city of Pusan. During their two years there, Kim used Flame to help unload supplies from American ships.

By 1952, Seoul was considered safe, and Kim once again hooked Flame to a cart to return home. American troops had converted the racetrack where he had formerly worked, to a landing field. Kim lived in poverty, finding it difficult to earn enough money to feed his family and Flame. The mare hauled rice from the fields to a warehouse. Local children gathered grass for her to eat.

Chung Soon, Kim's sister, worked in the rice paddies. One day, a worker near her stepped on a landmine. The explosion damaged Chung Soon's left leg. When his sister's leg had to be amputated, Kim was determined to find a way to provide her with an artificial one.

Flame was fast. Kim's plan was to develop her into a successful racehorse, so he could earn enough money to help his sister. He began training and conditioning the horse for the track. Maybe soon she could begin the racing career that had been interrupted by the war.

One October day in 1952, Flame was resting in her stall after completing a workout. Kim spotted four Americans heading his way. Fearing they were looking for horses, Kim wanted to hide Flame, but there wasn't time. His friend led the men straight into the barn. Lieutenant Eric Pedersen had a good eye for horses and passed by several before reaching Flame.

Kim hated to part with the mare he dearly loved. They had been through so much together. But Chung Soon meant even more to him. The $250 Pedersen offered was more than enough to purchase an artificial leg for his sister. Kim tearfully agreed to sell Flame.

The four-year-old mare's life was about to move in a direction she never could have imagined. When Pedersen returned to his base with a horse, the other men were puzzled. What was their lieutenant thinking?

Two Marines, Monroe Coleman and Joe Latham, were assigned to care for and train Flame. The mare's first meal at the camp was a loaf of bread and uncooked oatmeal.

Flame hadn't been purchased as a mascot; Pedersen hoped she could be trained to haul their heavy guns and ammunition. The Marines gave her a new name—Reckless—after their dangerous weapons: recoilless "reckless" rifles. Each gun was seven feet long and weighed 115 pounds. It took two to four men to move the guns into position at the top of a hill. The rifles didn't use ordinary bullets. Each round weighed twenty-five pounds.

The men built a special bunker for Reckless, although the mare didn't always use it. Horses are herd animals with a strong desire to live in a group. Since there were no other horses around, the Marines became Reckless' herd. She bonded with them and would do whatever they asked. The men grew to love Reckless as well, sharing their food and treats with her.

Once Reckless adjusted to her new home and life as a Marine, she had free rein to wander around the camp. Winters in Korea were bitterly cold with temperatures dropping below zero degrees. On those cold or rainy nights, Reckless often shared a tent with one of the men, warming herself at the his stove.

Her favorite place was the cook's tent. When the cook was late getting up in the morning, Reckless would enter his tent and lick his face to remind him it was time for breakfast. Having spent most of her life with little to eat, the horse had an insatiable appetite and would consume just about

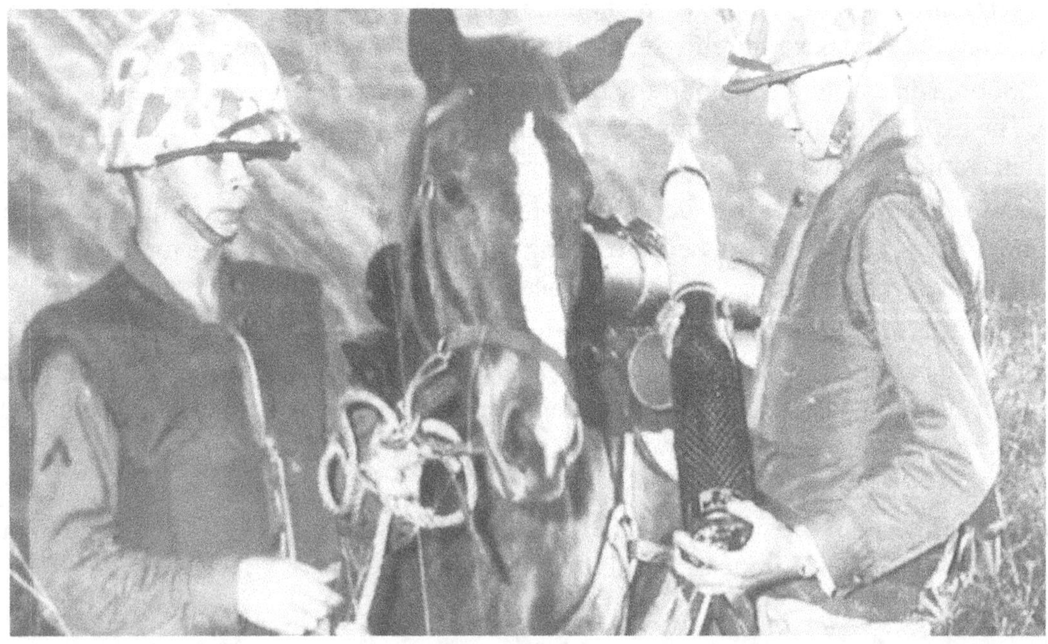

anything—scrambled eggs, coffee, peanut butter sandwiches, fruit pies, hard candy, chocolate bars, cereal, graham crackers, and bread with jam. Reckless could even drink Coca-Cola or milk from a cup. One Marine told the story of a time he bought a pack of cookies and hid them in his tent. He returned to find his tent a disaster. Reckless' keen sense of smell directed her to food however well hidden. She'd eaten not only his cookies, but the wrapper as well.

Joe Latham became Reckless' drill instructor, putting her through boot camp—or as he called it—hoof camp. In order to be useful to the Marines, Reckless had a lot to learn. Latham trained her to come when he whistled, to step carefully over barbed wire, and to lie down when Latham tapped her front leg. Reckless sometimes rode in a small, open cart pulled by a jeep. She had to stand at an angle in order to fit in the two-wheeled trailer. When someone yelled, "Incoming, incoming!" indicating the enemy was about to fire on them, Reckless ran to her bunker or to the bunker of the closest Marine.

When a pack saddle arrived from the United States, Reckless began more serious training—carrying the large, heavy ammunition used by the reckless rifles. Normally, the horse could carry six rounds, but when needed, she could take eight to ten at a time. The men practiced leading Reckless, loaded with the shells, up and down the steep Korean hills.

Although Reckless excelled in her training, no one was sure how she would react in a real battle. In November 1952, the horse was put to the test. After lugging six shells up to a ridge, Reckless heard the deafening blast of a recoilless rifle for the first time. All four hooves left the ground, and Latham could see the whites of her eyes. Reckless began to sweat all over, an indication of her extreme fear. Latham did his best to calm her, and by the time the third round was fired, she was more relaxed. She delivered four more loads of ammunition up to the ridge that day. Reckless had passed the test.

When Lieutenant Pedersen received his third Purple Heart in battle, he was supposed to be transferred out of combat duty. However, he did not want to leave his platoon. Pedersen knew if he took Reckless with him, the Marines would lose a valuable teammate. He convinced the general to let him remain at the camp.

Reckless proved herself repeatedly in battle. And between battles, she performed other tasks, such as stringing communication wires. Not only was the mare a genuine help, but her quirky personality and fearless determination encouraged the Marines in her unit.

Reckless is best known for her heroic performance in the Battle of Outpost Vegas. During that battle, she was wounded twice—once above the eye and a second time on her left flank. But after being treated, the brave horse went right back to work.

> *During the Battle of Outpost Vegas (March 1953), on one day alone she made 51 trips from the Ammunition Supply Point to the firing sites, 95 percent of the time by herself. She carried 386 rounds of ammunition (over 9,000 pounds — almost FIVE TONS! — of ammunition), walked over 35 miles through open rice paddies and up steep mountains with enemy fire coming in at the rate of 500 rounds per minute. And as she so often did, she would carry wounded soldiers down the mountain to safety, unload them, get reloaded with ammo, and off she would go back up to the guns.[1]*

By the fourth day, the Marines were victorious. Reckless was awarded two Purple Hearts for her role in the battle, a turning point in the war.

Reckless had a history of being temperamental with farriers. When her hooves reached an awful state, Joe Latham took her to Seoul to find a farrier who would shoe her. They went to the racetrack where Reckless was born. The men there immediately recognized the horse they knew as Ah-Chim-Hai. It didn't take long for word to reach Kim Huk Moon, and he raced to the stable to see "Flame." The Marines left to get something to eat while Kim cared for Reckless, perfectly fitting her with a new set of shoes. When the Marines returned, Kim was nowhere to be found. It was the last time the young Korean would see the horse he loved.

Toward the end of the war, the men in Reckless' unit challenged that year's Preakness winner, Native Dancer, to race their mare. They called the proposed race the Paddy Derby, stipulating that it had to be held in Korea. Each horse would be riderless, toting four rounds of the ammunition Reckless regularly carried in battle. Unsurprisingly, Native Dancer's owner did not respond to the challenge.

---

[1] *Sgt. Reckless: America's War Horse,* Robin Hutton

The war ended with a cease-fire on July 27, 1953, four months after the Battle of Outpost Vegas. Joe Latham returned to the U.S. in October, however, he didn't want Reckless to be abandoned in Korea. The new marines who arrived to relieve the men who were returning home took an instant liking to Reckless and watched over her.

On April 10, 1954, Reckless received a promotion to sergeant. A special red, silk horse blanket with gold trim had been designed for the occasion. Of course, the always-hungry horse attempted to eat it. Major General Randolph Pate presented Reckless with her sergeant's stripes. Reckless' military decorations were added to her new blanket.

- Two Purple Hearts
- Marine Corps Good Conduct Medal
- Presidential Unit Citation
- Navy Unit Citation
- National Defense Service Medal
- United Nations Service Medal
- Korean Service Medal
- Republic of Korea Presidential Unit Citation

News spread quickly about the Marine's new sergeant when a four-page article about Reckless appeared in the Saturday Evening Post. Readers began a campaign to bring the mare to the United States—"Operation Bring Reckless Home." Ernest Gibson of Pacific Transport Lines cargo service generously provided for her private transport.

The Marines agreed, on the condition that they would retain partial ownership, along with her original owner, Lieutenant Pedersen. The horse was to be kept at Camp Pendleton. Any money generated from her public appearances would be donated to the families of Marines from their platoon who were killed in the war.

Once the terms were accepted, the Marines had to get Reckless from Korea to Yokohama, Japan, where she would board the transport ship. The Marine Aircraft Wing agreed to fly

her there in the same type of plane they used to move jeeps and other heavy equipment. Reckless didn't enjoy the flight, but she made it safely to Yokohama.

On October 22, 1954, she boarded the ship for her journey across the Pacific Ocean with fellow Marine William Moore. Her stall was on the deck, so she would have fresh air to help keep her from becoming seasick. During a violent storm, a wave knocked Reckless down and nearly swept her overboard. During the rough weather, she refused to eat—something highly unusual for her.

Eric Pedersen and two other men who had been at the camp when Reckless became a Marine, traveled to San Francisco. As they waited for the ship to arrive, they learned Reckless had regained her appetite. She had eaten much of her special blanket and the ribbons attached to it. Pedersen believed it was important for Reckless to have a blanket displaying her awards when she met the press. He scrambled at the last minute to find someone to make a replacement for her.

Olsen Nolte Saddle Shop provided not only a new blanket but also a leather halter, and other tack. Emerson Manufacturing, a flag company, halted their normal production in order to create the letters for the blanket.

On the night of November 9, 1954, Reckless docked in San Francisco. It was obvious she remembered Pedersen and the other men. The mare's credentials did not impress the U.S. Agriculture Department, who demanded blood tests be drawn. If Reckless was infected with a disease, she would have to be destroyed or returned to Korea. The next morning, the USDA administered the tests, and Reckless had her first press conference on board the ship.

After the conference, Reckless was lowered from the ship to the dock in a large, wooden crate. Later that day, a reception was held in her honor on the second floor of the Marine's Memorial Club. She rode the freight elevator to the tenth-floor banquet hall. Before her handlers could stop her, Reckless dove into a two-foot-high cake. She finished her dessert off by eating the floral centerpiece.

The following day, Reckless entered a trailer to travel 500 miles south to the Marine Corps base at Camp Pendleton in San Diego County. When she arrived, Reckless made her mark in the guest log—and tried to eat the pen. Since the results of her blood tests hadn't yet been received, Reckless was quarantined at Pedersen's ranch close to the base where she remained for a year. Then, on November 23, 1955, the Marines purchased Reckless

for one dollar, and she was moved to the base stables. The mare was seven, still young for a horse. One of the stipulations for her care was, "Never should she be ridden by oversized, leaden-seated, heavy-handed cowboy types." In fact, no one over 130 pounds was permitted to ride her. Later, that was changed to nothing heavier than her blanket could be placed on her back. The Marines charged with her care ran alongside her when she was exercised. When younger in Korea, dogs had attacked Reckless, which resulted in a lifetime hatred of them. No dogs were permitted near her.

The press couldn't get enough of the equine Marine. She had many offers for endorsements and movies; however, the Marines set high standards for the horse's appearances and how she should be portrayed.

But Reckless was lonely. In Korea, the horse had adopted the Marines as her herd-mates. Now in retirement, she no longer had that constant contact. One spring, a sign appeared on the fence around her pasture—"Mare-Ternity Ward." A colt was born on April 5, 1957. The identity of the foal's father was not revealed.

Colonel Rothwell announced a contest among the Marines to name the foal. Unhappy with all the entries, Rothwell named the colt himself—Fearless.

Two months later, Fearless was promoted to Private First Class, and Reckless received a second promotion—to Staff Sergeant. When full grown, Fearless served as a trail horse at the base, then was later sold to a nearby ranch.

On March 2, 1959, Reckless gave birth to her second colt. His sire was a gray Arabian, Mayr Nasr. Once again, a naming contest was held, and like the first time, no names pleased the current commander, Randolph Pate. He named the colt Dauntless.

Dauntless was enlisted as a private in the Marines on July 1, 1959. He was used in Marine Corps rodeos, in steer roping and as a pickup horse to rescue cowboys in the bronc riding event.

Reckless officially retired from the Marines on November 10, 1960, but she remained at Camp Pendleton. On December 6, 1964, she gave birth to her third colt. This foal didn't continue the tradition of his mother and two brothers—with "less" at the end of his name. He was named Chesty, after Lieutenant General Lewis "Chesty" Puller. The sire was a registered, bay Thoroughbred. Chesty was the largest of Reckless' three colts. He was used for a while in the rodeo, then lived at two neighboring ranches.

Reckless passed her appetite on to her three colts. Like their mother, they were willing to eat just about anything. Reckless had her only filly in 1966, but the foal died at a month old.

In her later years, Reckless suffered from arthritis and laminitis. The mare died on May 13, 1968, at twenty, and was buried with full military honors. Her headstone reads, "In Memory Of Reckless, Pride of the Marines" along with her rank and dates of service.

Artist Jocelyn Russell sculpted a bronze statue of Reckless with ammunition strapped to her back. The statue, An Uphill Battle, was unveiled in 2013 at the National Museum of the Marines in Quantico, Virginia.

> *Reckless was a very special horse and undoubtedly bonded through a spiritual connection of love with her Marines. The noise and waves of concussion can't be described, but she endured it all. I believe an angel had to be riding Reckless, since she was alone and without a Marine to lead her. I have always cherished my horses. But after watching and learning more about that little mare of the Reckless Rifles, mine are even more special because I know they have the same Creator.[1]*

---

[1] *Sgt. Harold E. Wadley, USMC*

31

Swaps

In the 1930s, Rex Ellsworth set out to prove that successful racehorses didn't have to come from fancy Kentucky farms. Ironically, he got his start by purchasing six Thoroughbred mares and two weanlings from Kentucky, then, he hauled the horses in a rickety trailer back to his ranch in California.

In 1947, Ellsworth purchased the bay, four-year-old British stallion Khaled. In his second year at Ellsworth's ranch, Khaled sired forty-five foals, twenty-six of whom won as two-year-olds. Khaled continued to sire winners, the most notable being the chestnut Swaps, foaled in 1952, to the mare Iron Reward. Meshach "Mesh" Tenney trained Swaps. Ellsworth and Tenney had been friends from the time they were eight-year-old Mormon schoolboys. They were born a day apart, November 15 and 16, 1907.

Swaps proved Ellsworth's theory—a great racehorse could be raised in California. Ridden by Willie Shoemaker, Swaps beat the favorite Nashua in the 1955 Kentucky Derby. A son of the stallion Nasrullah, Nashua was trained by Sunny Jim Fitzsimmons and owned by Claiborne Farm in Kentucky. Swaps gained the nickname "The California Comet." He was the second California horse to win the Derby, after Morvich in 1922.

After the Derby, Swaps returned to the West, where he broke or equaled six track records. Back East, Nashua won both the Preakness and the Belmont.

Fans clamored for a match race between the two champions. The race, held on August 31 in Chicago, was disappointing. Swaps ran despite aggravating a leg injury the day before. Nashua won easily by over six lengths and was voted the 1955 Horse of the Year. Swaps did not race anymore that season to allow his leg to heal. Of nine starts in 1955, the match with Nashua was his only loss.

Footage of Swaps winning the Kentucky Derby was used in the movie *Glory* about a filly who wins the Derby. They applied a star and small snip via makeup to the live horses that played Glory to match the markings of Swaps. The movie's female lead, Margaret O'Brien, rode Swaps bareback while the movie was being filmed.

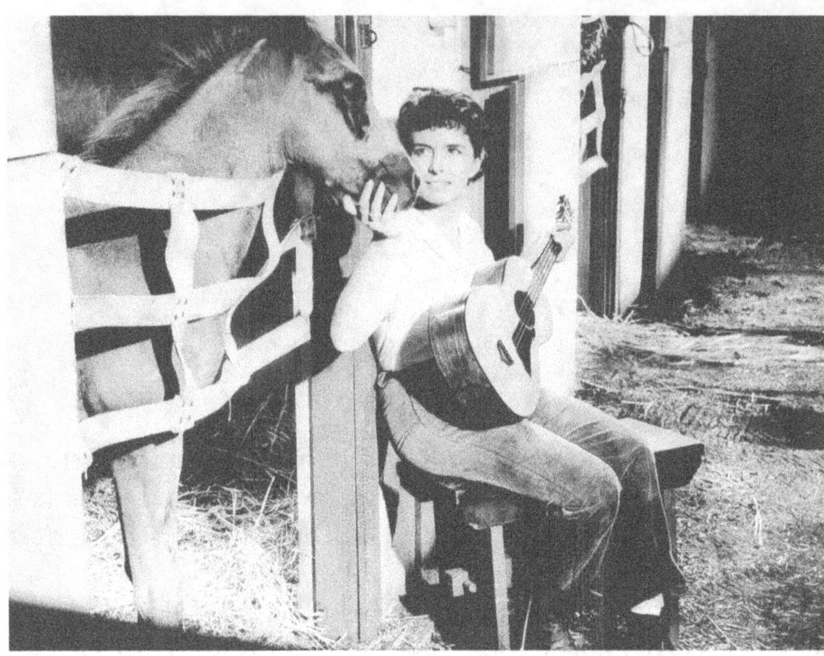

While I was making Glory, we were out at Hollywood Park, and they let me ride Swaps. He was very gentle —not too high-strung like so many racehorses. You could get hold of him and he wouldn't go too fast if you didn't want him to.[1]

The following year, Swaps raced ten times as a four-year-old with eight wins and one second. He received the 1956 Horse of the Year award.

Nashua and Swaps never faced each other again. In October 1956, while training in New Jersey, Swaps fractured his left hind cannon bone. A broken leg is usually a death sentence for a horse. In a desperate attempt to save his life, a veterinarian fitted Swaps with a cast, and the horse was confined to a stall. However, a week later, he broke the cast and extended the fractures.

When Jim Fitzsimmons, trainer of Swaps' rival, Nashua, heard of the dire situation, he sent a sling to use on the colt. Swaps spent weeks suspended by the device and lost 300 pounds. But the sling and the vigilant care provided by Mesh Tenney saved the horse's life. In December 1956, Swaps was well enough to be flown back to California.

Swaps retired from racing with nineteen wins in twenty-five starts and earnings of $848,900. John Galbreath, of Darby Dan Farm in Kentucky, purchased a half-interest in Swaps in 1956.

---

[1] *californiahorsehistory.blogspot.com/2024/07/beyond-news-reels-swaps-in-hollywood.html*

Galbreath believed the stallion deserved better accommodations than he had at Ellsworth's Chino ranch. He purchased the other half of Swaps the following year. The California horse, who had his origins in Kentucky, would spend his final years there as well—at Darby Dan and Spendthrift Farms. At Spendthrift, Swaps lived in the same barn as his old rival Nashua.

When criticized for selling his star horse, Ellsworth said, "I had no more fondness for Swaps over the rest of my horses than I have fondness for one of my five children over the other four."

One of Swaps' most successful offspring was a chestnut colt, Chateaugay, who won the Kentucky Derby and Belmont Stakes in 1963. The colt missed the Triple Crown by finishing second in the Preakness. Swaps' most famous filly was a dark bay named Affectionately, listed as eighty-first in Blood-Horse's Top 100 Racehorses of the 20th Century.

Khaled, Swaps' sire, died in 1968. Swaps died in 1972 at Spendthrift Farm at the age of twenty. He was originally buried there; however, in 1986, his remains were moved to the grounds of the Kentucky Derby Museum at Churchill Downs. In Blood-Horse's Top 100 Racehorses, Swaps ranks twentieth and his rival Nashua twenty-fourth.

Unfortunately, Iron Reward's last years weren't spent in the comfort and leisure her son experienced. In

January 1975, neighbors alerted the Society for the Prevention of Cruelty to Animals (SPCA) to the poor condition of the horses at Ellsworth's California ranch.

When they arrived, the SPCA found 130 horses, mostly broodmares. Two were dead. Three died a few days later. Others were neglected and starving. The SPCA impounded the surviving horses. One of the dead mares was Iron Reward. The mother of Swaps had just passed her twenty-ninth birthday.

Ellsworth's son Kumen, a veterinarian, lived at the ranch. He stated, "We had a financial problem and were in the process of moving the horses to our farm near Tucson, Arizona, where we raise our own feed. We had cut down on the feed but don't believe they were starving."[1]

The California Thoroughbred Breeders Association, of which sixty-seven-year-old Rex was still a member, covered the expenses incurred by the SPCA in caring for the horses.

Ellsworth later pled no contest to ten counts of mistreating animals. He received a $5,000 fine and was given a year of probation. Ellsworth continued in the horse business. He was the owner of California Jade, who raced in 1988. Rex Ellsworth passed away in 1997 at eighty-nine.

---

[1] *The Palm Beach Post, West Palm Beach, Florida, January 23, 1975*

32

Annie Wilkins

Many who have taken long-distance horseback journeys have done so for the sheer adventure of it. Mesannie (Annie) Wilkins' story is a little different. In September 1954, at sixty-two, the Minot, Maine, resident was alone and in poor health. After discovering a spot on her lung (cancer or tuberculosis), her doctor's prognosis was grim. She had two to four years left to live—if she took it easy.

Annie's last surviving family member, her father's brother, Waldo,[1] had passed away earlier that year. She was forced to sell her livestock to pay medical bills. Her only companion was a small dog, Depeche Toi (de-PESH twah, French for "hurry up"). The year-old dog was an odd combination of Spaniel and Dachshund.

Considering Annie's poverty, her doctor recommended she spend her final years in a state-funded facility. But Annie had other ideas. She would soon face her first winter alone, and she didn't want to spend it in her drafty farmhouse, nearly a mile off the main road. Annie's mother had always wanted to visit California, but she never made it there. Annie decided she would. But it wouldn't be by car or plane.

> *I would buy the cheapest horse I could find, ride him south until my money gave out, find a job, save a few dollars, and then ride on. The goal would be my mother's goal: California.*[2]

First, she needed some money to get started. Annie raised cucumbers and sold homemade pickles. Although she hadn't ridden a horse in thirty years, Wilkins was no novice. Earlier in life, she had ridden horses bareback as part of a circus act. Later, she rode a mule or donkey back and forth to her job at a shoe factory.

She shared her plan with Mrs. Williams, an old friend of her mother's, who was in her nineties. The woman reminded her she hadn't been on a horse in years and there were no longer any safe roads to travel by horseback. Mrs. Williams advised her not to tell anyone else of her plan or she might end up in the local insane asylum.

Next, Annie tried another of her mother's friends, Mrs. Miller. Her response was much more positive. It struck the woman as a wonderful idea. Mrs. Miller recounted the story of Annie's grand-mother, Libby, who had ridden 180 miles at the age of eighty.

> *So this sort of thing is in your bloodstream, and if I were your age and a Libby, I'd have a notion to join you. … I think you're doing something wonderful, Mesannie. You can do it, so long as you*

---

[1] *Some accounts say Waldo was not a blood relative.*
[2] *Last of the Saddle Tramps, Messanie Wilkins, 10*

Inspired by Mrs. Miller's encouragement, Annie set out looking for a horse. She found Tarzan at a riding stable that was selling some horses for the off-season. The fourteen-year-old gelding, possibly a Morgan, was brown or rusty black, and stood a little over 14 hands. The first time Annie mounted him, she felt right at home. When they delivered him to her farm, the horse and Depeche Toi bonded immediately.

In addition to practical supplies, Annie purchased a diary to record her experiences along the way. She would fill eight over the course of her trip. She'd planned to depart on November 7, but the night before, Annie felt uneasy. Maybe it was a crazy idea after all. She wanted God's assurance that she was doing the right thing.

I know You are busy, but if I toss a coin five times and it comes up heads three-out-of-five, will that mean I have Your approval?[2]

Annie climbed out of bed and began tossing a coin. When it turned up heads four out of five times, she believed she had her answer.

After a good night's sleep, the five-foot-one-inch, 150-pound, almost sixty-three-year-old woman set off with thirty-two dollars in her pocket. Dressed in a wool "union suit", wool shirt, blanket-lined vest, thick work jeans, lumberman's boots, and a hunting cap with ear flaps, Annie was often mistaken for a man. On the first day, she quickly realized she had a lot to learn about outfitting a pack animal. Each time her knots worked loose and something fell off, Tarzan stopped and waited patiently for Annie to dismount and reattach it.

That day, the trio traveled twenty-one miles. A family hosted them for an overnight stay. During their conversation at the dinner table, the father suggested Tarzan and Depeche Toi should each have a goal for the trip. Annie imagined what those would be.

Tarzan's goal should be to wash his feet in the Pacific Ocean. I daresay that no horse in history has ever walked from the Atlantic to the Pacific and washed his feet in both.[3]

---

[1] *Wilkins, 11*
[2] *Wilkins, 14*
[3] *Wilkins, 20 (Actually the Abernathy brothers accomplished this in 1911.)*

Depeche Toi wants to be the first dog in history to visit every bush, tree and telephone pole in America, from coast to coast.[1]

Word spread about Annie's unusual trip. Soon, she was featured on television, radio, and in newspaper and magazine articles. Mail from fans following her adventure awaited her at post offices along her route. The media exposure helped with accommodations along the way as people were able to predict when she would reach their area. She was happy to simply have the shelter of a barn overnight, but many not only put Tarzan up in their barn, they fixed her a special meal and allowed her to sleep in their homes. Others refused even their barn, urging Annie to keep going down the road. She sometimes stayed in inns and hotels or even in a local jail. Once, she slept in the same cell with a female prisoner.

Annie had left in November to avoid the Maine winter. She'd hoped to encounter warmer weather by riding south. But the northern states she rode through early in the trip were nearly as cold as Maine. They spent Thanksgiving with a family near Springfield, Massachusetts, where Depeche Toi received a pair of boots and Tarzan a set of rubber shoes.

Riding a horse alongside the highway in the 1950s meant continual encounters with motorized vehicles. In New York, during a sleet storm, a trucker couldn't see the light Annie wore backwards on her head until the last minute. He slammed on the brakes but skidded and hit Annie's left leg. Her horse and dog weren't hurt, but Annie's leg turned black and blue from the knee down. On December 13, her birthday, she was taken to a hospital. X-rays revealed she hadn't broken anything. Although the doctor didn't charge a fee for his services, he stated he would have to charge her for the X-rays. Annie handed him a ten-dollar bill. The doctor said, "Happy Birthday" and gave her thirty dollars in change.

---

[1] *Wilkins, 21*

Another encounter with a truck in Pennsylvania knocked Annie unconscious briefly, and left Tarzan limping for a few days. After that, she accepted an offer to haul them all to Kentucky, leaving the worst of the winter weather behind.

In Tennessee, fans who knew she couldn't afford another horse, gave her one. Rex was a twenty-year-old, 16-hand Tennessee Walking Horse. Annie, who was quite short, worried she wouldn't be able to mount the tall horse. But when his owner said, "Stretch," the horse spread his legs apart until his back was lower than Tarzan's.

It took several days for Rex to build up his endurance so he could take on his share of the work. Because of Rex's height and longer stride, the two horses had to learn how to maintain the same pace. Depeche Toi preferred walking rather than bouncing along to Tarzan's rough gait *(right)*. But Rex was so smooth, the dog enjoyed riding him.

In Arkansas, Annie was nearly left horseless when Tarzan and Rex escaped from a corral one stormy night. The two traveled fifteen miles down the road before stopping at an ice cream stand. The owner tied the horses to a fence and called the police. It wasn't difficult to determine who the animals belonged to, and Annie was soon reconnected with them.

Across Arkansas and Missouri, Annie encountered ticks, chiggers, cottonmouths, and rattlesnakes. By Memorial Day, they were in Kansas. Their next goal was to reach Cheyenne, Wyoming, in time for the Frontier Days rodeo. In Kansas, Annie became ill and made another trip to the hospital. She received medicine and was advised to rest for a week, but she stubbornly resumed her journey the following day. Annie was so dizzy, she strapped herself to the saddle so she wouldn't fall off. When she blacked out for a time, Rex turned around and traveled a mile back in the direction they'd come. After several days, Annie recovered, and they arrived in Cheyenne in time to join the opening day rodeo parade.

One night in Boise, Idaho, Annie was staying in the jail when she received a call from Art Linkletter, inviting her to be on his television show when she reached Los Angeles. Annie had no idea who Linkletter was. Although she owned a radio, she'd never had a TV and rarely watched one.

Annie spent Thanksgiving of 1955 in Oregon and planned to remain there until spring, but someone offered to haul her and the horses to Alturas, California. Annie turned sixty-four on

December 13. From Alturas, she rode 200 miles to Redding, arriving there on Christmas Day.

On New Year's Day 1956, they set out in a cold drizzle for the 550-mile trip to Los Angeles. One day, several wooden crates fell from a truck ahead of them and smashed on the road. Young people driving by in a car intentionally frightened Rex. The horse reared and came down on a piece of the broken wood. A nail went under Rex's shoe and into his hoof. A veterinarian removed the nail and assured Annie that a tetanus shot wasn't necessary.

But several days later, Rex began showing signs of infection. Annie located another vet who gave the horse a tetanus shot. However, it was too late. Annie nursed Rex for two weeks, but the horse faded away, dying just 180 miles short of their destination. Tarzan and Depeche Toi grieved for their lost friend. Annie blamed herself for Rex's death. The three continued in February, but for Annie, the heart had gone out of her trip.

When Art Linkletter heard of the tragedy, he purchased a part-Appaloosa horse, King, for Annie to use on the final leg of her journey. Twelve-year-old King had been a parade horse. Traffic and other noises didn't faze him. The new quartet arrived in Los Angeles in mid-March. The horses stayed at the Lone Ranger Stables, while Annie and Depeche stayed in a three-room suite at a Hollywood motel.

Tarzan developed an attachment to Silver, another horse at the stable, and didn't want to leave, so Annie took King with her to the Art Linkletter studio. After the show, Annie took Tarzan to Long Beach, where he dipped his hooves into the Pacific Ocean.

Annie figured that, including side trips, they had traveled nearly seven thousand miles, through eighteen states, over seventeen months. She'd even received a proposal of marriage from a lonely goat rancher in Wyoming. He'd promised to wait for her, but Annie never returned to the state.

Annie remained in California for at least a year. One day, Tarzan spooked at traffic as they rode near Santa Barbara. He injured his leg and never recovered, dying in 1957. It's unclear what became of King.

Arrive In California

Mrs. Annie Wilkins of West Minot and her horse Tarzan who have arrived in Alturas, Calif. after a transcontinental journey that started a year ago this month.

Horseback Annie To Skip Reno, Go To Los Angeles

Annie eventually returned to Maine, but she had lost her farm. She lived with a friend, Mina Titus Sawyer, in Whitefield. Since Annie only had a sixth-grade education, Mina helped her compile her diaries into a book. *The Last of the Saddle Tramps* was published in 1967.

Although her doctor had predicted Annie would die between 1956 and 1958, she lived until February 19, 1980, passing away at eighty-nine. Annie was buried in her family plot in Minot, Maine.

In October 2011, forty-six-year-old Sea G. Rhydr retraced Annie Wilkins' route in reverse, traveling from West to East with her horse, Jesse James, and a pack pony, Saint Finehorn, both fourteen.

33

Snowman

One cold, snowy day in February 1956, Harry de Leyer was on his way to a horse auction in New Holland, Pennsylvania, deep in Amish country. He hoped to purchase a horse for the New York school where he taught riding lessons. When a tire blew out on his station wagon, de Leyer worried he wouldn't make it to the auction at all. That annoying flat tire changed Harry's life forever.

The repair took so long that by the time Harry arrived at the auction, it was over. After making the long trip, he hated to return home empty-handed. All that remained from the sale were horses no one had bought. Those poor animals were packed into a large truck that would soon be headed for a slaughterhouse—the fate of unsold horses at many auctions. Harry couldn't see much through the slats of the truck, but the horses inside had a dull, lifeless look—all except one. A tall gray returned his gaze with what seemed like a hopeful look. De Leyer asked the truck driver to unload the horse so he could look him over.

Caked with dirt and manure, his mane and tail ragged, the gelding was so thin his hip bones stuck out. Harness marks were worn into his chest, and he had open sores on his legs. The horse was about 16 hands tall. Although not a draft, he had apparently been used for farm work. His hooves were overgrown and chipped, with one shoe missing. Harry estimated his age to be roughly eight. Someone had considered the gray used up at a relatively young age.

The gelding's gentle eyes convinced de Leyer he had potential. When the truck driver offered to sell the horse for $80, including delivery, Harry agreed. He drove home through the snow to wait for the horse's arrival.

When he made it to his farm, Hollandia, Harry's three children couldn't wait to hear what kind of horse he had purchased. Joseph (Chef) was six, Harriet four, and Marty two. Snow continued to fall as the horse arrived that evening and stumbled off the trailer. Harry's wife, Johanna, stood quietly, not sure what to think about the mangy-looking animal. The children, however, didn't notice his flaws. As they stood, watching the new arrival, snowflakes coated his back. Harriet said he looked like a snowman. And that's how the big gray got his name.

Marty walked over and wrapped his arms around one of Snowman's legs. Johanna hurried to rescue her youngest, but Snowman hadn't

budged. He seemed to like the children as much as they liked him.

Over the next few days, the family worked together to get the horse clean. Snowman was calm and gentle with the children. Under all the grime, they discovered he was a flea-bitten gray—gray with small dark flecks in his coat.

Each morning as Harry entered the barn, Snowman greeted him with three loud whinnies—always three. Once Snowman had gained enough weight, his training commenced with line driving. Harry

assumed the horse had been used for plowing long, straight lines, so he was a bit awkward when turning. Working him in small circles improved his flexibility.

When he first saddled Snowman, Harry was cautious, realizing the horse had likely never been ridden. Uncertain about this new experience, the big gray tensed at first, but it didn't take long for him to relax and accept his rider. The horse's quick progress made Harry feel confident he hadn't made a mistake by taking a chance on him. Snowman would make a wonderful lesson horse at the Knox School.

By March, Snowman was ready to begin his new career. Harry rode him the five miles to the Knox School. The stable at the school was shaped like a horseshoe. From their stalls, the horses could see each other across a central courtyard.

Knox was an all-girls boarding school with students from across the United States and abroad. The girls loved their young riding instructor—once they were able to understand him. Harry and Johanna had immigrated from Holland just a few years earlier, and he spoke English with a thick Dutch accent. If the students were surprised by the appearance of the new lesson horse, they didn't let on. The more timid riders loved Snowman. They weren't afraid to ride the big, gentle horse.

When the school closed for the summer, Harry moved his lesson horses to Hollandia; however, he didn't have enough stalls and couldn't afford to keep all of them. He tried to convince one of his students to buy Snowman. Riding the horse at the school had been one thing, but Snowman wasn't flashy enough for their tastes. He was broad and heavy-boned, not like the stylish Thoroughbreds the girls showed.

Early that summer, a doctor who lived six miles down the road appeared at Hollandia, looking for a calm horse for himself and his twelve-year-old son. At last, Harry had a buyer for Snowman. Dr. Rugen purchased him for $160. Harry would miss Snowman and his special greeting each morning, but he had a family to provide for. He'd doubled his money on Snowman. Horses were his business, and he couldn't allow himself to get sentimental about them.

Harry wasn't the only one who missed the horse. His children had also become attached to Snowman. The day after his sale, even the other horses in the barn seemed unsettled with the big gray gone. His gentle nature had been a calming influence on them. Harry figured it would just take everyone a few days to adjust.

As he went down the line of stalls, feeding each animal, he dreamed of having a horse

talented enough to compete in the elite jumping shows in New York. As a teen in his home country, Harry had been a likely choice for the Dutch Equestrian Olympic team, but World War II had changed all that. Now, although he was doing what he loved—working with horses—he struggled to make enough money to provide for his growing family. However, his vision of training and riding a champion jumper wouldn't go away. Maybe if he continued to make a profit by reselling horses, someday he would have enough money to buy just the right horse.

A few days later, as Harry was beginning to adjust to Snowman's absence, he received a call from Dr. Rugen. Snowman had gotten out and trampled the neighbor's yard. The doctor claimed the horse had jumped out of his pasture. Harry assured him that was impossible. After he hung up the phone, Harry thought no more of it, assuming the inexperienced horseman had simply forgotten to latch the gate or Snowman had discovered how to open it.

On his way to the barn several days later, a familiar triple whinny greeted Harry. He stopped for a moment, staring through the early-morning fog. Was he hearing things? Then, the big gelding appeared out of the mist, walking toward him. Harry grinned, delighted to see Snowman. He seriously regretted selling the horse, but a deal was a deal. The horse no longer belonged to him. He led Snowman to a stall, fed him, and returned to the house to phone the doctor.

When Dr. Rugen came to retrieve his horse, he assured Harry that he had checked all his fences. He insisted Snowman was jumping over them. Harry found that hard to believe and went to inspect the doctor's pasture himself.

For the next several days, this scenario was repeated. The doctor took Snowman home, only to have the horse reappear at Hollandia the following morning. Not only was Snowman jumping out of the doctor's pasture, he had to jump over a fence to get into the de Leyer barnyard.

Since Snowman seemed determined to remain at Hollandia, Harry suggested that the doctor board him there. Doctor Rugen agreed, but soon, he and his son lost interest in the horse altogether.

After a few months, Snowman was given back to Harry in exchange for his unpaid boarding fees. The de Leyer children were happy to have their favorite horse back. Snowman, delighted to be home again, was as patient with them as ever. He didn't object when young Marty tried to climb up his tail or all the children climbed on his back at once.

With the dream of a champion jumper in the back of his mind, Harry began working with Snowman. One

of the first training exercises for a jumper is trotting over cavaletti poles. The wooden poles were spaced four feet apart on the ground. In order to avoid hitting them, the horse learns to place his feet carefully. At least, most horses do. Snowman was an exception. He scattered poles every which way. Time and again, Snowman tripped. Snowman stumbled. Was this the same horse who had cleared those pasture fences?

Snowman made little progress at Hollandia that summer of 1956. In the fall, he returned with Harry to the school. In breaks between the girls' riding lessons, Harry continued trying to train Snowman to jump. When he failed to improve at the cavaletti poles, Harry moved on anyway to low jumps. But rather than jumping, the big horse would slow down and simply step over the rails.

One day, Harry prepared Snowman for another training session. A previous rider had left the jump in the ring at four feet. A stable boy joked with Harry, asking if he planned to jump his plow horse over the tall jump. Harry didn't hesitate long. The worst that could happen would be that Snowman would either stop dead in front of the jump or he would send the poles crashing to the ground. Harry turned Snowman toward the jump, and the horse gradually built up speed. They sailed over it—not even nicking a pole!

Harry was amazed. Had it merely been a fluke? He circled around and aimed Snowman at the same fence a second time. The horse flew over it again. Harry raised the jump to five feet, then six, then six feet six inches. Snowman soared over it each time.

Harry had discovered Snowman's secret. The big gray wouldn't put forth much effort unless he had a challenge. Harry had searched for years for a horse that could take him to the grand championship. And for the past year, Snowman had been trying to tell him he was that horse.

Harry worked with Snowman over the summer of 1957, and by September, they were ready for their first competition, the three-day North Shore Horse Show. All the other horses at the event were sleek, high-strung Thoroughbreds—some even Olympic hopefuls. Snowman looked like a clumsy plow horse in comparison. Harry stood out as well. No one else rode his own horse. Wealthy owners hired professionals to do that. Besides, Snowman was still a working horse—giving lessons to Harry's students.

Harry sat astride Snowman, outside the ring, waiting for their turn in the first class. He shrugged off the looks and laughter of some in the crowd. When it was their turn, horse and rider entered the ring, and Snowman broke into a lazy canter. Harry had a fleeting doubt. Was Snowman even awake enough to jump? But when he asked for more speed, Snowman got down to business and completed the course. He received just two faults for ticking one of the rails.

The next class was a knock-down-and-out with higher jumps. This time, it didn't matter if a horse hit a rail, as long as it didn't fall off. Once again, Snowman waited lazily for his turn. No one in the crowd paid any attention to the big lesson horse, but he jumped his first round clean.

The jumps were raised, and all the contestants with clean rounds continued. Snowman finished third in the class, not bad for his first show. Overall, he finished sixth out of twenty in the green jumper division. Snowman's performance gave Harry a taste of what was possible. The show season was wrapping up for the fall, but Harry dreamed of what he and Snowman could accomplish the following summer.

The first event of the summer 1958 season was the Devon Horse Show. Harry and Snowman missed that one. They were busy with graduation ceremonies at the Knox School. The girls had decorated the horse with pink ribbons. Harry considered it undignified for his gelding, but Snowman took it all in stride.

Once the school closed for the summer, Harry's focus turned to Snowman. Their first test would be the Sands Point show. On June 9, the entire de Leyer family rose early to travel to the show.

Snowman was entered in the Open Jumper division. There, it didn't matter what a horse looked like as he jumped, only that he jumped cleanly. Ticks and knockdowns received fault points. Harry couldn't afford a stylish fleece saddle pad as the other contestants had. He used an old blanket folded over several times so it would fit under the saddle.

There was no need to keep a tight rein on Snowman as the other nervous, prancing horses required. When it was his turn, the big gray calmly entered the ring, looking around at the crowd and seeming to smile at the de Leyer children watching from the rail. Snowman completed his round without a single fault, defeating several famous horses. When he was announced as the winner of the class, Harry trotted him into the ring with three of his children bouncing along on Snowman's back.

When Snowman cut his leg on the second day at Sands Point, his chance of becoming the show champion seemed to evaporate. Harry stayed up most of the night, icing the leg, and by morning Snowman was sound enough to compete. Harry and Snowman went on to win the championship. The next day, newspapers ran articles about the amazing win by the "Cinderella Horse," and Snowman's fame spread.

Points were awarded for each ribbon won at the shows. The points determined which horses would compete later in the year at Madison Square Garden.

Over the summer, Snowman finished first or second in each show he attended, quickly rising in the point standings.

When school started again, Harry was back teaching, and Snowman, the champion jumper, returned to giving riding lessons. They were limited to traveling to weekend shows, where Snowman continued to rack up points—enough to qualify for the National Horse Show at Madison Square Gardens. This was the event of the year for hunters and jumpers, lasting eight days, from November 4th to the 11th in 1958.

Since horse shows were always a family event, the de Leyer children were permitted to take the week off from school. With classes held each day, Snowman and another horse, First Chance, traded places back and forth for the show champion.

Toward the end of the event, Snowman had won two firsts, two seconds, and two thirds. He had become the crowd favorite. Harry even led Snowman down a busy New York street to tape a TV show at a local station. Snowman was oblivious to the noise and commotion of New York City life.

The points were so close that the winner of the final class at Madison Square Garden would be the U.S. Open Jumper Champion. Snowman had a spectacular round, jumping everything with room to spare. No other horse came close to matching his performance. He not only won the Open Jumper Championship, Snowman finished the year as the American Horse Show Association Horse of the Year and the Professional Horseman's Association Champion.

The thirty-year-old Dutch immigrant had only been in the US for eight years. And less than three years before, his mount had been an Amish plow horse. The story of Harry and Snowman really did seem like a fairy tale.

After the show, a wealthy man offered $35,000 for Snowman. At the time, Harry earned less than $4,000 a year teaching at the school. Harry hesitated, but he knew Snowman was more than a horse; he was part of the family. He'd already made the mistake of selling him once. Harry wouldn't sell Snowman again for any amount of money.

Snowman returned to the Garden the following year and won the AHSA and PHSA awards a second time. In 1960, he was the reserve champion. After competing several more years, Snowman

returned to being a family horse, teaching the de Leyer children, eventually eight in all, to ride. Harry, by then, had acquired a larger farm closer to the Knox School. The children loved riding Snowman to the Long Island beach. He enjoyed swimming with several of them on his back or he would stand patiently as the kids climbed up to use him as a diving board.

De Leyer returned to New Holland, Pennsylvania, to try to find out where Snowman had come from, but he was never able to learn anything about the horse. Snowman lived his remaining years happily at the Hollandia farm, sometimes jumping fences when he felt like joining friends in a different pasture. Or if he was bored in the pasture, he'd jump out and return to his stall. He knew when the children returned from school, and he would jump into the barnyard to wait for them.

With his jumping ability, Snowman could have escaped and run all over the countryside, but he never tried to leave the family he loved. As an adult, Harriet de Leyer said, "Snowman would do anything my dad asked of him, and I believe that's because Snowman understood my dad saved him."

Snowman died in the fall of 1974 at the approximate age of twenty-nine. No one knew exactly how old he was. Snowman was buried in his favorite corner of the pasture where he liked to stand under the pine trees.

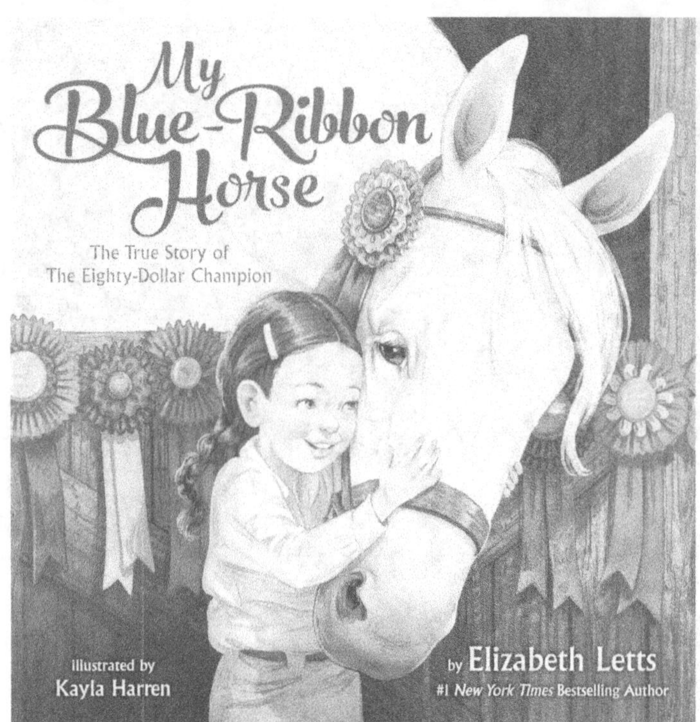 

Busloads of schoolchildren traveled to the farm to meet Snowman. Two children's books have been written about him. Breyer made models of Snowman in 2005 and 2013.

34

Kennedy Equines

The Kennedy children enjoyed many pets during their years at the White House.[1] One of the most special was young Caroline's pony, Macaroni. When John F. Kennedy became president on January 20, 1961, Caroline was three, and her brother, John Jr., was just two months old.

Caroline's gray cat, Tom Kitten, accompanied her to the White House. A regular menagerie of pets soon surrounded them. The dogs included Charlie, a Welsh Terrier, Clipper, a German Shepherd, Wolf, an Irish Wolfhound, Shannon, a Cocker Spaniel, and Pushinka who was a gift from Soviet Premier Nikita Khrushchev. Pushinka was the daughter of Strelka, a canine who had traveled on one of the Sputnik missions. Before the authorities accepted the dog, they extensively screened her to see whether she contained any spying devices. Pushinka later gave birth to four puppies known as the "pupniks."

Other small pets included Robin, a canary; two parakeets, Bluebell and Maybelle; hamsters, Debbie and Billie; and Zsa Zsa, a white rabbit.

John F. Kennedy was allergic to animal hair of any kind, but his wife was an accomplished horse-woman. Jackie's mother had introduced her to horseback riding when the girl was just a year old, and her early childhood revolved around her pony, Buddy.

At the time of Kennedy's election, Jackie had two horses—a brown and white pinto named Rufus and a bay gelding, A Bit of Irish. They were stabled at Glen Ora, a country home leased by the Kennedys in nearby Virginia.

In April 1962, the First Lady completed a goodwill tour of Pakistan which included horseback riding. Sardar *(right)*, a ten-year-old bay Thorough-bred jumper, impressed Mrs. Kennedy. Muhammad Ayub Khan, then president of Pakistan, gave her the horse, a

---

[1] *Although JFK was the youngest elected U.S. president at forty-three, Theodore Roosevelt was a year younger when he became president after the assassination of William McKinley in 1901.*

gift she later referred to as her "favorite treasure."

Khan told her, "It is my hope that every time you ride Sardar, you will remember with fondness the time you spent in Pakistan." After thirty-four days in quarantine, Sardar joined the other Kennedy horses. Later that year, Khan visited the United States and rode with Jackie and Sardar at Glen Ora.

As her mother had done with her, Jackie gave her own children an early start on horseback. She wanted a safe "baby sitter" pony for Caroline's first experience. Macaroni was perfect. A ten-year-old part-Shetland gelding, Macaroni was a stunning bay roan with four stockings and a star.

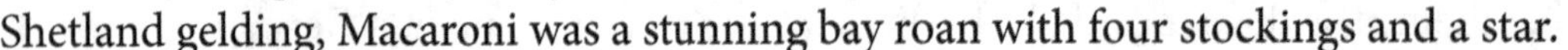

Macaroni spent time at Glen Ora but was also brought to the White House. He was ridden and grazed on the South Lawn where a temporary stable was erected. The pony was also ridden at the presidential retreat, Camp David, where President Kennedy had a bridle path cleared and a riding ring and stable built. Secret Service agents supervised the children on their rides.

The New York Times printed a photo of Macaroni, driven by Jackie, giving the Kennedy children and their friends sleigh rides. The cover of the September 7, 1962 issue of LIFE Magazine featured a picture of Caroline and Macaroni.

In 1962, Macaroni tried to steal flowers out of the hands of Queen Farah of Iran during an official visit. In 1963, Moroccan King Hassan II presented Caroline and Macaroni with the gift of a colorful, native saddle.

Although the most popular, Macaroni wasn't the only Kennedy pony. Vice President Lyndon B. Johnson gave Caroline a young bay named Tex.[1] Other children often rode Tex as Caroline rode Macaroni at the White House.

Although John, Jr. was too young to ride much, the people of Ireland gave him a Connemara pony named Leprechaun and a small saddle engraved with "JFK Jr."

Caroline was five days short of her fifth birthday when her father was assassinated on November 22, 1963. It's unclear what happened to the Kennedy horses and ponies after the assassination; however, given Mrs. Kennedy's love of horses, it's likely they were well cared for.

---

[1] *The breed is uncertain. Some sources say a Yucatan pony, others a Galiceno. A few sources state that Macaroni was a gift from Johnson. This seems incorrect.*

35

Black Jack

Black Jack is best remembered as the riderless horse at the funeral of John F. Kennedy. The Old Guard horse was a 15.1 hand, Morgan-Quarter Horse cross, black with only a small star. Foaled on January 19, 1947, the colt was named after World War I General John J. "Black Jack" Pershing.

With the disbanding of the mounted Cavalry, Black Jack was the last horse provided by the Army Quartermaster and the last with an Army serial number. He wore his Army brand on his left shoulder and his serial number, 2V56, on the left side of his neck. He was trained at Fort Reno in Oklahoma, but the spirited horse did not like to carry a rider or work in harness. He moved to Fort Myer in Virginia in 1953[1] where the beautiful horse found a job that suited him—the caparisoned or riderless horse.

The Caisson Platoon of the 3rd U.S. Infantry Regiment (the Old Guard) performs military funerals at Arlington National Cemetery in Virginia.[2] The Old Guard is the only remaining full-time equestrian unit in the Department of Defense. In addition to funerals, the Caisson Platoon takes part in parades and other military ceremonies.

In the past, horses pulled cannons and artillery (large-caliber weapons) using two-wheeled carts called caissons. These were equipped with ammunition chests, spare wheels, and tools used for the cannons. Now, at military funerals, the caisson has a flat deck which carries the casket.

---

[1] *Some sources say 1952 others 1953.*

[2] *Unsanitary living conditions, malnourishment, and a lack of open space for the horses led to the suspension of horse-drawn caisson funerals in May 2023. Two of the Old Guard platoon horses, Mickey and Tony, had to be euthanized due to negligent care. The horses had little grass in their fields and had eaten sand and gravel, resulting in colon impaction. Limited horse-drawn military funerals resumed in June 2025.*

A caisson funeral uses seven or eight horses, usually black or gray. The wheel horses are the two at the back, closest to the caisson. They are the strongest and most experienced horses and provide pulling and braking power. The two lead horses are the second-most experienced. Their job is to set the pace and maintain an appropriate distance behind the procession ahead of them. Swing horses are in the middle. Often the least experienced in the team, these two swing out wide to help turn the wagon. During funerals, the near (left) horse in each of the three pairs is ridden. In the past, the off (right) horses were used as pack animals and not ridden.

An additional horse, known as the section horse, is ridden at the front of the unit or alongside the lead pair. The section horse helps maneuver and lead the team. A caparisoned horse follows the casket of U.S. presidents and Army or Marine Corps officers holding the rank of colonel or above.

This riderless horse wears a decorative covering. For Abraham Lincoln's funeral, his horse Bob wore a blanket but no saddle. Today, the caparisoned horse typically wears a cavalry saddle with sword/saber, and boots that are placed backwards in the stirrups. The boots symbolize the fallen leader, who will never ride again, looking back at his troops one last time.

Black Jack served as the caparison horse in over 1,000 funerals. Pete Duda was Black Jack's favorite handler. The pair walked together in 200 funerals. But Private First Class Arthur "Andy" Carlson led Black Jack during John F. Kennedy's funeral.

Carlson was nineteen and had been leading the caparison horses with The Old Guard for nine months. Black Jack was selected over the other caparison horse, Shorty. Black Jack was high-spirited, but Shorty had a reputation as an evil kicker.

The assassination occurred on Friday, November 22, 1963. After the autopsy, President Kennedy lay in the East Room of the White House for twenty-four hours where family and high government officials paid their respects.

On Sunday, November 24, six gray horses pulled a caisson, accompanied by a seventh gray section horse, transporting the body from the White House to the Capitol where viewing hours were open to the public.

> *My first part in the funeral was to follow the caisson as it carried the casket from the White House to the Capitol Building, to lie in state. To reach the White House, Black Jack and I followed the caisson from the stable at Fort Myer, through Arlington National Cemetery, across Memorial Bridge, to the courtyard inside the Treasury Building.*
>
> *Black Jack was calm. It was the proverbial calm before the storm. When told to move out we exited through a narrow street-level tunnel, barely large enough for the horses and caisson. A*

*large steel grate was leaning against a wall
inside the tunnel, and the hub of the right
rear wheel of the caisson hooked it and
started dragging it along the cobblestone
paving and the stone wall. The noise inside
the tunnel was huge, and Black Jack went
wild. He stayed agitated for the next three
days, for the entire Funeral.*

*At the White House, instead of standing
steady, Black Jack constantly threw his
head and danced around me. After about
10 seconds people stopped crowding us and
gave us space.*[1]

On Monday, the 25th, the caisson platoon led
a procession from the Capitol to St. Matthew's
Cathedral for Kennedy's funeral.

*After the president had lain in state, we
went back to the Capitol. Black Jack
continued to act up. We moved the president's body to Saint Matthew's Cathedral
for the funeral service.*

*At the cathedral people again decided not
to crowd Black Jack and me. I tried to
stand at parade rest holding his bridle—at*

Kennedy, a torpedo boat commander during World War II, was buried in Arlington National Cemetery. When the casket was loaded one last time onto the caisson for the trip to the cemetery, young John-John Kennedy, almost three, gave a soldier's salute that was captured in an iconic photograph.

Andy Carlson delivered the saddle, blanket, boots, and saber to the White House. They are now part of the Kennedy Library and Museum in Boston, Massachusetts.

Black Jack also served as the caparisoned horse in the funerals of President Herbert Hoover (1964), General Douglas MacArthur (1964), and President Lyndon B. Johnson (1973).

After twenty-four years of service with the Old Guard, Black Jack retired to the 3rd U.S. Infantry Stables on June 1, 1973, at the age of twenty-seven. The staff decorated his stall in red, white, and blue. In his later years, Black Jack suffered from arthritis and other maladies. He was euthanized on February 6, 1976.

Members of the Old Guard served as the horse's pall-bearers. Fittingly, a caisson carried the old caisson horse to his burial place on the parade ground of Fort Myer. Black Jack even had a caparisoned horse in his own procession. A brass plaque engraved with his image marks

---

[1] *Black Jack: Americas famous riderless horse, Robert Knuckle, 11*

138

his grave. Black Jack is one of only four horses in U.S. history to be buried with military honors; the others are Chief (1968), Sergeant Reckless (1968), and Comanche (1891). Breyer made a model of Black Jack from 2003 to 2005.

Raven was another riderless horse who overlapped the final years of Black Jack. Also black, Raven was the horse used in President Eisenhower's funeral in 1969.

Sergeant York took up the caparison duties in 1997. Foaled on April 25, 1991, and named Allaboard Jules, the Standardbred colt's original career was harness racing, winning five of twenty-three races. After his career change, he was renamed in honor of the World War I soldier Alvin C. York. The equine Sergeant York served as the riderless horse in President Ronald Reagan's funeral procession in 2004 *(right)*. A unique aspect of Reagan's funeral was that the reversed boots in Sergeant York's stirrups were the former president's own brown riding boots provided by Mrs. Reagan. Sergeant York served twenty-five years, retiring in June 2022 at thirty-one.

Many other horses have served in the Caisson Platoon. As of 2024, the Caisson has forty-three horses in three squads. Each squad consists of eleven horses—six to pull the wagon, a section horse, and a caparisoned horse. The additional horses serve as alternates.

A horse named Hank served as the caparison horse during the funeral for General Colin Powell in

2021. Hank, known as Hank the Tank, served as a caisson horse for ten years, retiring in 2023. He is enjoying his retirement at Compassion Ranch in Alabama.

Horses that are injured or retire from the service are sometimes available for adoption. For example, after leaving the caisson unit, Herb, a 16-hand, 1400 pound, black Percheron gelding, became part of the Wounded Warrior riding program at Fort Sam Houston.

36

RCMP Horses

Burmese was a solid black, half Thoroughbred, half Hanoverian mare presented to Queen Elizabeth II after a Royal Canadian Mounted Police (RCMP) performance at the Royal Windsor Horse Show in 1969. Burmese became the queen's favorite mount.

Queen Elizabeth had loved horses from an early age. At four, she received her first—Peggy, a Shetland pony. It didn't take long for her to become an accomplished rider. In 1952, she inherited the racing stable of her father, King George VI. She continued to race horses under the family's registered colors—a purple and scarlet jacket with gold braiding and a black cap. In addition to Thoroughbreds, Queen Elizabeth raised Shetland, Fell, and Highland ponies at several stables in the UK.

Burmese was trained for service as a police horse, which required that she cope calmly with crowds, gunfire, loud noises, and obstacles or objects thrown at her. At five, Burmese took part in the RCMP Musical Ride, a performance of cavalry drills choreographed to music, dating back to the late 1800s.

The roots of the Royal Canadian Mounted Police are found in the North-West Mounted Police (NWMP) program, established in 1873 to enforce law in western Canada. The force was open to males eighteen to forty who could ride a horse, were of sound constitution and good character, and able to read and write in either English or French. They adopted blue pants and a scarlet jacket as their uniform. In 1920, the NWMP merged with the Dominion Police force of eastern Canada to form the Royal Canadian Mounted Police, Canada's national

Ronald Reagan on Centenial and Queen Elizabeth on Burmese.

police force. RCMP officers are sometimes known as Mounties.

In 1942, they established a remount ranch at Fort Walsh to raise horses for the RCMP. In the early days, the horses were primarily Thoroughbreds. Later, Hanoverians were introduced into the program. Burmese was born at the fort in 1962. Fort Walsh is now a Canadian national historic site.

Trooping the Colour is an annual celebration, part of the Horse Guards Parade in London, England, honoring the birthday of the current king or queen. Prior to receiving Burmese, Queen Elizabeth had ridden Tommy, Winston, or Imperial in the event. But from 1969 to 1986, she rode Burmese exclusively (sidesaddle) in Trooping the Colour.

During the 1981 event, someone fired six blank rounds at the queen from a starter pistol. Although Burmese startled, the queen kept her under control. Elizabeth continued to ride for pleasure into her nineties, but from 1987 on, she rode in a carriage for Trooping the Colour.

When not serving the queen, the Metropolitan Police Mounted Branch used Burmese. The beautiful mare retired in 1986 and was turned out to pasture at Windsor Castle's Great Park where the queen could see her. In 1990, at twenty-eight, Burmese passed away.

Other Police Service Horses given to British royalty by the RCMP include:

- Centenial (originally Jerry), 1973
- James, 1998
- George, 2009
- Elizabeth, 2012
- Sir John, 2016
- Kluane and Darby, 2019
- Noble (a mare) presented to King Charles III in 2023

The queen presented two horses to the RCMP— Golden Jubilee in 2002 and Victoria in 2018. Victoria was the foal of Elizabeth, the mare given to the queen in 2012.

To honor Burmese, Queen Elizabeth commissioned a bronze statue of herself riding the mare sidesaddle. The statue stands in front of the legislative building in Regina, Saskatchewan. Another statue, in Ottawa, portrays Queen Elizabeth[1] riding the gelding Centenial.

---

[1] *Elizabeth II, April 21, 1926—September 8, 2022*

37

Ride & Tie

Riding horseback was a common means of transportation in the days before automobiles. If two people had only one horse between them, they sometimes rode double. However, depending on the size of the people and the horse, the animal might tire quickly. An alternative was for one person to ride while the other walked. Rider and walker periodically switched places. That technique formed the basis for an interesting equine event—the Ride & Tie race.

Each Ride & Tie team consists of two people and a horse. When the race starts, teammate A rides the horse while teammate B runs. At some point, the horse and rider stop. Team member A dismounts and ties the horse to a tree or fence post, then starts to run. When B catches up to the horse, he unties it and rides. The teammates continue taking turns in this manner. The horse runs the entire route, but he rests periodically when tied. Each person runs about half the total race distance, and they can rest while riding.

Just because a runner or rider crosses the finish line first, doesn't mean they are the winner. A team's final time isn't recorded until all three members have finished.

The first official Ride & Tie race, twenty-five miles long, was held in California in 1971. To be sanctioned, a race must be twenty miles or longer. Recent Ride & Tie races have distances up to thirty-five miles. Levi Strauss & Co., known for its Levi's jeans, sponsored the first event. In 1886, the company had introduced their two horse trademark, which depicts two horses attempting to pull apart a pair of Levi's jeans. The logo symbolized the strength of the clothing.

One section of the first race crossed a state park. Park rangers informed the race organizers they had killed seventeen rattlesnakes in the area a week earlier. Apparently, the pounding hooves scared any remaining ones away as no snake bites occurred during the race.

In the first race, the teams didn't all start simultaneously (a shotgun start). They left in a staggered start, six groups at a time. A helicopter monitored the participants. Despite

Rules of the Race

having several vet stations, two horses died. In the weeks after the event, some called it the Ride & Die. Organizers were uncertain whether they would ever hold another race.

Jim Steere, a veterinarian and endurance rider, who participated in the first race, believed it could become a great event. He offered suggestions for improving the veterinary procedures to make the race safer for horses. No serious horse problems occurred in the second race, although two people were hospitalized with exhaustion.

The location of the Ride & Tie championship race changes from year to year. Awards are given in three categories based on the composition of the team members—two men, two women, and male/female.

Although horses must be at least five years old, no minimum age is listed in the Ride & Tie rules for human participants. The youngest winner to date was fifteen-year-old Sara Howard, who teamed up with her father in 2008. Nine-year-old Madison Trocha is the youngest to complete a race, thirty-four miles in 2007. Madison also participated with her father.

The race length, challenging terrain, hot weather, and unpredictability of excited horses all increase the possibility of mishaps and injuries. Many contestants over the years have inadvertently run right past their tied horse. Mary Tiscornia had the honor of being the first to do so. When she was two miles beyond the animal, she realized her mistake and ran back to retrieve the horse. Despite that setback, she was part of the first all-female team to finish.

Some participants tie brightly colored ribbons to their horses to make them easier to spot. One team even tied a radio to the saddle and turned it on at each tie to make their horse more noticeable. In 1978, Tiscornia's horse, Gus, broke loose from a tie and ran off. She and her partner didn't find him until after the race.

Scrapes, bumps, and bruises are common—and considered minor inconveniences. Marty Jensen was knocked down by a horse and broke her thumb. At the next vet check, she had it splinted and continued the race. One person described fellow competitor Joyce Taylor. "She looked like she had fought a war single-handedly, and lost … badly. A maze of scratches covered her thighs and numerous small chunks of flesh had been removed from her lower legs. There was a large cut on the back of her neck and her left wrist sported a deep, jagged gash."

Taylor's response. "Branches and bushes. They just wouldn't get out of my way."

Sometimes, more serious injuries occurred. A horse named Snicker kicked her owner, Pam Wagner, in the face during a pre-race vet check (held the day before the start). The following day, Pam was back to ride, with twenty-three stitches above her right eye. Marsha Groth was thrown from her horse and fractured her skull. She was flown by helicopter to a nearby hospital, recovered, and participated in the race in later years.

As Debra Pack rode past the tied horse Zar, he kicked her leg and broke it. Zar had a ribbon tied to his tail, a customary way to notify others that a horse kicks, however Pack ventured a little too close. Later in the same race, Zar stepped on his rider Bill Johnson's foot. Johnson twisted his leg in a

desperate attempt to free himself. He completed the race, but afterwards, X-rays revealed his ankle was broken.

The Ride & Tie website[1] displays information and race results from 2010 to the present. The information includes the date, location, length of the race, number of teams, teammate names, horses' names, finish times, and team placings.

---

[1] rideandtie.org

38

The Great American Horse Race

July 4, 1976 was the 200th birthday of the United States. However, the official bicentennial celebration began much earlier. On April 1, 1975, the American Freedom Train, a traveling American history museum, started its tour of the forty-eight contiguous states. Reenactments, parades, fireworks, and other festivities were held across the country.

One of the lesser-known events, for those outside the world of horses, was The Great American Horse Race. The race was the idea of thirty-two-year-old Randy Scheiding, who described his enjoyment of an 800-mile ride he'd taken from Illinois to Kansas.

> *It was the highlight of my life. You have a chance to become part of the landscape. It's a feeling of freedom I had never experienced.*[1]

Scheiding's friend, Chuck Waggoner, helped with organization and promotion. They hired journalist Curt Lewis to photograph the race. Scheiding placed an ad in Western Horseman magazine. "The adventure of a lifetime for the common American who regards his horse as something special. Longest horse race in history." The ad produced over 600 responses, many with a check for the $500 entry fee.

The race started on Memorial Day in Frankfort, New York, and finished on Labor Day at the California State Fairgrounds in Sacramento, California. In total, it was a 98-day journey of 3,200 miles through thirteen states, incorporating sections of the Oregon Trail and the Pony Express route.

The format wasn't that of a typical horse race. All the riders started together at dawn and followed a designated route, typically covering thirty-five to forty miles each day. Officials recorded each rider's daily time. The rider's total time when everyone reached Sacramento would determine the winners.

Each rider could use two horses, riding one while ponying the other and switching between the two as needed. The team also had a support crew, usually two or three people. Veterinarians performed health checks throughout the day. If a horse showed signs of poor condition, he was required to ride in a trailer until he

---

[1] *The Charlotte Observer, Thu, Apr 29, 1976*

returned to normal. The time a horse spent in a trailer was counted as double time for the team. If one equine member was withdrawn, a rider could continue with the remaining animal as long as he remained healthy. Teams did not receive a time penalty for withdrawing a horse.

Riders came from forty-seven states and ten foreign countries—Australia, Austria, Belgium, Canada, Denmark, England, France, Germany, Italy, and Japan. On May 31, 1976, ninety-four teams met at the starting line of the GAHR, competing for the first-place prize of $25,000. An additional $25,000 would be divided among the next nine finishers.

Arabian horses dominate endurance racing. According to Curt Lewis, "If you're not riding an Arabian, you're following an Arabian." However, a variety of other breeds were entered in the GAHR, including Mustang, Morgan, Standardbred, Icelandic, Orlov trotter, Appaloosa, Thoroughbred, Quarter Horse, Connemara, Paso Fino, and several mules.

When the Icelandics began to suffer from the heat during the race, their riders, an Austrian named Johannes and a German, Walter, decided to clip them. The only place they found to plug in their clippers was the bathroom in a state park. Park rangers weren't pleased with the horse hair flying everywhere, and ordered the men to leave. Even though neither rider spoke English, it must have been pretty clear what the rangers wanted. However, by the time they acknowledged comprehension, their four ponies were fully clipped.

There were nearly as many women in the race as men, including six husband-wife teams. Riders ranged in age from seventeen to seventy. The youngest was Valorie Briggs from Oregon. Her main horse, actually pony-sized, was a spunky 13.2 hand buckskin, Mustang-Arabian cross called Tiki. Valorie's other horse was Chuluck, a larger bay Thoroughbred cross. Valorie's mother, Mary Lou, also competed on her horse, Daniel. Although Mary Lou dropped out after a week, Valorie completed the race with Tiki, finishing fourteenth. One of the hardest things for Valorie was coping with the weather.

Places like Kansas, Missouri … they have hailstorms and rainstorms that are so bad, you can see 'em coming from miles away, a wall of black coming, and you know you'll have just a couple of minutes before it hits you. You'd put your poncho on, and pull it down so you could barely see out of the eyehole, and it would still drench you. Drenched. It would hit so hard it would almost knock you and the horses over. One rider got knocked off the horse by the lightning coming close by.[1]

Although this was a "horse" race, two teams rode mules. Virl Norton had entered with his main mule, Lord Fauntleroy (Leroy) and his backup, Lady Eloise. Leroy was a veteran of the 100-mile Tevis Cup race. Both mules were out of Thoroughbred mares. They were tall, each about

---

[1] theequestrianvagabond.blogspot.com/2011/02/great-american-horse-race-wild-terror.html

148

16 hands. The Arabians did not intimidate Norton. From the start, he was confident his mules would not only finish but would win. At shorter distances, the horses had an advantage over his mules, but he approached the race as a marathon, not a sprint.

Norton, one of the oldest GAHR riders, was a steeplejack[1] from San Jose, California. Born in Wyoming in 1916, he was an experienced horseman, having caught and trained wild Mustangs from the time he was a teen.

Most of the riders had two or three people to help them along the way. Virl's support crew was his sixteen-year-old son, Pierce, who had only recently received his driver's license. Pierce drove his father's pickup truck and horse trailer from one encampment to the next without incident.

A quarter of the way into the race, in Kankakee, Illinois, Virl Norton and his plain-looking mules took the lead, ahead of the fancy Arabians. After that, Norton was never lower than third in the race. When they reached northern Nevada, Lady Eloise became lame and had to be withdrawn. Norton continued on with his remaining mule at a slow and steady pace. Leroy confidently announced his victory as he crossed the finish line in Sacramento.

Owner Virl Norton of San Jose, Calif. was in the saddle as Leroy galloped into the California State Fair, stopped at a ring before about 200 spectators, and gave forth with a victorious hee-haw.[2]

---

[1] *steeplejack (one who paints or repairs tall things)*
[2] *Quad-City Times, Davenport, Iowa, Thu, Sep 16, 1976*

Norton provided hay and water for Leroy while he waited for the remaining riders to finish. Then, the organizers totaled everyone's ride time, factoring in any penalties, to determine the winners. Norton, Leroy, and Lady Eloise came in first with a total ride time of 315.47 hours, ahead of the second-place, Arabian team by nine minutes. Newspapers loved it, featuring headlines such as, "Mule Runs Away With Great American Horse Race."

Fifty-four teams completed the GAHR. After Virl Norton, the other nine in the top ten included six Arabians, an Appaloosa, a Connemara, and another mule, Hugo, ridden by Eva Taylor, who finished tenth.[1]

One entrant, Sonny Parker, dropped out two-thirds of the way through the race because his mare, Warsaw, kept gaining weight. The day after the race ended, Warsaw surprised everyone with a foal who was given the name GAHR Fiasco.

Virl Norton passed away in 1995. A friend, Maryben Stover, had promised Virl she would take care of Leroy, then twenty-five years old. The mule lived another twelve years at her place, just a mile from Virl's old ranch.

Top 10 Finishers

1st: Virl Norton, Lord Fauntleroy (Jack Mule, 7), Lady Eloise (Molly Mule, 5)

2nd: Juel Ashley, Hammon's Pride (Arabian stallion, 6), Granny (Arabian mare, 7)

3rd: Rhonda Utt, Ali Basa (Arabian gelding, 8), Checuke (Anglo-Arabian gelding, 10), only rider in the top 10 to finish with both mounts healthy

4th: Smokey Killen, Bandit (Arabian gelding, 6), Shablaze (Arabian gelding, 8)

5th: Diane Clagett, Rush Creek Dan (Arabian gelding, 7), Valentina (Arabian mare, 7)

6th: Irene Burd, Colty (Arabian Quarterhorse gelding, 6), High Hopes (Anglo Arabian mare, 10)

7th: Roger Justice, Spot (Appaloosa mare, 6), Unnamed Appaloosa gelding, 8

8th: Sam Garner, Bogam's Dude (Arabian stallion)

9th: Marian Molthan, Bridgit (Connemara pony mare, 14), Heather (Connemara pony mare, 14)

10th: Eva Taylor, Hugo (Jack Mule, 11), Sugar (Molly Mule, 8)

---

[1] *The race route ran from Frankfort, NY to Lisbon, OH; to Kanakee, IL; to Kansas City, MO; to Alma, NE; to Rawlins, WY; to Deeth, NV; and to Sacramento, CA.*

Reported numbers for the race vary. Sources say anywhere from 91 to 104 entries were at the starting line. Total miles were 3,200 or maybe 3,500. The number of states/nations represented also varied. Youngest to oldest riders, 17 to 70 or 18 to 69. Virl was described as anywhere from 54 to 60.

39

Man vs. Horse

One evening, a Welsh pub owner, Gordon Green, found himself arguing with a customer who believed that over a long distance, people were as fast as horses. Green believed they were not. The two agreed on one thing–a race was the best way to resolve the matter.

In June 1980, fifty runners and fifteen horses lined up for the first Man vs Horse race, in Llanwrtyd Wells, a small town in Wales. The twenty-two-mile race covered rough terrain across rivers and through steep ravines.

Rider Glyn Jones won the first race easily on his horse Solomon. The event was so popular it became an annual race. Bicyclists were permitted in the race from 1985 to 1992. For safety, runners start fifteen minutes ahead of the horses, and the time is adjusted for that at the finish.

Sue Thomas was the first woman to win (1982) riding Simon. It wasn't until the twenty-fifth race that a human beat the horses. In 2004, London marathon runner, Huw Lobb, finished in two hours and five minutes, beating the fastest horse by two minutes. Lobb won twenty-five thousand pounds. The prize money

increases by a thousand pounds each year a human does not win. The 2004 race had the highest number of participants—500 runners and forty horses. Additional human winners are Florian Holzinger (2007), Ricky Lightfoot (2022), and Daniel Connolly (2023).

Trophies are awarded to the top three finishers in the categories: male runner, female runner, and horse and rider. Veterinarians check all horses at the beginning, midpoint, and end of the race. Any that fail the vet check are not permitted to continue.

An American version of this concept is the Man Against Horse race in Prescott, Arizona. The first Arizona race was held in 1983, the result of a bet made in a bar. Gheral Brownlow bet cowboy Steve Rafters that he could outrun Steve's horse.

The race is held in October over steep, rocky trails that traverse Mingus Mountain. The course begins at an elevation of 5,200 feet, climbs to the top at 7,700 feet, then drops down toward the finish line. There are a variety of race distances—fifty-mile, twenty-five-mile, half marathon (thirteen-mile), and a kids' quarter-mile race.

Horses are vet checked roughly every five miles. The humans are on their own. Horses must be at least five to enter the fifty-mile race and four for the twenty-five-mile one. Because of the rough terrain, all horses have to be shod or wear hoof boots. There is no minimum age for riders; however, those under sixteen must be accompanied by an adult.

Time spent at vet check stations is subtracted to determine a horse's final race time. Everyone who finishes the fifty-mile course under a specified time receives a buckle. Additional awards go to the first-place finishers in each category, and to the top ten riders and runners.

In 2022, the Steel Cup was created for the horse finishing in the top ten who is in the best condition at the end of the race. The award is in memory of 2021 Man Against Horse winner, Steel, an Arabian owned by Susie Kramer. Steel died after a fall in July 2022, during the 100-mile Tevis Cup ride in the Sierra Nevadas.

Kim Abbott was the first to win the Steel Cup in October 2022, on her Arabian Justa Strike of Fire, nicknamed Goat. Abbott has won the race on horseback four times, the first in 2008 on Sea Spot Run.

Humans have an advantage over the horses on the steep downhill sections of the course. Hopi Dennis (Danny) Poolheco was the first runner to win the race. He won the race six times, from 1999 to 2004, and finished second in 2005.

Susie Kramer on Steel

40

Secretariat

The result of a coin toss in 1969 produced results that extended far beyond what the two participants could have imagined. Ogden Phipps and Penny Chenery Tweedy were flipping for rights to the foals from two Meadow Stable mares.

Penny's father, Christopher Chenery, had entered into the two-year agreement with Phipps. Chenery owned some of the best Thoroughbred broodmares, and Phipps had one of the top stallions, Bold Ruler. Two mares would be bred to Bold Ruler each year. The winner of the coin toss would get his choice of the first two foals. The loser of the toss would get the second foal that first year, and then first pick from the foals produced the second year.

In 1968, Christopher Chenery was hospitalized due to Alzheimer's disease. Penny kept the Meadow's part of this unusual deal to honor her father, but she planned to discontinue the arrangement after the 1970 foals were born. Penny's brother and sister thought it best to sell the Meadow, but Penny was determined to save the farm. Although she'd loved and ridden horses from her childhood, she hadn't been involved in the business side of things. Because of her father's condition, she began to intensely study the world of Thoroughbred horse racing. That's how Penny found herself at the coin toss.

In the spring of 1969, the Meadow's mare Somethingroyal produced a filly, The Bride. The second mare, Hasty Matelda, had a colt, Rising River. The half dollar was tossed into the air, and Ogden Phipps called, "Tails." The coin landed on the floor, tails up. Penny had lost. Or had she?

Phipps chose The Bride, by then a weanling, leaving Penny with Rising River, who was never successful as a racehorse.

Another mare, Cicada, replaced Hasty Matelda for the second year of the agreement. But Cicada had not conceived, meaning there would only be one foal in 1970.

Since Penny had first choice in the second year, she would receive Somethingroyal's foal. Although Phipps had won the toss, he received one foal. Penny, the loser, received two, and her second one just happened to be Secretariat. You have to wonder whether Ogden Phipps regretted calling "tails" that day.

The following spring, on March 30, 1970, Somethingroyal (eighteen at the time) gave birth to a chestnut foal with three white stockings (all but his left front) and a star/stripe. Secretariat wasn't the first choice for his name. Initial ideas were Sceptre, Royal Line, Something Special, Games of Chance, and Deo Volente (God Willing). Those were all rejected by the Jockey Club as they were already in use or were too similar to existing names. Finally, Elizabeth Ham, secretary at the Meadow, suggested Secretariat. That had been a title used when she worked as a secretary at the United Nations.

The young Secretariat had a huge appetite. The colt kept growing and growing. Some considered him fat—and awkward. While Secretariat was starting his yearling training with Bob Bailes, another Meadow colt began racing as a two-year-old.

Trained by Lucien Laurin, in Florida, the bay Riva Ridge would be overshadowed by Secretariat most of his life. The Disney movie, *Secretariat*, never mentions him at all. But it was Riva Ridge's success that began to turn things around for the financially strapped Meadow. Riva Ridge's wins convinced Penny's siblings not to sell the farm.

After a couple of disappointing starts in 1971, Laurin switched to Ron Turcotte as Riva's jockey. Turcotte realized the colt had a fear of being bumped by other horses. The jockey spent a month working with him to overcome his fear. Riva Ridge then returned to racing, winning five stakes races that year, earning the title of Champion Two-year-old Colt. Before the 1972 Kentucky Derby, Riva Ridge won two out of three races. He went on to win the Derby, leading the entire way. Riva Ridge finished fourth in the Preakness and then won the Belmont Stakes by seven lengths. If there hadn't been heavy rain the day before the Preakness, Riva Ridge might have won that, too and become a Triple Crown winner; however, the colt never raced well on muddy tracks.

At the time of the Derby, Christopher Chenery was in a nursing home with advanced Alzheimer's and did not speak. A nurse, feeding him, had the race on the television in his room. When she saw Riva Ridge had won, she said, "Mr. Chenery, your horse has won the Kentucky Derby!"

The nurse later told Penny that tears had dripped down her father's cheeks when he heard the news. Although he couldn't speak, he apparently understood that his lifelong dream of winning the Derby had finally come true.

Despite winning two-thirds of the Triple Crown, public attention was already shifting from Riva Ridge to the two-year-old Secretariat. Both horses raced

under the blue-and-white checked silks of the Meadow Stable. Lucien Laurin was also Secretariat's trainer. At first, he was skeptical about the big colt. He gained the nickname, Ol' Hopalong, for his youthful awkwardness.

In his first race, in July 1972, at Aqueduct in New York, Secretariat was bumped. His jockey, Paul Feliciano, believed the bump would have knocked a smaller horse down. Secretariat recovered to finish fourth. Feliciano rode Secretariat in the next race, which they won by six lengths. After that, Ron Turcotte would ride Secretariat in all but his last race.

Secretariat established a habit of starting slow, then coming from behind to win. At times, even his jockey was skeptical about the horse's ability to make up the ground he'd given away at the start. After that first loss, Secretariat lost only once more that year. In the Champagne Stakes at Belmont, he finished first, but the win was disallowed because he brushed against the horse Stop the Music. He finished the 1972 season with seven wins in nine starts. That year, Secretariat became the first two-year-old to be named Horse of the Year.

After Christopher Chenery's death in January 1973, the Chenery family faced financial problems once again—how to pay the taxes on his estate. Penny decided to syndicate Secretariat. Seth Hancock, owner of Claiborne Farm, assisted with the process. They sold thirty-two shares of Secretariat for a total of $6,080,000—all before the horse had entered a single race in 1973. The syndication required Secretariat be retired from racing at the end of his three-year-old season.

1973 started out well with Secretariat winning his first two races. Then, he finished a disappointing third in the Wood Memorial Stakes two weeks before the Kentucky Derby. First in that race was Angle Light, another Lucien-trained horse. Second was Sham, trained by Frank "Pancho" Martin and ridden by Laffit Pincay.

Secretariat's loss may have been due to an abscess that was later discovered in his mouth. Many still considered him the favorite to win the Derby; however, after the Wood Memorial loss, some began to doubt.

Secretariat faced both Angle Light and Sham among the thirteen entries in the Derby. He started the race in last place while Shecky Greene and Sham battled for the lead. Shecky Greene faded, leaving Sham out front until the "Red Ball Express"[1] passed him, winning by two and a half lengths. Sham, in second, was eight lengths ahead of third-place finisher, Our Native.

---

[1] *Red Ball Express is how Shecky Greene's jockey, Larry Adams, described Secretariat rushing past him on the outside in the Derby.*

Two weeks later, six horses competed in the Preakness Stakes. Secretariat again broke last out of the gate but won by two and a half lengths. Sham, who finished second, was his stiffest competition. After the race, the track manager Chick Lang said, "It's as if God decided to create the perfect horse."

There was a discrepancy over Secretariat's time in the Preakness. The official electronic timer showed 1:55 2/5 (not a record), while others had clocked the race at 1:53 2/5, which was a record. It wasn't until 2012, that videos of the race established the time as the record-setting 1:53 2/5.

After Sham's second-place finishes in the Derby and the Preakness, his trainer declared the horse would not run in the Belmont Stakes. "I don't want any more part of my horse looking at that big behind."

Martin later changed his mind, and Sham faced Secretariat again in a field of five horses. Unlike his previous races, Secretariat didn't start slow. He and Sham fought for the lead early on. Sham was briefly in front. Then, Secretariat pulled ahead and began increasing his lead to an unbelievable thirty-one lengths at the finish. The race announcer was amazed. "He is moving like a tremendous machine!"

Twice a Prince finished a distant second. Sham faded badly, finishing last. That day, Secretariat became the ninth Triple Crown winner, the first in twenty-five years. Citation was the previous winner in 1948. Secretariat's records in all three races still stand today.

It would be hard to have a more impressive demonstration of Big Red's abilities than his Belmont win. Perhaps he should have been retired after that victory. But Big Red raced six more times in 1973, winning four and finishing second twice.

He was beaten in August by a four-year-old unknown gelding named Onion, in the Whitney Stakes, one of the biggest upsets in horse racing. It was reported that Secretariat had been running a fever and was in the early stages of a viral infection.

He was defeated again by Prove Out in the Woodward Stakes in September. Prove Out also beat Riva Ridge that same year. Allen Jerkens, was the trainer for both Onion and Prove Out, gaining him the nickname "Giant Killer."

The first running of the Marlboro Cup Invitational was supposed to be a match race between Secretariat and Riva Ridge, but given recent losses by both horses, the race was opened to others. There were seven in the field. Early in the race, Onion battled Riva Ridge for the lead, but Secretariat once again came from behind to pass both, winning by three and a half lengths. Riva Ridge finished second, and Onion was fourth.

For Secretariat's last outing, he traveled to the Woodbine track in Ontario for the Canadian International, on October 28, 1973. Secretariat's trainer, Lucien Laurin, and his regular jockey, Ron Turcotte, were both Canadians. Turcotte had recently received a suspension and couldn't ride Secretariat in his final race. Eddie Maple, who had ridden Riva Ridge in the Marlboro Cup, was chosen to ride in place of Turcotte. The change in jockeys didn't bother Secretariat who won the race easily by six and a half lengths.

Secretariat finished his career with earnings of $1,316,808. On November 6, 1973, thousands of people turned out at Aqueduct in New York for a Farewell to Secretariat Day, the horse's last public

Secretariat by Nadina Ironia, ironia-art.com, used by permission

appearance. Secretariat appeared confused and maybe a little angry when he was ponied out only to find there was no one there to race. He was the only horse on the track.[1]

Riva Ridge's earnings ($1,111,497) nearly equaled those of Secretariat. Both retired to serve as stallions at Claiborne Farm where Penny Chenery often visited them.

> *As time passed, I'd call to Secretariat, and he wouldn't acknowledge me. I was just one of a hundred people calling his name every day. But right up until he died, Riva Ridge would perk up when he heard me call him. That's why when I talk about the two horses, I say Secretariat belonged to the people, and Riva Ridge belonged to me. Secretariat had millions of people who cared about him. He didn't need me. But Riva Ridge only had me. He was my hero and I knew I meant something to him.[2]*

---

[1] *Many people were involved in Secretariat's life. Too many to fully credit here. A book by Lawrence Scanlan, The Horse God Built: Secretariat, His Groom, Their Legacy, features Eddie Sweat, Secretariat's main groom.*

[2] *americasbestracing.net/the-sport/2025-meadow-stables-true-hero-riva-ridge*

41

Secretariat's Descendants

Surprisingly, Secretariat's first foal had spots! When he retired from racing, Secretariat was tested as a sire with three non-Thoroughbred mares, producing two colts in 1974. His first foal, named First Secretary, was born to Leola, an Appaloosa mare. The chestnut colt strongly resembled Secretariat except for the white blanket on his hindquarters. First Secretary grew to almost 17 hands and became an influential sire in the Appaloosa world. He died of colic in 1993.

Secretariat's stocky second colt, Statesman, was from an unnamed Percheron nurse mare at Claiborne Farm. A lawyer in Ohio purchased Statesman. The athletic horse never reached the height of his half-brother. He matured to a solid 15.3 hands and was trained for dressage. As a sire, Statesman was crossed with Thoroughbreds to create successful warmbloods and sport horses. Later, he became a polo pony and jumper. He spent his last years in Arizona. Statesman died in early 2003 at twenty-eight.

Secretariat sired 663 Thoroughbred foals. He wasn't considered a great sire of colts; however, he became a leading broodmare sire. One of his notable daughters was Secrettame, whose descendants included Smarty Jones, the 2004 Kentucky Derby and Preakness Stakes winner.

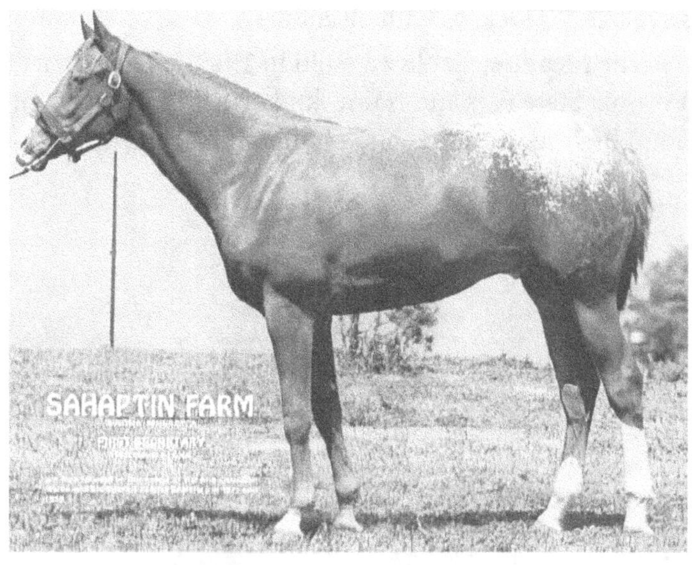

At nineteen, Secretariat suffered from severe laminitis.[1] When treatment didn't improve his condition, he was euthanized on October 4, 1989, and was buried at Claiborne Farm. After his death, an autopsy revealed Secretariat's heart was two and a half times larger than that of an average horse.

Riva Ridge had died in his paddock on April 21, 1985, at sixteen. He was thought to have had a heart attack. Billy Silver was a lesser-known equine connected with Secretariat and Riva Ridge. The Appaloosa was the track "pony" that led Secretariat and sometimes Riva Ridge out for races. He also served as a reassuring companion to both. After those two retired from racing, Billy Silver spent his remaining years as a 4-H horse.

On July 13, 1978, in a race at Belmont Park, Ron Turcotte was riding Flag of Leyte Gulf when a horse named Small Raja came too close. The horses clipped heels. When his mount stumbled, the jockey was thrown. His injuries left Turcotte a paraplegic. He remained a racing fan and became an advocate for jockeys with disabilities.

The Meadow Stable was sold in 1988. In 2009, part of the original farm became the home of the Virginia State Fair and is now known as Meadow Event Park. The park offers a Secretariat Birthplace Tour, highlighting sites and memorabilia from the horse's life.

---

[1] *Laminitis is a painful condition involving inflammation of the tissues that bond the hoof wall to the coffin bone. Since horse's legs and hooves bear so much weight, horses suffering severe laminitis are usually euthanized.*

42

Ruffian

Ruffian was a dark bay, almost black filly, foaled on April 17, 1972, at Claiborne Farm in Kentucky. She was a granddaughter of Bold Ruler (Secretariat's sire) on her father's side and Native Dancer on her dam's. Ruffian grew to 16.2 hands. Many thought she looked more like a colt than a filly. Unfortunately, this beautiful filly would grow up to be part of what has been called one of horse racing's saddest moments.

In her first race, on May 22, 1974, Ruffian won by fifteen lengths and equaled the Belmont track record. In the Spinaway Stakes at Saratoga Springs, N.Y., her fifth race, Ruffian won by nearly thirteen lengths. As a two-year-old, she won all five of the races she entered.

After that race, Lucien Laurin, Secretariat's trainer, commented that Ruffian might be better than Big Red. In the Spinaway, Ruffian suffered a hairline fracture in her right hind ankle. The filly didn't race for the remainder of the season.

The following spring, she was not entered in the Kentucky Derby, as her owner, Stuart Janney, believed the one and a quarter-mile distance was too much too early in the year for her. She would cruise to victory five times in 1975, with an average winning margin of over eight lengths. Although Janney and trainer Frank Whitely weren't thrilled with the idea, the public was clamoring to see the great Ruffian challenge the colts.

Her eleventh race was somewhat of a publicity stunt, reflecting the feminist revolution of the seventies—a match race pitting female against male— the country's best filly against that year's Kentucky Derby winning colt, Foolish Pleasure. Another such battle had been held two years earlier—the tennis match in which Billie Jean King defeated Bobby Riggs. Horse racing fans wore "The Great Match" buttons

with a picture of their favorite, Ruffian or Foolish Pleasure. Other buttons simply contained the text "HIM" or "HER."

The race, attended by over 50,000 spectators, was held on July 6 at Belmont Park. After a quarter mile, Ruffian, wearing number one, was ahead by a nose. It looked like she was about to break away when two bones in her right foreleg snapped. The filly refused to stop running, further damaging her leg.

The best veterinary surgeons were assembled to perform emergency surgery. But as Ruffian woke from the anesthesia, she struggled violently, smashing her cast and re-injuring her leg. She was euthanized and is buried at Belmont Park. In 2000, Dr. Edward Keefer said that the techniques to treat injured horses have improved so much that today, Ruffian might have been saved. Keefer was a cardiovascular surgeon rather than a veterinarian; however, he had been part of the team which attempted to save Ruffian's life. Now, a horse awakening from anesthesia after surgery is lowered into a pool filled with warm water for recovery. The water's resistance lowers the risk of reinjury if the horse thrashes about.

In her brief career, Ruffian won ten consecutive races, including three that were known as the Triple Tiara or Filly Triple Crown.[1] Her final contest was the only race she ever lost. She set track records in eight races and equaled the records in the other two. Her jockey, Jacinto Vasquez, rode Ruffian in eight of her races. Vasquez had ridden Foolish Pleasure in the colt's 1975 Kentucky Derby win, but he chose to ride Ruffian in the match race, believing her to be the faster horse.

Among her many nicknames, Ruffian was known as "Queen of the Century," "Queen of Racing," and "Queen of the Track." Ruffian received the 1974 Eclipse Award for Outstanding Two-year-old Filly. After her death, she was also awarded the 1975 Eclipse Award for Outstanding Three-year-old Filly. In 1976, she was inducted into the National Museum of Racing and Hall of Fame.

Sports Illustrated magazine ranked her as fifty-third in their 2000 list of the top 100 female athletes of the century, the only non-human in the list. Blood-Horse ranked Ruffian at number thirty-five in their list of the top 100 American Racehorses of the 20th Century, making her the top-ranking filly or mare.

---

[1] At the time, the Filly Triple Crown consisted of the Acorn Stakes, Mother Goose Stakes, and Coaching Club American Oaks. Currently, the Alabama Stakes replaces the Mother Goose race.

43

Alydar

The story of the racehorse Alydar has been called "a sweeping saga of greed, fraud, and almost unimaginable cruelty."[1]

Alydar's story is intertwined with Calumet Farm. In 1924, William Monroe Wright, owner of the Calumet Baking Powder Company, established a horse farm on 762 acres in Lexington, Kentucky. Calumet Farm initially raised harness racing horses. Warren Wright Sr. took over the farm in 1932 after his father's death and began replacing the Standardbreds with Thoroughbreds. A pivotal early decision was the purchase of a yearling Thoroughbred, Bull Lea, in 1936. Although he had a less-than-stellar racing career, Bull Lea was a top sire in the 1940s and 1950s.

In 1941, Whirlaway (1938–1953) achieved the first Kentucky Derby victory for Calumet. That year, he became the fifth Triple Crown winner. Calumet repeated that honor in 1948 with Citation (1945-1970), the eighth Triple Crown winner. Citation, a son of Bull Lea, won sixteen consecutive races and was the first Thoroughbred to win a million dollars. Calumet Farm was on its way to becoming one of the most successful stables in Thoroughbred racing history.

Over the years, Calumet produced ten Kentucky Derby winners: Whirlaway (1941), Pensive (1944), Citation (1948), Ponder (1949), Hill Gail (1952), Iron Liege (1957), Tim Tam (1958), Forward

Pass (1968), Strike the Gold (1991), and Rich Strike (2022).

After Warren Wright Sr. passed away in 1950, his wife, Lucille, managed the farm for the next thirty-two years. The widow married Admiral Gene Markey in 1952.

On March 23, 1975, a dark chestnut colt was born at Calumet. Mrs. Markey named him Alydar,

Alydar victory over Affirmed, 1977 Champagne Stakes

short for "Aly Darling," the nickname she used for her friend, the Aly Khan, Pakistan's ambassador to the United Nations. Alydar had a small star and stockings on his left front and right rear legs.

In 1977, as a two-year-old, Alydar beat Affirmed twice, in the Great American Stakes and the Champagne Stakes, both at Belmont Park. Toward the end of his career, Alydar would achieve another victory over Affirmed, in the Travers Stakes at Saratoga in August 1978. Affirmed actually won that race by two lengths, but the horse was disqualified for interfering.

However, Alydar is best remembered in his racing career for finishing second to Affirmed in each of the 1978 Triple Crown races, narrowing the gap with each race. Affirmed won by a length and a half in the Kentucky Derby, by a neck in the Preakness, and by a head in the Belmont Stakes—less than two lengths total for the three races.

Alydar retired in 1979 with fourteen wins in twenty-six starts and earnings of $957,195. In the Blood-Horse magazine ranking of the Top 100 U.S. Thoroughbreds of the 20th Century, Alydar ranked #27 and Affirmed #12. However, in his retirement, Alydar outperformed Affirmed, becoming a highly desirable Thoroughbred sire. One of Alydar's most famous foals was

2nd to Affirmed, 1978 Preakness Stakes

Alysheba, winner of the 1987 Kentucky Derby, Preakness, and the 1988 Breeders' Cup Classic. It was his success as a sire that ultimately led to Alydar's demise.

Just a few years into his retirement, things changed dramatically at Calumet Farm. Lucille (Wright) Markey passed away in July 1982 at eighty-five. The farm passed to the heirs of her only son, Warren Wright Jr. (who had died in 1978). Warren Jr.'s oldest offspring was Lucille "Cindy" Wright. Her husband was forty-one-year-old John Thomas "J.T." Lundy.

2nd to Affirmed, 1978 Belmont Stakes

The elder Lucille had never liked Lundy. However, after the matriarch's death, J.T. became Calumet's president. When Lundy took over in 1982, Calumet Farm was debt-free and valued at a hundred million dollars.

Although Calumet won the 1990 Eclipse Award for Outstanding Breeder, Lundy's foolish choices and reckless spending had pushed the farm toward bankruptcy. He borrowed millions to pay bills, then borrowed from another bank to pay off the previous loan. The farm's finances flipped. In eight short years under Lundy's control, they had become more than a hundred million dollars in debt. The farm had fallen behind on payments, including insurance premiums for Alydar, their star stallion.

Equine mortality policies on Alydar, totaling $36,500,000, made him the most heavily insured horse at that time. Two policies were held, through Lloyds of London and Golden Eagle Insurance. In 1990, both companies threatened to cancel their coverage because of Calumet's continued late payments.

Authorities caught up with J.T. Lundy's financial shenanigans through Frank Cihak, vice chairman of Houston's First City Bancorporation. The unscrupulous Cihak granted large loans to undeserving clients in exchange for kickbacks after the loan was issued. In 1988, Lundy had agreed to pay Cihak a million dollars if he would approve a fifty million dollar loan to Calumet. When bank officials discovered that loan and other nefarious deals, Cihak was fired, prosecuted, and sentenced to twenty-two years in prison.

In October 1990, First City demanded Lundy make a fifteen million dollar payment. Lundy hadn't made a single payment in the two years since the loan had been granted. The bank threatened to foreclose if payment wasn't received in a few months. They would seize Calumet Farm and its assets, including the horses.

A few weeks later, at 10 p.m. on Tuesday, November 13, fifteen-year-old Alydar was discovered in his stall with a broken right hind leg. Alton Stone, the watchman that night, called Calumet's resident veterinarian, Dr. Lynda Rhodes. Upon her arrival, she wrapped the leg and called Dr. William Baker. A third vet, Dr. Larry Bramlage, arrived around 11 p.m. Bramlage, an equine orthopedic surgeon, tranquilized Alydar and applied a splint. They agreed to re-evaluate the horse at seven the following morning. Ironically, Alydar's rival, Affirmed, had been leased by Calumet and was stalled in the same barn. Sedated, Alydar lay in his stall all night with his head held alternately by Dr. Rhodes, Sandy Hatfield (a farm manager), Cowboy Kipp (night watchman), and Michael Coulter (Alydar's groom).

On Wednesday, November 14, everyone agreed that although there was little chance surgery would be successful, it was their only option. They moved Alydar to Calumet's clinic. Dr. Bramlage set the broken coffin bone, reinforcing it with a metal plate and multiple pins. He covered the leg with a fiberglass cast, and Alydar was placed in a sling in a recovery stall.

The next day, Alydar showed signs of colic and had to be released from the sling. With his first steps, he lost his balance, fell, and broke his femur. The horse was euthanized and later buried in the Calumet cemetery.

Tragic accidents are not uncommon in the horse world, but from the start, some suspected Alydar's death was not accidental.

J.T. Lundy claimed Alydar had broken his leg by kicking his door hard enough to break the metal roller bolted into the concrete floor outside his stall. On the night of the 13th, the broken roller was found in the barn aisle.

The three veterinarians didn't question whether the injury was an accident; however, they disagreed as to how it might have happened. Dr. Bramlage insisted there was no way it was by kicking the door. He didn't think a horse could generate enough force from a kick to cause the type of break Alydar had. Bramlage's theory was that Alydar's kick had pushed the door outward enough to get his leg caught in the temporary opening between the door and the wall. Then, the break occurred as the horse struggled to free himself.

Tom Dixon, the representative for Lloyd's of London, believed the injury was from a straight-on or angled kick. Lloyds held the larger of the two insurance policies on Alydar. Dixon took a few photos that night and submitted a claim. Lloyds paid Alydar's insurance benefit within a month.

Golden Eagle had a smaller, five million dollar policy. That company's representative was Terry McVey. McVey never believed Lundy's account of what happened to Alydar that night. He also found Lundy surprisingly unemotional about the prize stallion's death. However, after three months, Golden Eagle also paid Calumet's claim.

Lundy used part of the insurance money to make a payment to First City Bancorporation to hold off the foreclosure. But Calumet's finances were unraveling. In April 1991, Lundy resigned as the farm's president. Portions of the property and some of the horses were sold to further reduce Calumet's debt.

Ultimately, the once-great horse farm went through foreclosure anyway and was sold at auction in 1992. Polish-born Canadian Henryk de Kwiatkowski purchased Calumet for seventeen million.

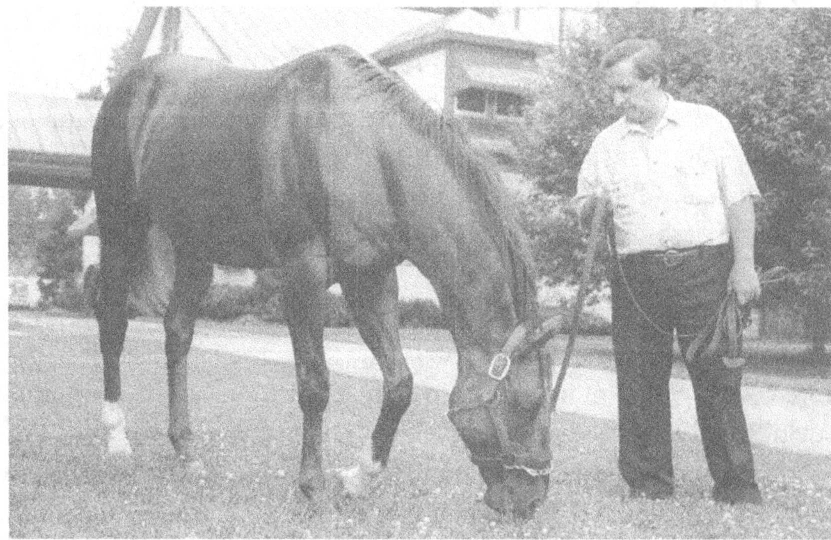

J.T. Lundy with Alydar

In 2000, J.T. Lundy was convicted on federal charges of bank fraud, bribery, and conspiracy. He received four and a half years in prison and was ordered to pay back twenty million dollars. In addition to his financial crimes, federal prosecutors Julia Tomala and James Powers, and FBI agent Rob Foster, believed Lundy was responsible for Alydar's death. They discovered many suspicious circumstances surrounding the horse's injury.

- Golden Eagle had notified Lundy that they would not renew Alydar's insurance policy, which was due to expire in December 1990.

- Lundy insisted Alydar was a known kicker, although marks in the stall didn't show evidence of recent kicking.

- Alydar's grooms and his trainer, John Veitch, contradicted Lundy, saying he was not a kicker. They claimed the marks on his stall door were from pawing with his front legs. The grooms agreed he was a biter but not a kicker.

- Five days prior to Alydar's injury, the farm's regular night watchman, Harold "Cowboy" Kipp, was ordered, by an unknown person driving Lundy's car, to take the night of November 13 off.

- Alton Stone claimed Kipp asked him to fill in for him on the 13th. Kipp denied asking Stone or even wanting the night off.

- Stone reported he found Alydar injured in his stall, but another watchman, Keed Highley, was actually the first to discover the injured stallion.

- Highley claimed he saw Alton Stone leaving the stallion barn in a truck right before Highley went inside and found Alydar injured. He also saw lights on in the farm office in the stallion barn that night.

- Alton Stone called Dr. Rhodes, but she stated that he never indicated Alydar's condition was serious, only that she should come up when she had a chance.

- At 2:00 p.m. on November 14, the day after the injury, Golden Eagle insurance investigator McVey arrived. He found Alydar's stall spotless. It had been cleaned and possibly painted, and a new roller bracket was bolted outside the door.

- Journalist Carol Flake testified that Alton Stone told her J.T. Lundy "knew something was going to happen to Alydar."

- Dr. Lynda Rhodes, Calumet veterinarian, reported that Alydar's X-rays mysteriously disappeared from the farm clinic.

- A grand jury indicted Alton Stone on two counts of perjury for lying about the time frame of where he was that night and about Kipp asking him to fill in for him. Stone was convicted and sentenced to five months in prison and five months of home confinement.

- If Alydar's leg had been stuck in the door, he likely wouldn't have been able to remove it without causing extensive injuries. Alydar's external injuries were not substantial. Only a small spot of blood was present when the horse was discovered.

- In the past, another Calumet horse, Tim Tam Aly, had kicked his door so hard he splintered it, breaking the entire lower half of the door. Similarly, Alydar's door should have broken before the metal bolts on the roller did. Some believe the bolts were sheared from a force outside the stall.

• Early the next morning, a Calumet maintenance worker replaced the broken stall roller and disposed of the broken pieces.

• MIT engineering professor George Pratt, hired by federal investigators, believed Alydar's injury was not an accident. According to Pratt, a kick would never have produced enough force to shear off the bracket's bolts. In a letter to the Federal Bureau of Investigation, Pratt stated that he believed Alydar's leg was broken in the stall and the scene staged to look like an accident.

• Alydar's stall door was secured in several places—the track above the door, a hook latch at the middle, right edge, the bottom roller, and metal edge guards at the bottom left and right sides of the stall. These render Bramlage's theory of "entanglement" impossible, since nothing other than the roller was damaged. It would be impossible for the door to have opened even a small amount with all the other guards remaining in place. It seems unlikely that a kick from inside the stall could shear bolts and break the roller but leave a small hook-and-eye latch unharmed.

• Dr. Susan Stover, veterinary surgeon and professor at UC Davis School of Veterinary Medicine, concluded from observing a photograph of Alydar's X-ray, that it was possible the break was due to a strike from an object such as a crowbar.

• J.T. Lundy refused to testify at his trial.

Prosecutor Tomala stated that only Lundy had "the motive and opportunity" to have the horse killed. U.S. District Court Judge Sim Lake admitted Alydar's injury was suspicious, but he did not believe the evidence was conclusive.

> *I conclude, based on the evidence admitted during the trial and the arguments raised in the briefs, that although there is evidence Mr. Lundy had a motive to injure Alydar, to collect the insurance proceeds, and that he had an opportunity, that I am not able to conclude by a preponderance of the evidence that Mr. Lundy is responsible for the death of Alydar.[1]*

J.T. Lundy was released from prison in 2005. The truth about what really happened to Alydar may have died with Lundy when he passed away on December 27, 2023, at eighty-two.

---

[1] *texasmonthly.com/true-crime/the-killing-of-alydar*

44

Insurance Fraud

We may never know the truth about Alydar's death, but from the 1970s to the mid 1990s, a number of expensive horses were insured against death, accident, or disease, and then cruelly killed to collect the insurance money. Unbelievably, in most of those cases, it was the owner who hired his horse's killer. The animals were killed in a variety of ways, all designed to look accidental.

The discovery of the equine murders was a result of an investigation into the disappearance of Brach Candy heiress, Helen Brach, in 1977. The sixty-five-year-old Brach may have been killed because she was about to report the horse killings to authorities. Brach's disappearance, and assumed murder, were never solved, however, the resulting FBI investigation led them to Tommy Burns, the most prolific of the horse killers. He confessed to killing fifteen, including three in one week in 1989. It's believed Burns may have actually killed fifty to one hundred horses over those years.

Burns committed his first equine murder in 1982 when he was twenty. The victim was a show jumper, Henry the Hawk. Seventeen-year-old Lisa Druck showed Hawk, but her father, James Druck, was the official owner. James hired Burns to kill the horse, so he could collect on the $150,000 insurance policy. The teen found her horse dead in his stall.

Druck taught Burns how to electrocute a horse, and that became the killer's preferred method. It was supposed to be quick and painless, and it was almost impossible to detect. The electrocution deaths were usually attributed to colic. James Druck died of lung cancer in 1990 before he could be charged for the death of Henry the Hawk.

For ten years, Burns continued killing horses. His fee was ten percent of the insured value of the horse. "I was a one-man crime wave. … Basically, I was just a piece of garbage."[1]

Burns had to change his method for a horse named Streetwise, a seven-year-old chestnut jumper. The owner, Donna Brown, a prominent

Henry the Hawk and Lisa Druck

____

[1] *Hot Blood, Ken Englade, 239*

horsewoman on the show circuit, insured Streetwise for $25,000. She hired Burns to kill the gelding for $5,000. The horse had suffered from colic in the past, so his insurance policy did not cover that. Since electrocution could not be used, Brown instructed Burns to break her horse's leg.

Tommy Burns had a slim remnant of a conscience and didn't want to kill the horse in such a brutal way. His accomplice, Harlow Arlie, agreed to do it. The plan was to make it look like a shipping accident, claiming the horse slipped off the side of a trailer ramp.

Florida investigators received a tip about Burns and were nearby on February 2, 1991. But they didn't arrive in time to prevent the injury to the horse. When informed of the "accident," a vet and the insurance company ordered Streetwise euthanized. The horse's regular veterinarian, Dana Tripp, knew of the plan with Burns to kill the horse but did not report it. She was convicted of concealing a felony, lost her veterinary license, and served four months of house arrest.

Although they hadn't been able to save Streetwise, the Florida Highway Patrol caught Burns and his accomplice as they tried to escape. Arlie pled guilty and served eight months of an eighteen-month sentence. Burns began to cooperate with the authorities. In exchange for serving as an informant, he received a light sentence for his crimes—a year in prison, of which he served only six months in a county jail.

Donna Brown and her husband, Buddy, were implicated in the death of another of their show jumpers, Aramis, who was insured for a million dollars and died under suspicious circumstances. Donna Brown was convicted but only served seven months in prison.

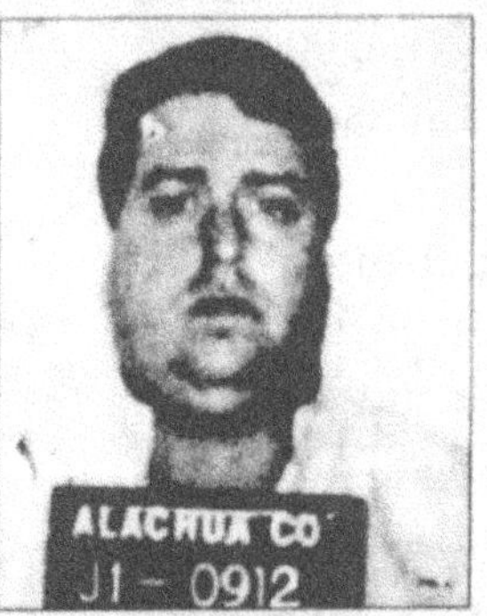

George Lindemann Jr., shown above competing in a show jumping event at the Palm Beach Polo & Country Club, is the son of one of America's wealthiest families and a top rider. He is accused of hiring Tommy Burns, top left, to electrocute one of his horses to collect $250,000 in insurance. He says he's innocent. Harlow Arlie, below left, was sent to prison for breaking a horse's leg with a crowbar.

In the ritzy world of show jumping, a saddle can cost $3,400, a top horse $1-million. The standard price for having your horse killed: $5,000.

Tampa Bay Times, Sept. 18, 1994, p. 27

Barney Ward of Castle Hill Farm in New York was one of the top show jumper trainers in the country. He sometimes acted as a middleman for Burns. In 1994, he was charged with arranging the killings of four horses. Ward served three years in federal prison, followed by three years of probation. The American Horse Show Association (AHSA) banned him for life. After his release from prison, Ward had the audacity to sue the AHSA; however, the Supreme Court of New York upheld the ban.

Another of Burns' clients was George Lindemann Jr., an accomplished Grand Prix equestrian and son of the founder of US Cellular One. He had his champion hunter, Charisma, killed in 1990. Lindemann was sentenced to thirty-three months in prison and was ordered to pay a $500,000 fine and $250,000 restitution to the insurance company.

Trainer Paul Valliere of Rhode Island hired Burns to destroy his horse, Roseau Platiere, in 1989. Valliere served four years of probation and paid a $5,000 fine. A few of the other horses killed by Burns whose names are known, include Rub the Lamp, Condino, Empire, Belgian Waffle, Rainman, and Emili's Choice.

Burns was known as "The Sandman" because many in the elite horse show world knew that horses "went to sleep" after he visited a stable. Burns recalled one woman who approached him at a show.

> *"Do you think you could kill my horse for $10,000?" So I did. She bought another horse with the insurance money and came up to me two months later and asked me to kill her new horse. She didn't like it.[1]*

Through information gained from Tommy Burns, thirty-six owners, trainers, veterinarians, and riders were indicted on charges related to the killing of horses for insurance payments. Thirty-five were convicted.

---

[1] *vault.si.com/vault/1992/11/16/blood-money-in-the-rich-clubby-world-of-horsemen-some-greedy-owners-have-hired-killers-to-murder-their-animals-for-the-insurance-payoffs*

45

Scamper

Barrel racing is the only women's event in modern professional rodeo. Only bull riding is more popular. Women's Professional Rodeo Association (WPRA) members compete for millions of dollars in total prize money at sanctioned rodeos in the United States and Canada.

In a barrel race, the horse runs around three barrels set up in a triangular layout, resulting in a cloverleaf pattern. To achieve a fast time, it's important to circle each barrel closely, but knocking one over results in a time penalty. Winning times for the American standard pattern length average sixteen to seventeen seconds.

Charmayne James started riding at three. By six, she was running barrels, and at nine was competing on her horse Bardo. Charmayne was heartbroken when Bardo shattered a bone in his leg in 1981 and had to be euthanized.

The following spring, Charmayne's father suggested she look at a horse that had been demoted to working at a feedlot because of his habit of bucking. She rode the small, five-year-old bay gelding in the pen. When she asked for a canter, he bucked, but she stayed on. Charmayne felt a connection with the horse and bought him for $1200. Her dad thought that was way too much money for a horse who had never barrel raced. Charmayne worked with Gills Bay Boy on barrels for two weeks before they entered their first competition—which they won. Her father commented, "He sure wants to scamper around those barrels." That's how Gills Bay Boy became Scamper.

After many wins on the amateur circuit, Charmayne decided to turn pro. She won her first world title in 1984 at fourteen. Charmayne and Scamper dominated professional barrel racing in the 1980s and early 90s. They won National Finals Rodeo (NFR) championships in 1984, 1986, 1987, 1989, 1990, and 1993.

During an event in 1985, as they rounded the first barrel, Scamper's bridle came unfastened. It dangled from his head,

but he held the bit in his mouth. As they circled the final barrel, he opened his mouth and the bit dropped out, causing the bridle to fall completely off. Scamper never slowed down. They won the round, bridleless.

The pair won ten consecutive WPRA championships from 1984 through 1993. Scamper was named the AQHA/WPRA Barrel Horse of the Year five times. Scamper and James earned over a million dollars together, making her the first rodeo cowgirl to reach that mark. In 1992, James was inducted into the National Cowgirl Hall of Fame and in 2012, the Pro Rodeo Hall of Fame. In 1996, Scamper was inducted into the Pro Rodeo Hall of Fame, the first barrel horse inductee.

To preserve her horse's genetics, James paid $150,000 to an Austin company, ViaGen Inc., to clone[1] Scamper, then twenty-nine years old. She believed, "If there was ever a horse to be cloned, Scamper's the one." The result was Clayton, born August 6, 2006. Clayton had bold facial markings, where Scamper had only a small star. Otherwise, the colt closely resembled Scamper. James said, "He looks so much like Scamper, when I walked into the stall and looked at him, the hair on the back of my neck stood up."

AQHA rules prevent cloned horses and their offspring from being registered or competing in Quarter Horse shows, but they can compete in rodeo events such as barrel racing. Clayton's first foals were born in 2009.

Scamper passed away in 2012, at thirty-five. He was buried at Charmayne's Texas ranch.

Clayton and Scamper

---

[1] *The first cloned equines were the mules Idaho Gem (May 4), Utah Pioneer (June 9), and Idaho Star (July 27) in 2003. The first cloned horse in the U.S. was a bay colt named Paris, Texas, born March 13, 2005 at Texas A&M University.*

46

Reagan and His Horses

While a sports announcer in Iowa, in the 1930s, Ronald Reagan wanted to pursue his love of horses. He figured joining the Cavalry was a good way to improve his horsemanship skills. He never thought he would actually be involved in combat. Certainly, after the "Great War," there would not be another one. He enlisted in the Army and was assigned to the 322nd Cavalry Regiment in Des Moines. In June 1937, the Army transferred him to the 323rd Cavalry in Los Angeles, California.[1]

Reagan became an accomplished horseman; however, he was wrong about there being no more wars. When World War II broke out, the 323rd Cavalry horses were never used in active duty. By then, tanks had replaced U.S. Cavalry horses. Because of poor vision, Reagan never saw combat, either. He served in administrative roles and helped make training films for the Army.

Reagan liked to joke that the real reason he ran for president was to bring back the Cavalry. He often quoted the saying attributed to Winston Churchill. "There is something about the outside of a horse that is good for the inside of a man."

After WWII, Reagan's riding ability made him a popular choice for Hollywood westerns; the first was the 1947 film *Stallion Road*. He rode a three-year-old black Thoroughbred mare named Baby (Tar Baby). The producers leased the mare from her owner, Nino Peppitone. Reagan enjoyed the horse so much, he bought her.

There is an old horseman's saying, "Never marry a horse," but nearly everyone does—at least their first one.[2]

Reagan purchased an eight-acre farm with a stable for Tar Baby on the outskirts of Los Angeles. Nino, a former Italian Cavalry officer, and his wife, Ruth, taught Reagan the husbandry aspects of owning a horse that he hadn't learned in his Cavalry years. Even as president, he insisted on grooming and saddling his own horses. Reagan almost always rode in an English saddle with English riding attire.

---

[1] *In 1942, Reagan transferred from the Cavalry to the Army Air Forces (AAF).*
[2] *Ronald Reagan's Own Story: Where's the Rest of Me?, Ronald Reagan, 187*

Tar Baby appeared with Reagan in other films, including *The Last Outpost* (1951) and *Law and Order* (1953). He referred to the mare as his "first leading lady." Tar Baby had two foals, the dapple gray, Nancy D. (named after Mrs. Reagan) and a black colt, Little Man. Tar Baby and her foals carried Reagan through thirty-seven years of riding.

As Los Angeles grew and Reagan's acting career became more lucrative, he purchased a three-hundred-acre ranch in Malibu. Reagan built jumps across each fence so he wouldn't have to dismount to open and close gates as he rode Nancy D around the ranch.

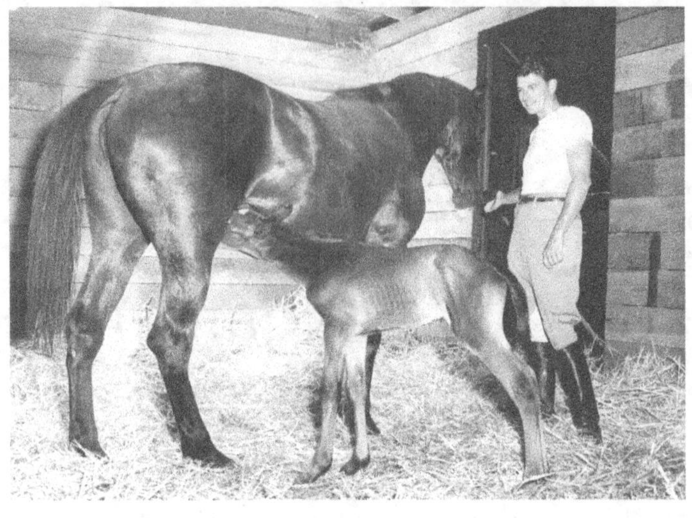

In 1976, Reagan challenged Gerald Ford for the Republican presidential nomination. Ford became the nominee by a narrow margin, eventually losing the election to Democrat Jimmy Carter. In 1980, the political tide shifted, and Reagan won the presidency in a landslide.

During the end of his second term as governor of California, Reagan had purchased a 688-acre ranch in the Santa Ynez Mountain Range northwest of Santa Barbara. Rancho del Cielo means Sky's Ranch or Heaven's Ranch. The president and Mrs. Reagan often spent time there to briefly escape Washington, D.C. It became known as the Western White House or the Reagan Ranch. Reagan liked to say of the place, "If it wasn't heaven, it was in the same zip code."

Reagan had many horses over the years. During his presidency, he kept seven at his ranch. He liked fast, athletic horses. One of his favorites at the time was El Alamein, a 16-hand, gray Anglo-Arabian[1] given to him in 1980 by Mexican president, Lopez Portillo. Reagan's staff did not view El Alamein as favorably. One day, Dr. Doug Herthel, the veterinarian who cared for Reagan's horses, rode El Alamein. When asked what he thought of the horse, the vet replied, "I can't believe you let the president of the United States ride this dingbat."[2]

Nancy Reagan often accompanied her husband on rides at the ranch. She preferred a more sedate equine partner. Her favorite was the Quarter Horse No Strings. The ranch was also home to Dormita (Quarter Horse), El Primero Teniente, known as First Lieutenant (Peruvian Paso), and the Arabians Gwalianko, Catalina, and El Saraff (Alfie).

When Reagan didn't have time to go to the ranch, he rode at Camp David, the presidential retreat, a two-hour drive from the White House or thirty minutes by

---

[1] *A Thoroughbred—Arabian cross. After El Alamein, Reagan's primary horse was a Quarter Horse he called Sergeant Murphy.*
[2] *Riding with Reagan: From the White House to the Ranch, John Barletta, 59*

176

helicopter. His primary mount there was Giminish, a 17-hand Hanoverian. He also rode a 17-hand bay Thoroughbred named Gimcrack, a U.S. Park Police horse.

Reagan's love of riding presented a challenge to his Secret Service staff, most of whom had no experience with horses. They simply could not keep up with the president. Between the election and the inauguration, an agent riding at the ranch with Reagan fell off and broke his arm. The president-elect jumped off his horse to help. At that point, the Secret Service realized something had to change. Their job was to protect the president, not the other way around.

After a frantic search for an agent who knew how to ride, they found John Barletta. He was in Washington, D.C., protecting outgoing president, Jimmy Carter. The following day, Barletta was sent to the Santa Barbara ranch to become Reagan's primary riding partner.[1] Three other agents accompanied them on their rides.

When a trip to the ranch or Camp David was planned, Barletta arrived four days ahead to ride the horses, so they weren't too fresh for the president.

At the ranch, Reagan usually rode El Alamein while Barletta often rode a nearly identical gray Arabian, Gwalianko. The two horses wore similar tack, and the riders dressed the same. That was all intentional. From a distance, it was difficult to distinguish the two men, thus making a sniper attack against the president more difficult.

During their rides, the president and Barletta rode out front, followed by Mrs. Reagan and her Secret Service agent. Next were two more agents on horseback, then a military aide carrying the "football" which contained the codes to launch a nuclear attack. Behind the horses was a Jeep or Hummer with more Secret Service agents and the president's physician, Dr. John Hutton. At the back of the procession was another vehicle containing communication personnel and equipment.

There was an attack on the president's life, but it didn't occur at the ranch. On March 30, 1981, after the president had spoken at the Washington Hilton Hotel, John Hinckley Jr. fired six shots at him. One bullet ricocheted off the presidential limousine and hit Reagan under his left arm, breaking a rib and puncturing a lung. At first, even Reagan didn't realize he'd been shot.

After two weeks in the hospital, he returned to the White House, initially working only half days. He made a rapid recovery, and two months after the shooting, he was back at the ranch, doing what he loved best—riding.

---

[1] *Horsewoman Barbara Riggs was another Secret Service agent who rode with Reagan.*

During a 1982 visit to England, Reagan enjoyed an eight-mile ride with Queen Elizabeth II, touring the grounds of Windsor Castle. The Queen rode her favorite mare, Burmese, while President Reagan rode Centenial, a black gelding.

In November 1982, representatives of the Spanish Riding School conducted a special performance of the Lipizzaner horses on the South Lawn. They presented the president with Maestoso Blanca, a twelve-year-old Lipizzaner stallion. Reagan referred to the horse as Amadeus. Legally, presidential gifts cannot exceed

$140 in value, so the president could not keep the horse. Friends of the president paid to have the stallion boarded at a private stable in Maryland. Later, after a trip to South America, the Brazilian president tried to give him a six-year-old bay Thoroughbred, Gymnich.

Reagan's presidential term ended on January 20, 1989. He was two weeks away from his seventy-eighth birthday, but that didn't keep him from riding. In July, he rode horseback on a hunting trip at a friend's ranch in Mexico. His horse bucked on a rocky, downhill slope and stumbled. Reagan was thrown. The former president was placed on a backboard and taken by helicopter to Fort Huachuca Army base in Arizona. Doctors treated him for minor scrapes and bruises and advised him to stop riding. When he experienced lingering effects from the fall, doctors at the Mayo Clinic discovered fluid or a blood clot on Reagan's brain. That September, they performed surgery to successfully drain it.

On November 5, 1994, five years after leaving office, Reagan announced, through a letter, that he had Alzheimer's disease. Although he continued to ride with Barletta for a time, the disease gradually affected his ability to tack up and ride a horse. His last visit to Rancho del Cielo was in 1995. The ranch was sold in 1998 to the Young America's Foundation.

During his final years, he lived out of the public view. The former president died on June 5, 2004. The Old Guard selected Sergeant York to be the caparisoned, or riderless, horse at Reagan's military funeral. Traditionally, riding boots are placed backward in the riderless horse's stirrups. Reagan's funeral was unique in that those boots were his own.

Sergeant York, a Standardbred, was born in 1991. He raced in New York under his original name "Allaboard Jules." In 1997, he was donated to the U.S. Army and given a new name in honor of World War I soldier, Alvin C. York. The equine Sergeant York served with the Caisson Platoon until retiring in 2022 at thirty-one to the Equine Advocates Sanctuary in New York. In 2023, he received the Animals in War & Peace Distinguished Service Medal.

47

Sefton

Sefton was the worst injured and I knew that we had to get him back if there was to be any chance of saving him.

—*Major Noel Carding, veterinarian*

At four, Sefton was purchased by the British Army. He had been born in Ireland in 1963 to an Irish Draught mare and a Thoroughbred stallion. By 1967, the black gelding with a wide blaze and four socks had grown to an impressive 16 hands. He was assigned to the Household Cavalry Mounted Regiment and sent to London for training.

He earned the nickname Sharky for his tendency to bite. Although his training took longer than the average horse, Sefton finally passed his course in June 1968. With his reputation for being difficult increasing, Sefton was deployed to Germany. There, he became a popular mount for hunting and show jumping.

In 1975, large, black horses were needed for ceremonial duties in London, so Sefton returned to England and his old regiment. In addition to his regimental duties, he continued to compete in jumping until the age of eighteen.

On a sunny summer day, July 20, 1982, Trooper Michael Pederson and Sefton, along with fourteen other mounted soldiers, rode along South Carriage Drive to the Changing of the Guard in Hyde Park.

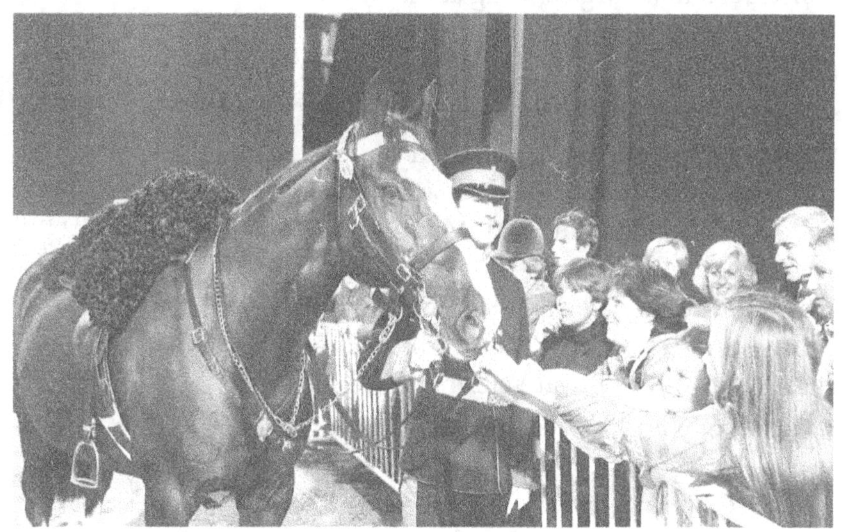

Sefton and Michael Pederson

At 10:43 a.m., someone remotely detonated a bomb in a car parked on Carriage Drive as the regiment passed by. The bomb contained twenty-five pounds of explosives and thirty pounds of nails. The explosion killed two soldiers immediately. Two other men died later. All fifteen horses were injured; seven so severely that they were euthanized at the scene. The seven who died were Cedric, Epaulette, Falcon, Rochester, Waterford, Yeastvite, and Zara.

Sefton's injuries were the most serious of the surviving horses. His jugular vein was severed, his left eye wounded, and he had thirty-eight wounds from the nails and shrapnel.

The explosion alerted soldiers from a nearby barracks, including regimental commander Andrew Parker Bowles and veterinarian Noel Carding. Bowles ordered a soldier to remove his shirt and use it to apply pressure to Sefton's neck to stop the bleeding.

Carding performed the first ninety minutes of emergency surgery on Sefton before civilian veterinarians joined him. The nineteen-year-old horse underwent an additional eight hours of surgery. The vets gave Sefton a fifty percent chance of survival. Thousands of well-wishers sent cards to the horse. Monetary donations were made in his name. Sefton made steady progress and eventually a full recovery.

He was named "Horse of the Year" and received a standing ovation at the 1982 Horse of the Year Show. The money that had been donated for Sefton was used to construct a new surgical wing at the Royal Veterinary College; named the Sefton Surgical Wing.

Most of the other horses who survived the bombing were too traumatized to return to work. But within three months, Sefton was back on duty with Michael Pedersen, bravely passing the exact spot

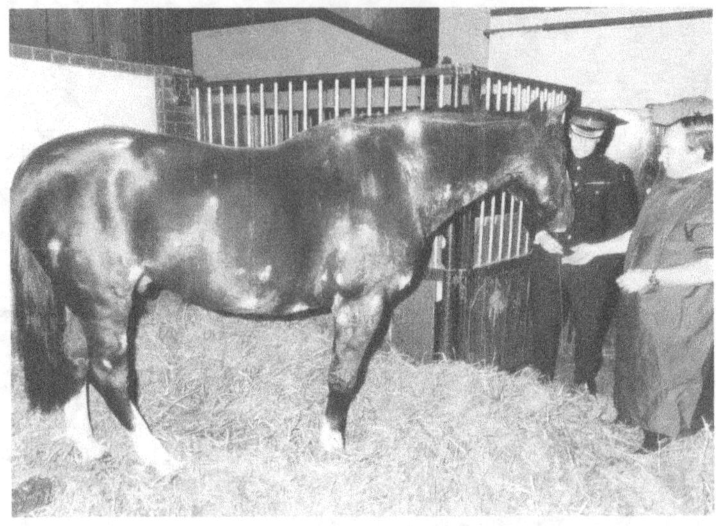

Sefton and Echo, also a victim of the attack, in retirement at The Horse Trust's Home of Rest

where the bomb had exploded. In 1984, after seventeen years of service, Sefton retired to the Horse Trust sanctuary, where he lived from the age of twenty-one to thirty. Today, a bronze statue of Sefton stands outside the Royal Veterinary College.

A second attack occurred later that same day at 12:55 p.m. A bomb exploded under a bandstand in Regent's Park. Six people were killed immediately. A seventh died later. Eight others were injured. No horses were involved in this second attack. Both attacks were the work of the Irish Republican Army (IRA) which wanted to free Northern Ireland from British control.[1]

---

[1] *The United Kingdom consists of four countries: England, Scotland, Wales, and Northern Ireland. The Republic of Ireland is not part of the UK.*

Nationalists or Republicans believed Northern Ireland should leave the UK and become part of a united, independent Ireland. Fighting between the groups occurred from the late 1960s into the 1990s. Thousands died on both sides. The conflict ended with the signing of the Good Friday Agreement in 1998.

48

Shergar

The mystery of Shergar began on March 3, 1978, when the bay colt with a blaze, four socks, and one blue eye was born in Ireland. The Thoroughbred's billionaire owner, Karim al-Husseini, held the title Aga Khan IV, a high Islamic spiritual leader.

Michael Stoute trained the horse in England in 1979 and 1980. Shergar had a mild temperament and was easy to break. He raced twice in 1980, with first and second-place finishes. Lester Piggott rode Shergar in those first two races. After that, nineteen-year-old Walter Swinburn became the horse's jockey.

Swinburn rode Shergar to his most famous victory—the Epsom Derby. England's Epsom Derby is the equivalent of the U.S. Kentucky Derby. Today, the race is also known as the Derby Stakes or the Betfred Derby. Shergar won the 1981 Epsom by ten lengths—the greatest margin in the race's history.

In his last race of the year, Shergar finished fourth, and the Aga Khan retired the three year old to the Ballymany Stud Farm in Ireland. The Khan sold forty shares of the horse to a syndicate for a total of ten million pounds, keeping six shares for himself. In 1982, Shergar produced his only crop of foals—seventeen colts and nineteen fillies.

On February 8, 1983, at 8:30 p.m., someone stole Shergar from the Aga Khan's farm. His groom, James Fitzgerald, reported that six to nine men in ski masks captured the horse at gunpoint. They locked Fitzgerald's family in a room, then the groom was forced to load Shergar into a trailer. Several men escaped with the horse while the others drove Fitzgerald around for hours in another vehicle. They released him thirty miles from the farm, threatening the groom with death if he contacted the police.

The Aga Khan was in Switzerland and couldn't be

reached until 4:00 a.m. He directed them to contact the Irish police immediately. But by then, Shergar had been gone for nearly eight hours. The Aga Khan refused to pay a ransom for the following reasons.

- The horse was owned by a syndicate of thirty-five people. One person alone couldn't decide how to handle the situation. All the owners would have to agree.
- Paying the ransom was no guarantee Shergar would be returned alive.
- Paying the ransom would encourage more horse kidnappings.

One of the kidnappers told Fitzgerald that he would use the phrase "King Neptune" to identify himself in any communications. That night, he phoned Jeremy Maxwell, a horse trainer, and demanded a ransom of $2,600,000. Although Maxwell tried to keep him talking, the man hung up before police could trace the call.

The syndicate hired a risk consulting firm to negotiate with Shergar's kidnappers. Another call was received the next day at the Ballymany Stable. The owners demanded proof that their horse was still alive. On Saturday, February 12, the kidnappers left several Polaroid photos of Shergar's head at a hotel. Not convinced, the negotiators demanded more conclusive proof that Shergar was alive.

In one last phone call, the kidnapper said, "If you're not satisfied, that's it."

Nothing more was ever heard from them, and the horse's body has never been found.

The case was never officially solved; however, years later, a former Irish Republican Army (IRA)[1] member, Sean O'Callaghan, stated Shergar's kidnapping had been an IRA operation to raise money for weapons. O'Callaghan claimed that soon after the abduction, Shergar panicked and injured one of his legs. Then, he was killed by the kidnappers.

All the shareholders had insurance policies on Shergar, but the policies of fifteen members were based on the horse's death not his theft. The Aga Khan was one of the fifteen that received no money since it could not be proven that Shergar was dead.

Walter Swinburn won the Epsom Derby twice more, in 1986 and 1995. Unfortunately, he died in 2016, at fifty-five, after a fall from a window. He suffered from epilepsy after a nearly fatal accident in a 1996 horse race left him in a coma for four days. It's believed a seizure may have been a factor in his fall.

In 1999, the Shergar Cup was started in the horse's honor. The race is now held at the Ascot track in England. A film, titled *Shergar*, loosely based on the true story, was released in 1999.

---

[1] *See the note about the IRA in chapter 47.*

49

Harvey Wallbanger

In 1986, Energy Downs in Gillette, Wyoming, sponsored an unusual horse race. In the match race, a Quarter Horse faced a different kind of opponent—a one-ton bison named Harvey Wallbanger. The hulking six-year-old sprinted 110 yards and finished two and a half lengths ahead of the horse, earning the bison a victory in his first race[1].

Harvey raced ninety-three times in the U.S., Canada, and Mexico, winning seventy-nine times. In 1990, his best year, Harvey won $108,000 in twenty races.

Harvey's owner, T.C. Thorstenson, claimed the bison thought he was a horse. Whether Harvey was actually faster than the horses he faced is debatable. Some believe the races were fixed; the horses were deliberately held back, allowing Harvey to win. The bison's victories brought publicity and crowds to the tracks. But perhaps it was simply that his massive size, horns, strange smell, and the peculiar sounds he made frightened the horses so much that they couldn't hit their usual stride.

Golden Gate Fields

---

[1] *Some sources list Harvey's first race as 1985. The most reliable sources indicate 1986.*

Thorstenson was no stranger to bison. He'd grown up around them. His family raised cattle and bison on their ranch near McLaughlin, South Dakota. His father, Calvin, had been killed by one. When Calvin and a ranch hand were driving the animals through a gate, one bison turned and charged, tossing him into the air. Despite that, T.C. continued raising the animals. In 1980, he found an orphaned bison on the ranch. Poachers had killed his mother. T.C. bottle fed the days-old calf, keeping him in his car for a time.

The calf quickly bonded with T.C. He became agitated when his surrogate mother left him and would bang into the walls of his pen. That's how the bison earned his name. Harvey's wild nature made him difficult to train. T.C. stated he could have trained forty horses in the time he spent training one bison.

Harvey hit the California tracks in 1989. At Golden Gate Fields, he raced Two Eyed Burt, a Quarter Horse. Harvey beat Burt by half a length, finishing the 110-yard sprint in less than ten seconds for his twenty-first win.

Two years later, eleven-year-old Harvey died after eating hay contaminated with oleander, a poisonous weed. T.C. sued the hay supplier and was awarded $475,000. After losing Harvey, T.C. trained another bison, Harvey Wallbanger Jr. Racing didn't appeal to Junior, but he enjoyed performing in exhibitions and wild-west-type shows.

Today, some fairs and racetracks offer "extreme" race days in which camels, ostriches, and zebras compete. These animals are generally not as dedicated to the sport as Harvey Wallbanger was. It seems one of their main goals is to eliminate their rider rather than cross the finish line first—or at all!

Later events cast a shadow over T.C. Thorstenson. In October 1996, at thirty-nine, he married Margaret Lesher, a multimillionaire heiress. Lesher was twenty-five years older than T.C. She purchased a small ranch in Arizona for him. Six months later, Margaret drowned at Bartlett Lake while on a camping trip with her new husband. The county sheriff ruled Lesher's death an accident. Although T.C. was never arrested or officially named a suspect in her death, some, including Lesher's daughters, remain suspicious.

50

Sweetwater Oak

It appears the expression "holding on for dear life" was in use as far back as the 1700s, but there can be no better illustration of it than a ride by four-foot-eleven-inch, 108-pound apprentice jockey Nate Hubbard.

Sweetwater Oak was foaled on April 1, 1985. If you go back far enough in her pedigree, you'll find War Admiral and Man o' War. However, Sweetwater never achieved the success of those ancestors. The closest she came to victory was on February 3, 1989. Nineteen-year-old Hubbard rode the four-year-old in a claiming race on a sloppy track at Golden Gate Fields in Albany, California.

Later in the race, Hubbard steered Sweetwater to the outside. The filly was coming up strong behind the frontrunner Current Lady. Just when it seemed Sweetwater might pass her for the win, the filly stumbled. It's not clear whether she clipped heels with Current Lady or simply tripped. Fortunately, the horse didn't go down. With about a hundred yards to go, Sweetwater regained her balance and kept running. However, the stumble launched her jockey out of the saddle onto the horse's neck. Hubbard grabbed frantically for Sweetwater's mane. He found himself sliding down the horse's right side, eventually dangling under her neck.

As Sweetwater Oak continued down the stretch, track photographer Peg Grueneberg saw the fear on the jockey's face. Her zoom lens captured the iconic photo of Hubbard literally "hanging on for dear life."

One can only imagine what Sweetwater Oak thought about the situation. This was her twelfth race. In all previous ones, her jockey had remained perched on her back, in the saddle. Never before had she raced with a human clinging to her neck.

Despite her confusion and the awkwardness Hubbard's position must have caused in her gait, the mare pressed on, crossing the finish line in second place. Coming up quickly behind them, fifth-place finisher Ron Warren on Lystra moved in front of Sweetwater Oak, slowing her so Hubbard could make a safe dismount.

After the race, a muddy Hubbard said, "I just tried to hang on so I wouldn't get run over. I saw those horses behind me, and I wasn't going to let go for nothing."

But, would Sweetwater's finish count since her jockey was not in the saddle? During a post-race inquiry, the stewards reviewed the video. Hubbard's feet had never touched the ground, so it was ruled Sweetwater had carried her jockey for the entire race. Her second-place finish was ruled valid.

Although Sweetwater's knees severely bruised his left thigh, Hubbard resumed racing the next day. 1989 was his best year, riding in 647 races with seventy-one wins, seventy seconds, and ninety-eight thirds, earning $815,146. He retired from racing in 1999.

Sweetwater ran in only two more races before being retired as a broodmare to raise six foals. In her fourteen starts, the mare's best finishes were two seconds and three thirds. She earned a mere $9,358 over her racing career (1987-1989).

Would Sweetwater have won if she had not stumbled? A victory would have been nice, however, with a win that day, we would almost certainly never have heard of Sweetwater Oak. Her stumble resulted in a level of fame for the unsuccessful racehorse and her jockey.

Even more unusual than Hubbard's finish was that of twenty-two-year-old Frank Hayes on June 4, 1923. Hayes rode the horse, Sweet Kiss, in a steeplechase race at Belmont Park in New York. In the home stretch, Sweet Kiss moved into the lead, crossing the finish line, first by a head. The race spectators were surprised by Hayes' relaxed position in the saddle.

When the horse's owner came to congratulate the jockey, Hayes tumbled from the saddle. He had died of an apparent heart attack in the latter part of the race. Belmont ruled his win official, making him the only jockey to win a race while deceased. Hayes was buried in his racing silks. It's said that Sweet Kiss never raced again. Some called her "The Kiss of Death."

51

Zippy Chippy

With a name like Zippy Chippy and a pedigree that includes some of the most famous racehorses of all time, his owner, trainer, and jockey were optimistic about the horse's future. The Thoroughbred colt was born on April 20, 1991, into the equivalent of a royal family in the racing world. His ancestors included such greats as Native Dancer, Bold Ruler, Northern Dancer, War Admiral, and Man o' War.

The bay with a small star was born at Capritaur Farm in upstate New York. Charles Frysinger purchased the colt as an investment. He had high hopes of making his fortune in horse racing. Knowing nothing about horses himself, he hired a trainer and manager to handle Zippy.

Zippy's first chance to show his stuff was as a three-year-old at Belmont Park on September 13, 1994. Jockey Julio Pezua rode Zippy to an eighth-place finish out of ten horses. After five races, Zippy had finished no higher than third. When Belmont closed that fall, Zippy raced at the Aqueduct track in New York. In his first race there, in October, Zippy finished ninth out of eleven horses. Two weeks later, he was dead last, eighth out of eight and fifty-four lengths behind the winner.

Zippy was demoted from the big-name tracks to the minor leagues of horse racing. Although he was running against horses of lower quality in his first race at the Finger Lakes track, he finished a disappointing fourth.

Zippy continued to rack up lackluster performances, but he never lost his enthusiasm. Zippy eagerly anticipated each race, and despite finishing third, fifth, or last, he left the track tail held high, prancing as if he'd just won the Kentucky Derby.

After eighteen races, Zippy managed to finish second three times, but by then Frysinger had given up on him. The horse had gained a reputation of being hard to handle and impossible to motivate. He was known for destroying stalls and water buckets. One of his favorite tricks was to snatch items from the hands or head of unsuspecting people passing by his stall. Zippy changed hands several times with his future looking bleaker each time.

A Puerto Rican trainer, Felix Monserrate, took a liking to Zippy. Wanting to keep the losing horse from ending up at a slaughterhouse, he traded his 1988 Ford pickup for him. Zippy had no way of understanding what had happened, so he didn't feel particularly grateful to Felix. One of the first things the temperamental horse did was to bite Felix on the back.

Zippy's new owner was also his trainer. Horses and racing were all the optimistic Monserrate knew. Under his care, Zippy's prospects began looking up. In his first seven races with Felix, the horse finished third twice. On September 23, 1995, Zippy came oh-so-close to winning. In a heartbreaking finish, the big gelding lost by a nose, a mere one-fortieth of a second behind the winner. Felix was pleased with his new horse's performance. Ever the optimist, he believed the next race would be the one.

On his next outing, Zippy was in last place for most of the race. He came on strong at the end and finished second, losing by a neck. After that, Zippy hit a bad streak, losing repeatedly. Felix tried everything—switching jockeys, exercise boys, saddles, even changing the horse's diet, but nothing made a difference.

Felix's devotion to the horse is puzzling. Most people who knew Zippy described him as moody and mean to people and other horses. Grooms scooted food into his stall with a rake or pitchfork, remaining at a safe distance, so he couldn't bite them. It was challenging to find an exercise boy to ride Zippy, since he bucked most of them off. He was hard to shoe and once kicked the farrier's truck with both hind legs. One day, Zippy trapped Felix in the back of his stall for close to an hour. Each

Zippy led for most of this race in September 2000, only to be nosed out at the finish for second place.

time the man tried to leave, Zippy threatened to strike him with a front leg or bite him. According to Felix, the horse never intended to hurt anyone; it was all a game to Zippy.

At six, when Zippy extended his record to eighty losses, Felix tried to retire him. But the horse was so miserable away from the track, Felix brought him back. Despite his lack of success, or maybe because of it, Zippy became a favorite with local spectators. Fans flocked to his races to cheer him on, rooting for the underdog to achieve his first win. The media, however, was not so kind. Newspaper headlines referred to Zippy as ugly and stupid. Felix was determined to help Zippy win in order to prove them wrong.

In the fall of that year, Felix waited at the barn with his seven-year-old daughter for her school bus. He was preoccupied with thoughts of his training plans for Zippy. The horse had hit a real racing low, even for him. Felix wasn't sure what to try next. Maybe he should give up and sell him. Suddenly, he realized his daughter, Marisa, was no longer beside him. He looked everywhere but couldn't find her. An awful thought occurred to him—Zippy Chippy!

Felix raced into the barn and stopped outside the horse's door, frozen in fear. Zippy faced away from him. The big horse had Marisa cornered in the back of the stall. Felix couldn't see her face, but he imagined the terror she must feel. The horse had trapped him more than once. His mind raced, trying to think of a way to rescue his little girl. He was afraid to do anything. If he startled the horse, Zippy would be even more likely to hurt Marisa. How could he have let her out of his sight?

Then, Felix heard something. He listened closely. It was Marisa—she was laughing. The girl stepped around the big horse, and Zippy carefully turned to follow her, lowering his head to nuzzle and nicker to her.

That day, Zippy became a member of the family. No matter how badly the horse raced, Felix would never sell him. He explained it this way, "Say you have three children. One is a lawyer, doing well. The other a doctor, very, very successful. But the third one, not so smart, so he's working at McDonald's. What do you do? Ignore him?"

Zippy had one more trick he hadn't yet played. This would be a costly one. In many of his previous races, he'd started slowly, then tried to come from behind. But on June 23, 1998, in a race at Finger Lakes, six horses flew out of the gates at the starting bell. The seventh decided not to. Zippy just didn't have much zip that day. His jockey finally got him going, but they finished last, his eighty-third loss.

Not leaving the gate or leaving very slowly is called dwelling. For obvious reasons, it's highly frowned on in racing. But, Zippy liked it so much, he tried it again a few weeks later. This got him banned from the track for sixty days. During that time, Felix supervised some remedial lessons with the horse, working on breaking quickly from the gate. In September, he returned to racing. Despite all the practice sessions, he dwelt in the gate again. Zippy received a permanent ban.

The horse was seven years old and had run eighty-five races. Most racehorses retire by the age of five, but Zippy liked to run. Felix really wanted the horse to have a win before retiring. The horse began getting a lot of attention in the media—just not positive attention. County fairs were the only racing venue were Zippy wasn't banned. A year later, Zippy finished third at a fair in Massachusetts.

Felix had an idea. Maybe his horse could outrun a human. He arranged a forty-yard race—Zippy against baseball player Jose Herrera. Nine thousand fans came to watch the event. An intense hunger pang gripped the horse just as the bell sounded. He grabbed a bite of grass before starting to run. Given the shortness of the race, he was never able to catch up to Herrera. But Felix put a positive spin on it, telling reporters Zippy had let the man win just to make him feel good.

The following year, with the race extended to fifty yards, Zippy beat two other ballplayers. Zippy also managed to win against two harness-racing horses: Paddy's Laddy, a pacer, and Miss Batavia, a trotter. However, wins against people and harness racers didn't count as official wins. Over the next few years, Zippy continued his quest for that elusive victory, racing at smaller tracks: Northampton Fair in Massachusetts, Penn National in Pennsylvania, and Thistledown in Ohio. Felix and Zippy's fans always believed his next race might just be the one.

On September 6, 2003, at Northampton, Zippy passed all the other horses early on and was six lengths ahead at one point. But Short Notice caught up with him, and the two fought back and forth for the lead. At the finish line, Zippy was edged out by a nose. The jockey of the third-place horse called foul, registering a complaint with the track steward. He claimed Short Notice had bumped his horse during the race. If the steward agreed, Short Notice would be disqualified, and Zippy would have his first win!

In order to decide, the official reviewed the race video. But it wasn't to be. The steward agreed Short Notice had bumped the horse, but he ruled it wasn't intentional. Short Notice was declared the winner, and once again, victory eluded Zippy.

The following year, fans crowded the Northampton track to cheer Zippy on in his 100th race. The atmosphere at the track was electric. Zippy's fans, decked out in Zippy hats and T-shirts, were convinced he would win this important race. But sadly, Zippy finished last that day. A disappointed Felix decided his horse had run his last race. Zippy Chippy finished his eleven-year racing career with eight seconds and twelve thirds, earning $30,834.

Knowing how much Zippy loved to be at the track, Felix thought working as a track pony would keep him happy. His job would be to ride alongside, leading a racehorse out to the track, helping the other horse remain calm. Zippy didn't last long in that role. He wanted to race the other horse or tried to bump or bite him.

For the next six years, Felix kept the horse with him, exercising him, but never again racing him. When Zippy was approaching twenty, Michael Blowen offered to buy Zippy for his Thoroughbred

retirement farm near Saratoga, New York—Old Friends at Cabin Creek. Blowen was aware of Zippy's popularity with his fans and the media. He figured the horse would be a wonderful ambassador and fundraiser for his farm.

At first, Felix refused. He had vowed never to sell Zippy and couldn't bear to part with him. But Felix was approaching seventy, and after several months, his family persuaded him that Zippy would be happy at Cabin Creek.

Felix trailered his horse to the farm in the spring of 2010. Zippy had never gotten along well with other horses, having spent nearly his entire life around people. Life at Cabin Creek would be a big change for the gelding. Over 500 people attended the farm's grand opening ceremony.

The owners had created a winner's circle from flowers and bales of straw, with a sign that read "Cabin Creek Winner's Circle." The plan was for Felix to lead Zippy into the circle, a place the winless horse had never

Haru Arara

entered. Then, everyone would take photos of Zippy and Felix. Apparently, Zippy was insulted by the idea. He kicked the sign over.

After some time at the farm, the cranky gelding made a friend, a chestnut named Red Down South. The two lived in the same pasture and became inseparable. Tourists visit Cabin Creek each summer to see the famous retired Thoroughbreds, but Zippy Chippy was one of the most popular. A best-selling item in the gift shop was a mug featuring a photo of Zippy and the caption, "Winners don't always finish first."

Zippy passed away in 2022 at the age of thirty.

Haru Urara (Glorious Spring) was another racehorse whose name exceeded her accomplishments. Racing in Japan from 1998 to 2004, the Thoroughbred mare racked up 113 losses and zero wins.

52

Black Ruby

Mules are well-known for the vital roles they played in our past—towing canal boats, hauling borax out of Death Valley, and pulling supply wagons in war and peace, among other things. Their specialty has been their use as "beasts of burden." However, some mules today are known for their speed rather than their strength.

Mule races date back to at least the 1800s. Horse racing had long been the sport of the wealthy. Mule racing was something the commoners could enjoy. The races were popular events at county fairs, especially in the South, where the mule population was higher. Tennessee hosted races at the Maury County Fair in 1835 with slaves serving as jockeys.

Mark Twain described a mule race he observed in New Orleans.

There were thirteen mules in the first heat; all sorts of mules, they were; all sorts of complexions, gaits, dispositions, aspects. Some were handsome creatures, some were not; some were sleek, some hadn't had their fur brushed lately; some were innocently gay and frisky; some were full of malice and all unrighteousness; guessing from looks, some of them thought the matter on hand was war, some thought it was a lark, the rest took it for a religious occasion. And each mule acted according to his convictions. The result was an absence of harmony well compensated by a conspicuous presence of variety—variety of a picturesque and entertaining sort. …

It is great fun, and cordially liked. The mule-race is one of the marked occasions of the year. It has brought some pretty fast mules to the front. …

The riders dress in full jockey costumes of bright-colored silks, satins, and velvets. The thirteen mules got away in a body, after a couple of false starts, and scampered off with prodigious spirit. As each mule and each rider had a distinct opinion of his own as to how the race ought to be run, and which side of the track was best in certain circumstances, and how often the track ought to be crossed, and when a collision ought to be accomplished, and when it

ought to be avoided, these twenty-six conflicting opinions created a most fantastic and picturesque confusion, and the resulting spectacle was killingly comical.[1]

Mule racer Freddy Anderson described one unpredictable mule, Rodie.

When Rodie got to running, she'd stop all at once and make you come over her head see. So, I didn't want to be out there and some of the other mules running and run over you and hurt you and kill you. So I rode her one time and hung her up.[2]

In 1935, Larry Pryor held the first Pryor Derby on the Saturday after the Fourth of July at his Silver Lake Plantation in Mississippi. Pryor wanted to encourage people during the Depression years. "Bad times or not, something unusual should be done to commemorate the Fourth of July."

The Pryor Derby was so popular it led to races at Greenwood and Rosedale, Mississippi, as well. The mules were ridden bareback in the races, some of which continued into the 1960s. Winning mules from races at Greenwood in 1944 were Little Joe, Doughboy, Foots, Bazooka, Baby Buzzard, Miss Victory, and Pippin.

Although mule racing got its start in the deep South, the modern version of the sport is most popular in California where it's featured at several county fairs and the California State Fair. Mule races also occur in other states such as Nevada, New Mexico, Texas, Colorado, Wyoming, Idaho, Illinois, and Nebraska.

The American Mule Racing Association (AMRA), in Sacramento, California, regulates mule racing much as the Jockey Club does for Thoroughbred horse racing. Although Thoroughbreds race at two, mules don't start their careers until three. Mules cannot keep up their speed for the lengths

Greenwood races 1940s

that Thoroughbreds do. Their races are similar to Quarter Horse ones, sprints of 350 to 440 yards, with a few as long as 800 yards. At a distance of 440 yards, a horse would finish about two seconds faster than a mule.

Because of their later start into racing and the shorter distances, which reduce the chance for injuries, a mule often remains sound and healthy over a career of twelve years. The mule Loretta Lynn won a race at nineteen. In the Thoroughbred world, colts dominate fillies. However, most agree in mule racing that the females (mollies) are faster than the males (johns).

That was certainly true for a molly named Black Ruby.

---

[1] *Life on the Mississippi, Mark Twain, 133*
[2] *Mississippi Folklife, 29*

Ruby's sire was a 15.1 hand, black Mammoth Jack, and her dam was a Thoroughbred/Quarter Horse cross named My Satinette. Black Ruby was born in Utah on April 17, 1992. Despite her name, the mule was not black but a chestnut with a light mane and tail. At three, she was owned by Bob and Ronda Davis in Nevada. Ruby's training was delayed for a time when her right rear foot went through a rotted trailer floorboard. She eventually recovered from the injury with no long-term, harmful effects.

In her early races, Black Ruby twice beat Fancy, the top mule of Sonny and Mary McPherson. When Ruby's owners offered to sell her to the McPhersons, they jumped at the chance to buy the speedy mule. Her purchase price was never revealed.

Young Ruby was never fully trained and was difficult to work with. She despised the track starting gates. Once, her jockey fell off and broke his wrist as he attempted to force her into the gate. Despite her fits in the early moments of a race, once the gate sprang open, Ruby was focused on running. She won sprints of all distances, sometimes winning two races in the same day.

Black Ruby gained a reputation and fan base in her own right, but her rivalry with a john mule, Taz, put a spotlight on the little-known sport of mule racing. On September 8, 2002, a $10,000 match race in Del Mar, California, pitted the two against each other. Promoted as the Mule Duel, the race was never much of a duel, as Black Ruby beat Taz by two lengths.

Six days later, the two faced off again in Pomona for the Mule Heavyweight Championship: The Rematch. This time, Black Ruby won by half a length.

Their third and final match race was held the following May at Los Alamitos. Labeled "The Battle of the Titans," Ruby led the entire race, beating Taz again by half a length. At that point in her career, she had defeated Taz in twenty-three of their twenty-five encounters.

Black Ruby raced for the last time in 2008, at sixteen, the mandatory retirement age for a racing mule. She won 70 of 119 races with twenty-two seconds and earnings of more than $260,000. She spent her final years with the McPhersons in Healdsburg, California. The mule remained ornery until the end, often racing her pasture mates around the ranch for the sheer joy of it. She passed away in 2022 at thirty.

Known as the "Secretariat of Mule Racing," Ruby was inducted into the Mule Racing Hall of Fame and the Sonoma County Horse Council's Equus Hall of Fame.

Don Jacklin, owner of Taz, wanted to preserve his successful mule's genetics; however, mules, as hybrid animals, are almost always sterile. With no traditional way to perpetuate the mule's bloodlines, Jacklin turned to cloning.

In 2003, Idaho Gem became not only the first cloned mule, but the first cloned equine. Gem was produced using DNA from a fetus that would have been Taz's brother. Other clones from that line include Idaho Star and Utah Pioneer. Unlike Thoroughbreds, cloned mules are permitted to race. Although all three cloned mules raced, none were as successful as Taz.

53

Zenyatta

Zenyatta got a late start on her racing career. Most Thoroughbreds race as two-year-olds; however, Zenyatta was too busy growing. The average Thoroughbred racehorse stands 15.3 hands high. Zenyatta grew to 17.2 hands, two full hands taller than Seabiscuit and a hand taller than Secretariat.

Although Zenyatta was tall, the honor of the largest racehorse goes to Holy Roller in Australia. The giant Thoroughbred, born in 1992, stood 18.1 hands. Normally, a horse that tall would be awkward, but Holy Roller, towering over his competition, won twelve of his twenty-five races.

Jerry and Ann Moss, who worked in the music industry, purchased the yearling filly for $60,000. Her price was lower than most of the other yearlings, because she suffered from a skin infection at the time of the sale. The Mosses named her after the album "Zenyatta Mondatta" by The Police, a music group they managed.

Late in her three-year-old year, the filly finally grew into herself. On November 22, 2007, Zenyatta broke last from the gate in her first race, at California's Hollywood Park track. Despite being tenth of twelve horses after half a mile, Zenyatta came from behind to win by three lengths. She raced once more as a three-year-old, coming from behind again to win by a similar margin.

In April 2008, Zenyatta's owners switched jockeys from David Flores to Hall of Famer Mike Smith. Smith rode Zenyatta for the rest of her racing career. The filly became famous for her pre-race dance ritual. As she was led to the track, she pranced and pawed rhythmically, doing her Zenyatta "dance." On the track, it was a different story. The dancer became a racing machine known as Queen Z.

Her signature style was to start slow, often dead last, then make an amazing surge to pass all competitors for the win. Never was that more spectacular than in the Breeders' Cup Classic. In 2008, she won the Ladies Classic, but in 2009, Zenyatta faced the boys for the first time—twelve of the top Thoroughbred colts, such as Mine That Bird (2009 Kentucky Derby winner) and Summer Bird.

Coming into the Breeders' Cup, Zenyatta was undefeated in thirteen races. Early on, it looked grim. She trailed by as much as fifteen lengths. She was still seven lengths behind with just a quarter-mile left in the race. It seemed impossible, but Zenyatta slowly made up ground, then wove through a narrow gap in the pack of horses ahead of her.

Race announcer Trevor Denman described the move well, "Zenyatta is flying on the grandstand side! This. Is. Un-be-liev-ABLE! What a performance! We will never see another like this!"

Zenyatta won by a length, becoming the first female to win the Breeders' Cup Classic. Mine That Bird finished ninth. Second-place finisher Gio Ponti's trainer Christophe Clement commented, "She's a freak, what can I say? My horse ran a great race but he couldn't beat her."

Jockey Mike Smith described the noise from the grandstand as Zenyatta pulled into the lead. "It was almost like an earthquake. I've never experienced anything like it."

It's believed her size contributed to Zenyatta's slow starts. She didn't like to touch the gate when she came out, so she waited until she was fully clear before really starting to run. Zenyatta raced six times in 2010, at the age of six, winning all but her last race. She returned to the Breeders' Cup Classic in 2010 in an attempt to repeat her amazing win of the year before–and she came within inches of doing so.

Zenyatta #4 starting slow

To no one's surprise, Zenyatta started last in the race. But this time, she could not pull it out, finishing second by a head to Blame. After the race, Mike Smith, in tears, blamed himself for the loss. "I got away slow and got squeezed out of there. If you have to blame anyone today, it would be me."

Even the winning horse's jockey, Garrett Gomez, paid tribute to Zenyatta. "Zenyatta's been an ambassador for racing. We had a lot of people out here supporting her. She was going for twenty for twenty and she came up a head short. I'm glad I was able to give her the defeat, but at the same time I wish she could have gone out twenty for twenty at someone else's expense."

Zenyatta and Rachel Alexandra, born a year apart, were two of the greatest fillies to race. Each had their fans who claimed their favorite was the better of the two. Many wanted a match between them to decide once and for all who was better. Both horses planned to race in the Apple Blossom Handicap on April 9, 2010, at Oaklawn Park in Arkansas for a $5 million purse.

However, when Zardana beat Rachel Alexandra on March 13, her owner decided not to enter Rachel in the Apple Blossom. Zardana was a stablemate of Zenyatta, whom Queen Z routinely blew past in workouts. Zenyatta won the Apple Blossom by four lengths.

Rachel Alexandra's best year was as a three-year-old, while Zenyatta continued racing strongly to the age of six. She was named Horse of the Year in 2010 and three times Champion Older Female (2008-2010). The rivalry between the two great mares has never been resolved. Perhaps it's better that way.

Zenyatta was a gentle horse, enjoying visits with her fans. She especially liked children. Her jockey, Mike Smith, said of her, "She was as close to perfect as perfect can be."

In 2010, Zenyatta retired to Lane's End Farm in Kentucky with nineteen of twenty wins and career earnings of $7,304,580. She began a relatively unsuccessful career as a broodmare, producing the following foals.

Zenyatta and Nymue

2012 — A dark bay colt, Cozmic One, raced poorly twice and switched to show jumping.

2013 — A chestnut colt, Ziconic, raced twelve times with no wins, two seconds, and six thirds.

2014 — A dark bay filly, Z Princess, was injured as a weanling and had to be euthanized.

2016 — A colt who died at two days old.

2017 — A bay filly, Zellda, never raced.

2018 — Zenyatta lost an unborn foal.

2020 — A chestnut filly, Zikha, never raced.

2021 — Zenyatta lost an unborn foal.

2023 — At nineteen, Zenyatta had her last foal, Nymue, a dark bay filly.

Nymue closely resembles Zenyatta. It remains to be seen whether this daughter will achieve the success of her mother. Zenyatta retired as a broodmare to live her remaining years relaxing at Lane's End Farm.

54

Rachel Alexandra

When the dark bay filly was born on January 29, 2006, at Heaven Trees Farm near Lexington, Kentucky, her dam, Lotta Kim, wanted nothing to do with her. She was a large foal with a curious facial marking that resembled a reversed question mark. She had socks on her left front and right rear legs. Later, her owner, Dolphus Morrison (Dolph) named her Rachel Alexandra after his granddaughter. Lotta Kim never developed any maternal feelings for Rachel, so an Appaloosa nurse mare raised the filly.

The filly didn't impress Dolph either. He considered her an ugly duckling, large and awkward. Not believing she would amount to anything, he planned to sell her that fall as a weanling. When a veterinary examination revealed some joint issues in the filly, Dolph had to scratch her from the sale.

The following year, he sent Rachel to the Diamond D Ranch in Lone Oak, Texas, for yearling training by Scooter Dodwell. Dodwell had trained Lotta Kim as well. He wasn't fond of Rachel's ornery mother; however, as training progressed, he liked the filly's intelligence, temperament, and long stride. Rachel was the fastest of the group of yearlings he had at the stable. X-rays revealed Rachel had outgrown the abnormality she'd had as a weanling. Now, her legs were clean and strong. Her owner again planned to sell her, but Dodwell was so impressed with the big filly, he advised Dolph to hold on to her.

Next, Rachel was sent to trainer Hal Wiggins at Churchill Downs in Louisville, Kentucky, for race training. Wiggins loved the filly and was quick to realize her potential. He fed her peppermints every morning when he went to the barn. Rachel began her racing career as a two-year-old in 2008. Jockey Brian Hernandez Jr. rode her to two wins in five starts. Wiggins believed the big filly was better than that. He didn't think Hernandez and Rachel were connecting. For the last race of 2008, Wiggins switched riders. Forty-two-year-old veteran jockey Calvin Borel rode Rachel Alexandra to a first-place finish in the Golden Rod Stakes that November.

The pair went undefeated in 2009—nine wins in a row. The Oaks, a race for three-year-old fillies, takes place the day before the Kentucky Derby. Derby winners receive a garland of roses. Oaks winners receive one made of lilies, known as "lilies for the fillies." Rachel won the Kentucky Oaks by an amazing twenty and a quarter lengths.

After the Oaks, Rachel Alexandra was sold to Stonestreet Stables, owned by Jess Jackson. Although Calvin Borel continued to ride her, Steve Asmussen replaced Hal Wiggins as her trainer. The loss of the filly devastated Wiggins, but he knew Dolph Morrison had received an offer he

Winning the Kentucky Oaks

couldn't refuse, reportedly more than $10,000,000. Wiggins retired from training with the satisfaction of seeing the filly he had trained win the Oaks in a victory reminiscent of Secretariat's thirty-one length win in the 1973 Belmont Stakes.

Dolph had refused to race his filly against colts; however, Jess Jackson believed Rachel would do well against them. Since she had run in the Oaks, the filly was not entered in the Kentucky Derby. Rachel Alexandra's jockey, Calvin Borel, won the Derby on Mine That Bird.

Rachel's first test against the boys was the Preakness Stakes, the second race in the Triple Crown. This presented a dilemma for Borel. Both horses he'd recently ridden to big victories were entered in the Preakness. Which one would he ride?

Mine That Bird was the only horse that year with a chance at a Triple Crown win. But, Borel thought Rachel Alexandra was the better horse. He chose to ride her. In fact, he later claimed Rachel was the best horse he'd ever ridden.

On May 16, 2009, Rachel was the only filly in the race, facing twelve colts, including the Kentucky Derby winner. She also had the disadvantage of starting from position thirteen on the far outside of the track. However, Rachel moved to the front of the pack early on and led for most of the race, winning by a length over Mine That Bird. She became the first filly in eighty-five years to win the Preakness.

Next, Rachel defeated two other fillies by over nineteen lengths in the Mother Goose Stakes. Rachel developed quite a fan base with women and girls who otherwise had no interest in horse racing. This filly who could beat the colts appealed to them. They wore T-shirts or carried signs with messages like "Girl Power" and "I run like a girl." Rachel didn't disappoint them. When she faced colts again in the Haskell Invitational, she won, beating the Belmont Stakes winner Summer Bird by six lengths.

Rachel, now known as the "Super Filly," finished the season by running in the Woodward in Saratoga, New York, a race that a filly had never won. Rachel pulled out another victory, winning by a head over second-place finisher Macho Again. The Woodward was her eighth win of the year and her

ninth consecutive victory since the fall of 2008, when Calvin Borel took over as her jockey. Rachel Alexandra was named 2009 Horse of the Year and was featured in Vogue magazine.

It would have been fitting for Rachel Alexandra to retire after the Woodward victory; however, Jess Jackson decided to race her as a four-year-old in 2010. She raced five more times, finishing first twice and second three times. She was retired to Jackson's Stonestreet Farm in Lexington with career earnings of $3,506,730.

At Stonestreet, Rachel had two foals, both bays. Her first was a colt named Jess's Dream in 2012. Her second was a filly, Rachel's Valentina. Rachel Alexandra suffered internal injuries during the delivery of her second foal. She recovered after a six-hour surgery but had no more foals after that. She is enjoying her retirement and was inducted into the Racing Hall of Fame in 2016.

Besides Rachel Alexandra, Ruffian, and Zenyatta, there have been several other notable Thoroughbred racehorse fillies.

Fillies who have won the Kentucky Derby include Regret (1915), Genuine Risk (1980) and Winning Colors (1988). Genuine Risk was the filly who came closest to a Triple Crown win, finishing second in both the Preakness and the Belmont. Winning Colors finished third in the Preakness and sixth in the Belmont.

Fillies who have won the Preakness Stakes include Flocarline (1903), Whimsical (1906), Rhine Maiden (1915), Nellie Morse (1924), Rachel Alexandra (2009), and Swiss Skydiver (2020)

Fillies who have won the Belmont Stakes include Ruthless (1867, the first running of this race), Tanya (1905), and Rags to Riches (2007).

Personal Ensign, a bay filly, raced from 1986 to 1988 and retired undefeated with a perfect thirteen wins in thirteen races.

Kincsem, however, holds the record as the longest undefeated racehorse, male or female. She was foaled in Hungary on March 17, 1874. Her name means My Precious or My Treasure. Kincsem raced in Europe from the ages of three to six. She won every one of the fifty-four races she entered, against both colts and fillies.

Rachel in retirement

Kincsem

55

Magna Fortuna

Despite a racetrack policy that horses who have raced are not to be sold at low-end auctions, some unfortunate animals find themselves at these sales where they are purchased by "kill buyers." Although no equine slaughterhouses operate in the United States, thousands of U.S. horses are exported each year for slaughter in Canada and Mexico.

After changing hands several times, a bay Thoroughbred mare ended up at the Shipshewana Livestock Auction in Indiana. The mare had already been purchased by a kill buyer when Gail Vacca spotted her. Vacca, president of the Illinois Equine Humane Center (ILEHC), suspected the mare was a Thoroughbred, and the tattoo inside the horse's lip confirmed it. She convinced the buyer to sell the mare to her for $300. On June 6, 2009, the horse, Lulu, became one of the fortunate few to escape Shipshewana.

Lulu suffered from laminitis and was fitted with corrective shoes. As the ILEHC volunteers nursed the lame mare back to health, they were surprised to find they'd rescued not one horse but two. Lulu was in foal. Initially, they couldn't identify the mare because a dark spot on her lip obscured part of the tattoo.

Lulu foaled on April 15, 2010, a dark bay colt Vacca named Taxi (for tax day). After spending three months on a foster farm, the mare and foal returned to ILEHC. Impressed with the foal's conformation, Vacca renewed her efforts to determine Lulu's identity and that of the colt's sire. She learned the mare was Silver Option, born in 1997. After a short, unimpressive racing career, she became a broodmare.

Vacca called the previous owner to inform him about the colt and to get more information about Silver Option. Taxi's sire was Magna Graduate, winner of $2.58 million over his racing career (2004 to 2008). While still with her previous owner, Silver Option was thought to be carrying twins (rare and often dangerous in horses). A veterinarian removed one of the foals. At a later examination, the vet believed Silver had lost the other foal as well. At that point, the frustrated owner just wanted to get rid of the mare, and that's how she ended up at Shipshewana.

When informed of Silver Option's foal, the previous owner pressured Vacca to sell him the colt.

Vacca's response–"Are you out of your mind? Buddy, there's not enough money on the planet for me to sell this horse to you. You threw his mama away like yesterday's garbage."

As the colt grew, Vacca wondered whether Taxi could become a racehorse, not for the money, but to serve as a representative who would help get better treatment for discarded Thoroughbreds.

She formed a racing partnership called Rescue Me Racing. Fifteen others bought shares of the colt. Vacca was determined to take care of him whether or not he became a success on the track.

First, they had to register Taxi with the Jockey Club. They obtained the stallion certificate from Darby Dan Farm in Kentucky, where Magna Graduate was standing as a stallion. A DNA sample from the colt confirmed his pedigree. The partners settled on Magna Fortuna (great fortune or luck) as his registered name.

Michele Boyce trained Magna. He placed ninth in his first race on December 26, 2012, wearing yellow and black and ridden by jockey Julio Felix. In 2013, Magna won two of four races, one of them by ten lengths.

With the victories came trouble. According to Gail Vacca's attorney, "The worst thing that ever happened to Taxi was that he began winning."

In late 2013, Magna suffered an injury to a ligament in his left front leg and was rested for several months. He resumed training in April 2014 and ran in two early races. After one training session, he was found bleeding from his nose. A veterinarian diagnosed the problem as a severe exercise-induced pulmonary hemorrhage.

Vacca believed they should retire Magna before the condition became worse. Eleven of the Rescue Me Racing partners disagreed. They thought with rest, antibiotics, and oxygen therapy, Magna could run again. The partners voted Vacca out as the equine welfare manager of the group and filed a lawsuit against her.

After two years of legal wrangling, the conflict was resolved. Magna's ownership was transferred back to ILEHC. The gelding was later adopted by Alex Haser and embarked on a new career as a dressage horse. His mother, Lulu or Silver Option, died at the rescue on June 1, 2015.

56

White Bliss

I magine Peter Congilose's surprise on May 6, 2012, when he saw the Standardbred colt foaled by his bay mare, Coochie Mama. The foal's sire, Art Major, was also a bay, by far the predominant color of Standardbred horses. Even white facial or leg markings are uncommon in the breed.

Coochie Mama's foal was startlingly white. On closer inspection, Congilose discovered a light sprinkling of reddish-brown hair between his ears and a few, small dark spots on his otherwise pink skin. He named the colt White Bliss.

Standardbreds are the lesser-known racehorse breed in the United States. They descended from some of the same ancestors as their more famous Thoroughbred cousins. The breed traces back to Messenger, a gray Thoroughbred foaled in England in 1780 and imported to the U.S. in 1788. His great-grandson, Hambletonian 10, foaled in 1849, is considered the Standardbred's foundation sire.

Standardbreds are usually smaller and a little heavier than Thoroughbreds and are considered more even-tempered. They are harness racers, racing at either a trot or a pace, with pacers slightly faster than trotters.[1]

---

[1] *At a trot, the legs move in diagonal pairs; the right foreleg with the left hind, and vice versa. At the pace, each foreleg moves with the hind leg on the same side. You can see this in the photos of White Bliss (a pacer) and Via Lattea (a trotter).*

Although most often bay, less frequent colors include brown, black, chestnut, and gray—but almost never white!

White Bliss had no white relatives in his family tree. DNA testing confirmed his parentage. A gene mutation caused his rare coloring. The odds of the New Jersey colt being born white are believed to be 1 in 200,000. He is not an albino. There are no albinos in the horse world.

Congilose sold White Bliss at the Standardbred Horse Sale in Pennsylvania in 2013 for $240,000. He was the highest priced of the 297 yearlings in the sale. The average was $39,742. Swede Tristan Sjoberg bought the horse as a Christmas present for his mother who had always wanted a white Standardbred.

Trained by Ake Svanstedt, White Bliss was boxed in behind other horses in his first race in 2014 but finished third. His first win came as a three-year-old on July 25, 2015, at Vernon Downs in New York. The pacer raced seventy-three times over his career, with five wins, nine seconds, and nine thirds before retiring in 2019.

Lillbliss

On April 15, 2021, White Bliss' first foal was born. The white colt, Lillbliss, was also born to a bay mother, Bon Mot.

Sjoberg bought another white Standardbred, a filly trotter born April 4, 2014, in Italy. Her name is Via Lattea, meaning "Milky Way." Breyer made a model of Via Lattea in 2023.

Via Lattea

57

Recent Triple Crown Winners

Before Secretariat won the Triple Crown in 1973, it had been twenty-five years since Citation won the three races in 1948. Two more horses won the Crown in the seventies—Seattle Slew (1977) and Affirmed (1978). Then, there was a gap of thirty-seven years before American Pharoah won in 2015 and Justify in 2018.

American Pharoah, owned by Ahmed Zayat, of Zayat Stables, was born on February 2, 2012, in Lexington, Kentucky. The name "American Pharoah" was accepted by the Jockey Club even though the second word was misspelled. It should have been "Pharoah." Once registered, the misspelled version became permanent; however, the Jockey Club has reserved both spellings to prevent someone from using the variant form in the future.

In his first race, American Pharoah wore a hood with blinkers, the idea being to keep the horse focused on what was ahead of him. American Pharoah finished fifth in that race. His trainer, Bob Baffert, felt the limited visibility caused by the hood bothered the horse, so he didn't use it in later races. Instead, he placed cotton in the horse's ears to keep him calm by muffling the noise.

Although sometimes nervous, the colt was not aggressive and was unusually gentle. His owner described the horse as, "The kindest, friendliest, happiest, easiest, most brilliant horse I've ever seen in my life. He connected with people. He loves people."

Pharoah settled down and won his next two races as a two-year-old. A bruised heel on his left front hoof kept him out of any further races that season. His farrier devised a special shoe for Pharoah with a flat aluminum plate that covered the rear of the shoe and protected the horse's heel and part of the frog. A regular shoe was used on his other front foot. Farrier Wes Champagne said, "I'm not one of those who worries about balancing out the two front feet with the exact same shoes."

"""

Victor Espinoza rode Pharoah in the 2015 Kentucky Derby, finishing first by a length over Firing Line. In the Preakness, they won again, seven lengths ahead of Tale of Verve. In the final Triple Crown race, the Belmont Stakes, American Pharoah took the lead early and no one could catch him. He won by five and a half lengths over the gray Frosted, becoming the twelfth Triple Crown-winning horse. Victor Espinoza was the first Latino jockey to win the Triple Crown and at forty-three, the oldest.

American Pharoah would go undefeated for the rest of his career, except for a second-place finish in the 2015 Travers Stakes at Saratoga. By winning the Breeders' Cup Classic and the Triple Crown races, Pharoah became the first horse to win what is known as the Grand Slam of Thoroughbred racing. In 2015, he was American Horse of the Year and Champion Three-year-old Male Horse.

Bob Baffert was back three years later with another Triple Crown winner, Justify. Baffert is only the second person to train two Triple Crown winners. The first was Jim Fitzsimmons with Gallant Fox (1930) and Omaha (1935). In comparing Justify's temperament to that of the gentle American Pharoah, Baffert said, "You have to watch him. He likes to push you around. He's not a mean horse, but his patience level with people is, like, five seconds."

Justify was purchased as a yearling at the Keeneland sale for $500,000 by a partnership of WinStar Farm, the China Horse Club, and SF Racing. Rodolphe Brisset initially trained him, then he was sent to Baffert in California. Justify was a slow developer, as many big horses are. Because of this, he never raced as a two-year-old. The chestnut colt with a large blaze grew to 16.3 hands.

Jockey Drayden Van Dyke rode the three-year-old Justify in his first race on February 18, 2018. He won by nine and a half lengths. Mike Smith would be Justify's jockey for his remaining races. They won the second outing by six and a half lengths. Since he hadn't raced at two, Justify had to earn

enough points before May 2018 to qualify for the Kentucky Derby. On April 7, he reached that level by winning the Santa Anita Derby.

Despite having only raced three times, Justify finished the Derby in first place, a length and a half ahead of Good Magic. He was the first horse since Apollo in 1882 to win the Derby without racing as a two-year-old.

Heavy rains created a soupy track for the running of the Preakness Stakes. Justify held on to the lead to pull slightly ahead of a pack of four horses and win by half a length.

Justify had an easier time in the Belmont, leading for most of the race and winning by a length and three-fourths over Gronkowski to become the thirteenth Triple Crown winner. Mike Smith, at fifty-two, replaced Victor Espinoza as the oldest jockey to win the Triple Crown.

Justify retired, unbeaten, after the June 9, 2018 Belmont Stakes. He was the only Triple Crown winner who did not race after the Belmont. He joined American Pharoah in retirement at Ashford Stud in Kentucky.

Controversy erupted the following year. On September 11, 2019, The New York Times ran a story titled "Justify Failed a Drug Test Before Winning the Triple Crown."

After his victory in the Santa Anita Derby in April 2018, Justify tested positive for scopolamine. If the results had been made public at the time, Justify could have been disqualified from the Santa Anita. That would have made him ineligible for the Kentucky Derby. Therefore, he could not have won the Triple Crown. The article insinuated Baffert had intentionally drugged Justify, and the California Horse Racing Board covered up the test results.

Some believed scopolamine was a performance-enhancing substance that acted as a bronchodilator to enlarge a horse's airway and optimize his heart rate. They insisted it had to have been intentionally administered.

On the other side were those who claimed the scopolamine occurred naturally in jimson weed, an invasive plant that must have found its way into the feed or bedding used for the horse.

Justify's Triple Crown victory still stands. However, several other Bob Baffert horses have failed drug tests, and multiple mysterious deaths have been connected to the trainer.

Seven horses in Baffert's Hollywood Park stable died between November 2, 2011, and March 14, 2013, all from sudden, unexplained heart attacks. An investigation revealed that Baffert routinely gave the horses thyroxine, a thyroid hormone. No sanctions were issued against Baffert at the time.

In 2021, a Baffert-trained colt, Medina Spirit, finished first in the Kentucky Derby, but was disqualified when a post-race test was positive for the drug, betamethasone. In June, Baffert was banned from entering horses at Churchill Downs-owned racetracks for two years.

Three-year-old Medina Spirit collapsed and died at Santa Anita Park following a workout on December 6, 2021.

Churchill Downs extended Baffert's ban another year. It was lifted in July 2024. Baffert issued a statement regarding Medina Spirit's positive drug test. "I have paid a very steep price with a three-year suspension and the disqualification of Medina Spirit's performance."

Some estimate that seventy-five racehorses in Baffert's care have died since 2000. As recently as April 2025, two Baffert horses, Willy and Non Compliant, were euthanized after suffering injuries. With statistics like that, it's a wonder anyone sends their horses to him; however, because of his ability to produce winners, Baffert continues to get horses to train.

58

Almost Triple Crown Winners

No one remembers who came in second." That saying is attributed to professional golfer Walter Hagen. Unfortunately, it's usually true. To date, eight amazing horses have won the first two Triple Crown races (the Kentucky Derby and Preakness Stakes), only to finish second in the final one, the Belmont Stakes. These horses are recognized here for coming as close as possible to becoming Triple Crown winners. The year and the horse's losing margin in the Belmont are noted below.

- Pensive (1944, half a length)
- Tim Tam (1958, six lengths)
- Forward Pass (1968, one and a quarter lengths)
- Majestic Prince (1969, five and a half lengths)
- Sunday Silence (1989, eight lengths)
- Silver Charm (1997, three-fourths of a length)
- Real Quiet (1998, a nose)
- Smarty Jones (2004, one length)

Although the Crown eluded them, these second-place finishers deserve recognition for their performance and contribution to the world of horse racing.

Pensive was the first of this group to win the first two races and come in a disappointing second in the Belmont. He sired Ponder, the 1949 Kentucky Derby winner. Ponder sired Needles in 1953. Needles won the 1956 Kentucky Derby and the Belmont Stakes. Needles missed the Triple Crown by finishing second in the Preakness Stakes.

Pensive - Preakness Stakes

Toward the end of the the Belmont Stakes, **Tim Tam** fractured a sesamoid bone in his right, front leg. He gallantly continued the race, finishing second. Surgery was performed to remove bone fragments. He never raced again, but he became a successful sire. One of his grandfillies, Davona Dale (1976), won the 1979 Triple Crown for fillies. Ross Arnott, of Arnott's, an Australian food company, was so impressed by Tim Tam's victory in the 1958 Kentucky Derby, he named a chocolate biscuit after the horse. Although Tim Tam failed to win the Triple Crown, the biscuits carrying his name were a winner for Arnott's. Tim Tams have been the company's most popular product since 1963. The biscuits were first made available in the U.S. in 2008.

Tim Tam - Kentucky Derby

Forward Pass - Preakness Stakes

Forward Pass actually finished second in the 1968 Kentucky Derby. However, he was later declared the winner when first-place finisher, Dancer's Image, tested positive for phenylbutazone, a prohibited drug at the time. By 1974, the racing commission approved the use of the anti-inflammatory drug commonly known as bute. In 1977, Forward Pass was sold to Nishiyama Farm in Japan, where he died of colic in 1980.

When **Majestic Prince** injured a tendon in his right front leg, it was doubtful whether he would enter the Belmont. Both his trainer and jockey believed the horse should not race, but his owner Frank McMahon overruled them. Arts and Letters defeated him in the Belmont by five and a half lengths. Majestic Prince never raced again, finishing his career with nine wins in ten starts. One of his sons, Coastal, won the Belmont Stakes in 1979.

Majestic Prince - Kentucky Derby

It's a miracle **Sunday Silence** ever raced at all. He almost died twice before making it to the track. He suffered from an intestinal infection as a weanling and had to be fed intravenously. As a yearling,

he was cow-hocked and knock-kneed, so hopeless looking that Arthur Hancock purchased him at an auction for a paltry $17,000. By the age of two, his legs were straightening. One day, the driver of a van transporting the colt had a heart attack, and the van flipped. Fortunately, Sunday Silence suffered only cuts and bruises. He spent two weeks recovering at an equine hospital. Sunday Silence came up short in the third leg of the Triple Crown, losing to Easy Goer. But the handsome black horse won the Breeders' Cup Classic later that year (beating second place Easy Goer). He retired in 1990 after fourteen races, with nine wins and five seconds. He was sold to Zenya Yoshida's Shadai Stallion Station in 1991, where he came to be regarded as a superstar sire. One of his most famous colts was Deep Impact, who won the Japanese Triple Crown in 2005.

Sunday Silence - Kentucky Derby

Born jet-black, turning gray with age, **Silver Charm** was a rare color for a champion racehorse. Only eight gray horses have won the Kentucky Derby, and none have won the Triple Crown. At four, Charm won the 1998 Dubai World Cup (a race in the United Arab Emirates for world-class Thoroughbreds four and older). He also finished second in the 1998 Breeders' Cup Classic. He retired with earnings of $6,944,369. Charm was sold to Japan with a buyback clause. He spent the years from 2005 to 2014 at the Shizuanai Stallion Station. In December 2014, he flew home to enjoy retirement at the Old Friends Farm in Kentucky. As of 2025, Silver Charm, at thirty-one, was the oldest surviving Kentucky Derby winner.

Silver Charm - Kentucky Derby

Real Quiet, nicknamed "The Fish" because of his narrow frame, was the closest "almost winner" of the Triple Crown. Victory Gallop beat him in the last stride of the Belmont. The photo finish revealed Real Quiet was a mere four inches short of victory. He retired as a four-year-old with earnings of $3,271,802. He spent time at stud farms in the U.S., Australia, and Uruguay before returning to Penn Ridge Farms in Pennsylvania. Sunday Silence and Real Quiet were both honored by naming streets after them in Prince William County, Virginia. However, someone misspelled Real Quiet's name as Real Quite. The misspelling still appears on the street sign.

Photo finish of the Belmont Stakes showing the slim margin by which Real Quiet missed the Triple Crown

Smarty Jones was named after the mother of co-owner Pat Chapman. Her mother, Milly Jones, was called "Smarty" as a child. After their trainer, Bob Camac, was murdered in December 2001, the Chapmans sold most of their horses, keeping only two, one of which was Smarty Jones. In July 2003, under new trainer John Servis, Smarty reared in the starting gate. The horse hit his head and fell, bleeding and unconscious. He was alive, though X-rays showed he had fractured his skull. Swelling in his head made the veterinarian fear they might have to remove his left eye. Smarty spent three weeks in the hospital and a month resting on a farm. He made a full recovery, and by November 2003, was ready to race. He won both of his two-year-old races, the first by eight lengths, and the second by fifteen. Smarty still holds the record for the largest margin of victory in the Preakness, winning by eleven and a half lengths. Smarty Jones' only loss out of nine starts came in the Belmont, his last race. Oaklawn Park in Arkansas named the Smarty Jones Stakes after him.

Smarty Jones - Belmont Stakes

Some racehorses sold overseas today include a buyback clause, making their return to the U.S. possible. This practice came about after the tragic death of Ferdinand, winner of the 1986 Kentucky Derby and the 1987 Breeders' Cup Classic. Ferdinand was named the 1987 Horse of the Year. In 1994, he was sold to Japan. After his popularity as a sire declined, the champion ended up at a Japanese slaughterhouse in 2002. This resulted in the New York Owners and Breeders Association implementing a voluntary per-race charge called the "Ferdinand Fee." This money is used to help fund Thoroughbred rescue and retirement groups.

59

Paardenvissers

Over the years, horses have assisted people in many ways; one of the more unusual ones is shrimp fishing. For five hundred years, the practice was common along the coastal areas of the North Sea. Today, it only occurs in the small town of Oostduinkerke, Belgium. Each spring and fall, fishermen catch shrimp from the back of a horse. The locals call these fishermen paardenvissers.

In the morning, the horse is tacked up with a special pack saddle, then hitched to a cart to pull the fishing equipment to the beach. The fisherman rides on the side of the cart. During the tourist season, the paardenvissers parade through town with a crowd following them to the sea.

When they arrive at the shore, the fishermen put yellow rain suits on over their clothes. They bind the pant legs at the ankles to keep water out. The horse is unhooked from the cart, and a funnel-shaped, thirty foot long net is attached by chains to his harness. Two planks of wood keep the net open on each side.

The rider mounts, and the horse walks into the North Sea, until the water is chest deep, pulling the net behind him. As the net skims over the sand, the chains cause vibrations that make the shrimp jump up and land in the net. Horse and rider sweep back and forth parallel to the coastline, returning to the beach every half hour to empty their catch and give the horse a rest. Unwanted creatures such as crabs, small fish, and jellyfish are returned

to the sea. The shrimp are placed in wicker baskets carried on each side of the horse.

The craft appears deceptively simple as horses and riders wind slowly back and forth. But fishing on horseback requires skill and a good knowledge of the tides, shrimp, and horses. A fishing day lasts about three hours—an hour and a half before and after low tide.

> *The catching season usually starts in the middle of March or early April and runs to the end of June. The water is too hot in summer. We get back into the saddle from mid-September to mid-December. I think that October's the best month, but it's certainly not a precise science.[1]*

A trustworthy horse is essential, and when found, he often becomes a lifelong companion. Not all horses like trudging out into the waves. In the past, when smaller nets were used, small draft horses or mules were popular. Longer, modern nets require a stronger animal. A popular breed for fishing today is the Brabant draft horse. They are large, gentle, and strong. Male Brabants can reach 16 to 17 hands and weigh 2,000 or more pounds. Females are a little smaller. The Belgian horse in America traces its lineage back to the Brabants.

About seventeen horseback shrimp fishermen work in Oostduinkerke today. Their catch is too small to make a living from the practice. The shrimp are often cooked and handed out to tourists. Since demonstrations of horseback fishing are a popular tourist attraction, the village provides financial support for the paardenvissers. Tourists bring income to the village by patronizing the local hotels, restaurants, and other shops.

Nele Bekaert was the first officially recognized female horseback shrimper, working the sea with her horse Axel. Prior to that, it was a man's profession. Nele, a mother of three, works at a nursing home and enjoys shrimp fishing in her spare time.

UNESCO added horseback shrimp fishing to its Intangible Cultural Heritage list in 2013. The ICH hopes to safeguard cultural traditions and practices for future generations.[2] Preserving the craft of shrimp fishing has also helped protect the Brabant horse, which has dwindled in numbers over the years. The Navigo Museum offers a training course for those eighteen and older who would like to become paardenvissers. The training includes two years of fishing with an established horse fisherman. Trainees must carry liability insurance and provide their own horse, cart, tack, equipment, and clothing, as well as food and stabling for their horse.

---

[1] *Eddy D'Hulster, paardenvisser*
[2] *UNESCO United Nations Educational, Scientific and Cultural Organization*

60

Wadden Sea

The Wadden Sea National Park is a tidal basin at the southern end of the North Sea, stretching 300 miles from the northern part of the Netherlands, across Germany, and into Denmark. In the center of the park is Neuwerk Island, a 1.2 square mile island which is part of Germany. Neuwerk is home to twenty to forty year-round residents. Dikes surround the island to protect it from flooding. The Great Tower Neuwerk was built in 1310 for defense. It served as a lighthouse from 1814 to 2014. Tourists can climb 138 steps to the top of the historic lighthouse. It also now serves as a small hotel and restaurant. Cars are not permitted on the island. Neuwerk can be reached by ferry at high tide.

At low tide, the basin turns into a giant mud flat, and one can walk to the island from the village of Cuxhaven, Germany. The eight-mile trip takes about three hours on foot, but walkers have to watch their step. Sea life, including mounds of lug and sand worms, covers the exposed mud flat. Far off in the distance, the island can barely be seen at the start of the trip. A line of markers, visible at low tide, show the route to Neuwerk.

Rather than walking, a more popular means of reaching the island is riding on a Wattwagen. This is a sturdy carriage pulled by a team of two draft horses with names like Sidar and Meike or Nele and Otti. The bed of the bright yellow wagons is held up by leaf springs. The wagon bed sits about four feet above the ground to accommodate rising sea levels.

A line of Wattwagens travels to the shore from several inland stables. They assemble at a sandy turning area called the Wattwagenplatz where passengers board. A ladder is carried under the bed so tourists can climb into and out of the tall wagons. Three bench seats hold up to nine people–eight passengers and the driver. The water is deepest in the middle of the channel, often reaching the

horses' abdomens. They seem to enjoy walking in the water, and it's believed the salty water promotes health and healing.

The carriages run in all but the worst weather. Waterproof tarps and blankets are provided for the passengers' comfort. The mud flat is passable for the duration of low tide, about four hours. The Wattwagen journey takes an hour and a half one way. That leaves an hour to explore the island before heading back to the wagon for the return trip.

Those who walk may return by ferry the same day or spend the night on the island and walk back the following day. Occasionally, high tide catches a walker by surprise. Cages mounted on posts in the middle of the basin provide a safe perch for those unfortunate people. They can wait it out until the water is shallow enough to walk again or call for a rescue boat. Those who are rescued must pay a fine.

Each year, the mud flat becomes the wettest horse racing track in the world. The Duhner Wattrennen has been held annually since 1902. The festival includes racing on horseback and harness races, with a special cart race for minis.

61

Mule Train Mail

One of the most remote communities in the continental United States is Supai, the capital of the Havasupai Indian Reservation. The Havasupai are known as the "People of the Blue-Green Water." About 200 people live on the reservation, which consists of 188,077 acres of land near the Grand Canyon's South Rim. Although Supai is located inside the Grand Canyon, it is not part of the park and is governed by the tribe.

The only way to reach the village is by an eight-mile trek on foot, by mule, or by helicopter. There are no automobiles in Supai, but it has a church, school, lodge, cafe, and general store. Supai relies on tourism for part of its income. Approximately 20,000 people visit the village each year, hiking and camping in areas such as Havasu Falls.

Supai's post office is one of the things that makes the village unique. The village has the only official USPS mule route in the country. Mules have provided this delivery service since at least the 1930s. When mail is sent from the Supai post office, it receives a special Mule Train Mail postmark popular with tourists.

Mail delivery begins before sunrise with a truck containing outgoing Supai mail driving to Peach Springs, Arizona. Peach Springs is the closest post office—seventy-five miles from Supai. At Peach Springs, the driver leaves any outgoing mail and picks up mail addressed to Supai. The "mail" heading to the bottom of the canyon isn't usually letters. Villagers receive food, medicine, and other supplies through the postal service. Villagers are said to "eat more mail than they read." Because it processes so much food, Peach Springs is the only U.S. post office with a walk-in

freezer. Once the mail bound for Supai is loaded, the driver heads to Hualapai Hilltop on the canyon's rim. A hitching area at the trailhead contains a sign that reads, "U.S. Mail Delivery Zone."

Meanwhile, the mule wrangler began his day at about 3:00 a.m., feeding and watering the mules and horses. By 8:00, he and his team of eight or more mules have climbed to Hualapai Hilltop. There, he waits with his mules for the mail.

The arriving packages are stored in saddlebags or plastic USPS crates. The driver and wranglers work together to attach them to the mules' pack saddles. Each mule carries a maximum of 150 to 200 pounds, evenly distributed over his back and sides. When the mules are loaded, the last leg of the journey begins—down eight miles to the village post office. The first part of the trail is the steepest and includes a series of switchbacks. The trip down takes three hours, while the more strenuous journey up to the top takes nearly five.

The arrival of the mail at Supai is a social event, with residents gathering near the post office as everything is unloaded. Charlie Chamberlain, who rode the Supai mule route for twenty-five years, insists it's the most cost-effective way to deliver mail to the village.

In the past, some people became aware of cases of abuse and neglect of the pack animals. A group called SAVE Havasupai Horses was formed in 2016 to establish regulations for the humane care of the pack animals that serve Supai. There is concern that there isn't enough vegetation on the arid land to provide grazing for them. Transporting hay and grain is challenging. Some observed and photographed animals who were underweight, were loaded beyond the weight limit, had saddle or harness sores, or had neglected hooves. These cases may have been privately owned animals providing services to tourists, rather than the horses and mules working for the USPS.

Another mule delivery route operates nearby, carrying mail to a tourist lodge, the Phantom Ranch, also at the bottom of the Grand Canyon. However, the Phantom Ranch delivery mules are not part of the U.S. Postal Service.

Amazon has also found mules to be an effective delivery option to the area. Amazon packages arrive at a warehouse on the South Rim. From there, Phantom Ranch trucks carry the packages to the mule barn. After their breakfast, the mules are packed with the Amazon items. At sunrise, they start down the canyon to Phantom Ranch.

62

Rich Strike

On September 17, 2021, trainer Eric Reed claimed Rich Strike in a claiming race at Churchill Downs which the horse won by an amazing seventeen lengths. Reed claimed the two-year-old chestnut for owner Richard Dawson for $30,000. That might seem like a lot of money, but it pales when compared to the price of many racehorses. At Keeneland's Thoroughbred yearling sale in September 2021, a sale for untrained Thoroughbreds, the average price was $400,000, with a high sale of $1,400,000.

Every horse in a claiming race is available for purchase at a fixed price. The price varies depending on the caliber of the race. The person who wants to buy or "claim" a horse submits a form, before the start of the race, specifying the horse he wants. If more than one person submits a claim for the same horse, the winner is determined by a random drawing known as a shake. The claimer owns the horse after a post-race inspection. The claim can be voided if the horse dies, is injured during the race, or tests positive for drug use. Anything the horse wins during the claiming race goes to the owner who entered him in the race, not to the new claimant.

Claiming races are sometimes a way to unload horses who are not performing up to a trainer or owner's expectations. As a two-year-old, Rich Strike finished last out of ten horses in his first race—not a great start for his racing career.

For his new owner, Rich Strike finished third three times, fourth once, and fifth once. Rich Strike's less than spectacular performance seemed to match the misfortune of his trainer.

Eric Reed and his wife, Kay, experienced a tragic barn fire, thought to be caused by lightning, in December 2016 at their Mercury Equine Center in Lexington. Reed and his employees saved thirteen horses by leading them out of the burning barn, but twenty-three Thoroughbreds died in the fire. They would have lost fewer horses, but the fire department, located just five minutes away, didn't arrive until forty minutes after the first call for help. The tragedy made Reed consider leaving horse racing.

The next morning when we saw the devastation—because this happened in the middle of the night—I just

Overwhelming support from his friends and others in the racing industry convinced Reed to rebuild and continue training. It was after that fire that Reed claimed Rich Strike and began working with the colt.

Although his racing career hadn't been remarkable, Rich Strike, or Richie, as his new owner calls him, earned enough points to qualify for the Kentucky Derby as a three-year-old in 2022. However, the field for the race on Saturday, May 7, 2022, was full. Richie was first on standby in the "Also Eligible" list in case any of the entrants dropped out of the race (scratched).

At 8:45 a.m. on Friday, the day before the race, Reed was informed no horses had scratched. Disappointed, the trainer began calling friends to let them know Richie wouldn't be racing. But fifteen minutes later, Reed received another call. The owner of Ethereal Road had scratched his horse at the last possible moment. Rich Strike was in the Derby after all!

As an unheard-of horse, race experts gave Rich Strike 80 to 1 odds of winning. He was an extreme long shot—an underdog. No one other than Richie's owner and team thought the horse would do anything but fill the empty slot in the lineup.

Fortunately, Rich Strike was unaware of everyone's low opinion of him.

Twenty horses entered the race. The favorites were Epicenter and Zandon. As the last entry, Rich Strike was in the twentieth position on the far outside of the track, wearing number twenty-one. Running from the outer positions means covering a longer distance. It's important for the outside horses to quickly move to the

[1] *cnn.com/2022/05/07/us/ kentucky-derby-winner- trainer-barn-tragedy*

Rich Strike starting on the outside in the Derby.

inside of the track. But doing so means they may encounter a pack of horses that can be difficult to get past or through.

Rich Strike's jockey, Venezuelan Sonny Leon, was as well known at the Kentucky Derby level of racing as his mount—that is—unknown. Leon began racing at fifteen in Youngstown, Ohio. Prior to the Derby, his experience was limited to the Ohio area horse-racing world.

For most of the early race, Richie ran at the back of the pack. At a half-mile, he was in eighteenth place. At the mile mark, with only a quarter mile to go, he was fifteenth. Then, Sonny Leon maneuvered the horse toward the rail, and the pair began weaving in and out, passing horses in the pack who were tiring.

The race announcer, focused on the battle between the leaders, Epicenter and Zandon, missed the freight train that was Rich Strike coming up from behind. Richie pulled ahead of the favorites to win by three-quarters of a length over Epicenter, with Zandon in third.

Rich Strike lived up to his name that day, winning $1.8 million, becoming the first claimed horse to win the Kentucky Derby.

A Sports Illustrated article described the underdog's victory perfectly, stating that no one saw Rich Strike coming.

> *Not until the very end, when this nobody of a horse, with a nobody trainer and nobody jockey and nobody owner, came knifing along the rail a few strides before the wire to launch himself into history.*

Owner Richard Dawson skipped The Preakness, the second race in the Triple Crown, run just two weeks after the Derby. He didn't feel that was enough time for Richie to rest.

Rich Strike finished a disappointing sixth out of eight entries in the Belmont Stakes on June 11. Trainer Eric Reed took the blame for Richie's poor performance, claiming he had given the jockey a bad race strategy.

Later that year, Rich Strike finished fourth in both the 2022 Travers Stakes and the Breeders' Cup Classic.

Although Rich Strike never won another race, no one can take away his amazing come-from-behind victory in the 2022 Kentucky Derby. He retired from racing in 2024 due to leg injuries.

63

Mounted Search and Rescue

As mechanization has replaced horses in many areas, it remains to be seen what roles they will play in the future. A few things seem to have come full circle and moved back to horses. For example, many police forces have realized equines provide unique advantages over motorized vehicles, primarily in the area of public relations. Besides their specialties of crime deterrence and crowd control, police horses serve as ambassadors to their communities.

A related area where horses provide valuable service is search and rescue. Many counties across the country have mounted search and rescue teams (MSAR). Volunteers often make up these groups.

Not all horses are capable of being MSAR animals. They have to meet requirements such as the following to be accepted into search programs. Acceptable horses must be:

- in good health and condition, able to travel up to twenty miles in a day

- calm, not aggressive toward people or other horses

- able to be ridden away from other horses and work independently

- sure-footed, experienced on trails, able to cross streams and fallen trees

- accustomed to stressful sights and sounds such as cars, ATVs, helicopters, gunshots, alarms, sirens, and wildlife

- easily loaded into a trailer

- able to stand quietly while tied

The human members of MSAR teams also have requirements. Riders must be able to stay in the saddle for hours and be comfortable covering rough and steep terrain. Ability to control their horse and confidence between horse and rider is a must. Clothing and equipment that provide protection from the elements are required.

Mounted search and rescue has many advantages; horses:

- are able to search areas inaccessible to motorized vehicles.

- can cover more area, faster, than humans on foot.

- can carry equipment and supplies and transport injured individuals.

- elevate a rider's eyes eight feet off the ground, giving a better angle and wider field of vision than a person on foot or an ATV rider.

- can feed along the trail during a long search where an ATV will require refueling.

- are quieter than vehicles, allowing horse and rider to more easily hear voices and other sounds.

- are more cost-effective than deploying helicopters and may be deployed faster.

- allow riders to spot clues such as footprints or small items not visible from the air.

- have nearly 360-degree vision, allowing them to see almost all the way around themselves.

- have better hearing and sense of smell than humans.

- don't require constant steering, allowing the rider to focus more on looking for the missing person or clues.

As prey animals, horses are on the lookout for things that are out of place. They may detect something unusual even before the rider. Common advice when training mounted searchers is to "Look where the horse looks." If a horse detects something unusual, he will usually stop and look in that direction.

Dogs have long been used in search and rescue for their tracking ability. More recently, it's been recognized that horses have incredible scent abilities as well. Rather than tracking a scent on the ground, horses perform air-scenting. The horse can vary the level of his nose by raising and lowering his head. Trainer Terry Nowacki, author of *The Air Scenting Horse*, is the leading expert in this area.

In 2017, in Grapeland, Texas, Frank Roth, a seventy-year-old man who suffered from Parkinson's disease, went missing while taking the family dog for a walk. For two days, volunteers searched on foot, as well as using tracking dogs and a helicopter with infrared technology, but Frank was not found.

On the third day, the East Texas Mounted Search and Rescue offered to help. With all their trucks, trailers, and horses, it appeared as if the Cavalry had arrived. Once mounted, they split into two groups and began searching. It wasn't long before one rider spotted Roth's sweatshirt. An hour later, the team located Frank and his dog in an area of brambles and thorny vines. They had to cut away vines to reach him. Roth was scratched and dehydrated but had no serious injuries. He spent a few days in the hospital before returning home.

Rescues on horseback aren't always part of an organized MSAR unit. In early May 2020, two-year-old Jesse Dale Young went missing from his home near Salina, Oklahoma. Handlers provided Bloodhounds with a piece of the boy's clothing to give them the scent, then the dogs were commanded to find him. Besides the tracking dogs, hundreds of law enforcement officials and volunteers spread out on foot and with four-wheelers in the rugged, wooded area surrounding the family's home. They later added drones and a helicopter equipped with an infrared camera to detect body heat. Searchers worked through the night without finding the boy.

After hearing about the lost boy, Shane Best and his sixteen-year-old son, Seth, joined the search on the second day. Seth grew up riding horses on his family's ranch in nearby Strang. He competed in roping events at rodeos on his horse, Hass. Seth and his father ended up in a thick, brushy area two miles from the boy's home, an area searchers on foot hadn't entered.

Within half an hour, Seth and Hass heard a faint cry. They followed the sound and found Jesse halfway down a hill. By then, he had been missing for twenty-six hours. During his night in the woods, temperatures had dropped into the forties, and the boy wore only a pull-up and one shoe.

Seth scooped up Jesse who was shivering and covered in scratches. He wrapped the boy in a shirt and placed him on the saddle in front of him. With his arms around Jesse, Seth and his father rode to a nearby house where someone gave the boy a bottle of Dr Pepper. He was soon reunited with his family.

Seth revealed his insight into the rescue to reporters. "Horses and Dr. Pepper is what I believe he liked." The teen rejected the idea that he was a hero, claiming he was just in the right place at the right time.

Hurricane Helene devastated the mountainous area of Western North Carolina in late September 2024. Washed-out roads and downed power lines prevented conventional access—another case where equines could go where vehicles could not. This time, mules came to the rescue more often than horses.

Hannah Stutts, owner of Jak's Stables in Wendell, used her mules Kitty and Buck to check on area residents and to deliver medical supplies and other necessities.

Mountain Mule Packer Ranch in Mount Ulla also used mules to help the victims of the storm. Vader, Lil Wayne, Jeb, Max, and Smokie made multiple trips, each packing 150 to 200 pounds of donated food and supplies. The ranch is proud of its mules.

They call them beasts of burden, we call them our beloved mules. They are capable and willing to work in many conditions most won't. They are not stubborn … they are wise, and require respect.[1]

After their experience with the mules during the Hurricane Helene relief efforts, the ranch formed Mission Mules, an organization dedicated to using mules for disaster relief and community rebuilding. They are committed to faith-based service with "Pack it up and Follow the Lord" as their guiding principle. Since then, Mission Mules has assisted with recovery efforts in a variety of areas, including recovery from the 2025 catastrophic flash flooding in Kerr County, Texas.

---

[1] *Mountain Mule Packer Ranch Facebook 9-30-2024*

64

Equine Therapy

Equine therapeutic programs capitalize on the relational capabilities of horses. These programs come in two basic versions—equine-assisted therapy and hippotherapy.

Equine-assisted therapy focuses on healing mental health problems such as anxiety, depression, or issues caused by trauma. EAGALA (Equine Assisted Growth and Learning Association) uses a ground-based program they call Equine Assisted Psychotherapy (EAP). In this program, a mental health professional and an equine specialist work together with a client or patient. During an EAP session, both the client and the horse are free to move around in a pen or arena. As a sensitive, prey animal, the horse is quick to pick up on people's emotions. When the client attempts to interact with the horse, the animal's responses reflect that person's emotional state.

With the horse free to move around, he can avoid the client if he or she is not perceived as safe or trustworthy. The client must develop strategies to build trust, improve communication, and establish a strong, healthy relationship with the horse. Through these types of interactions, it's believed the client will receive insights into her own feelings and behavior. These insights will lead to solutions that extend to relationships with the people and situations in her life. EAP practitioners believe the absence of riding is a benefit rather than a shortcoming. Without the distraction of learning to ride, everyone becomes more focused on the emotional interactions. EAP programs are also able to use older horses or those who can no longer be ridden because of minor health issues.

Rather than addressing mental health, hippotherapy programs use riding to improve physical issues. The name comes from the Greek word "hippos" meaning horse. Clients with physical challenges, such as cerebral palsy, multiple sclerosis, stroke, or autism, engage in therapeutic activities on horseback. The motion of the horse helps improve the client's posture, balance, coordination, and strength. A physical therapist works with the client to help the rider perform specific exercises or movements. The focus is not on the client's riding ability but on the benefits provided by the rhythmic motion of the horse.

Branching out from hippotherapy are various equine-assisted programs which include riding and more extensive involvement with horse handling and care. These programs are often provided for children to help them develop desirable characteristics or skills, such as positive attitudes, confidence, responsibility, leadership, teamwork, problem solving, and communication.

The Professional Association of Therapeutic Horsemanship International, PATH, was founded in 1969 to provide guidance and certification for equine-assisted programs. As of 2024, there were 767 PATH-certified equine centers in the U.S. and over 4,525 certified professionals. These facilities use 7,694 equines, including 5,454 horses, 1,176 ponies, 565 minis, 183 donkeys, 41 mules, and 96 Mustangs.[1]

No particular breed is best suited for equine therapy. Instead, each horse's personality and temperament are the deciding factors. Older horses are well-suited for these programs. Serving as an equine therapist is often a second or third career for these horses.

A few of the horses at Equi-librium[2] in Nazareth, Pennsylvania, provide examples of the diverse backgrounds of these equine therapists.

George, a black Percheron-Morgan cross, weighing 1700 pounds, worked as a carriage horse in Canada. From there, he became one of the original horses serving with the Bethlehem Mounted Police, reestablished in 2010 after a hiatus of sixty-five years. George was a faithful and popular police horse from 2010 to 2022. He might have served longer if he hadn't developed mild arthritis. The Friends of the Bethlehem Mounted Police knew George would not be happy, retiring to pasture. They connected with Equi-librium, and George now continues to serve his community as a therapy horse.

Jackie is a 15.3 hand Percheron/Standardbred mare who used to pull an Amish carriage outside of Lancaster, Pennsylvania. Besides riding, the big mare pulls a wheelchair-accessible Thornlea wagon. Equi-librium is a PATH-certified center and the first to offer therapeutic carriage driving in addition to riding.

Lito, a 16 hand, bay French Trotter gelding, imported from France, had a lengthy harness-racing career before joining the program at Equi-librium.

Edward The Great "Eddie" is a 15.3 hand, gray Percheron gelding who used to take part in jousting events at Renaissance Festivals around the country.

Some therapy horses have themselves suffered abuse or neglect in the past. The fortunate few who are rescued seem to possess a special ability to connect with troubled children. Such was the case for Winston, a pony at Asheville Equine Therapy Inc.[3] in North Carolina.

---

[1] *pathintl.org/wp-content/uploads/2025/01/PATH-Intl-Facts-2024.pdf*
[2] *equi-librium.org*
[3] *asheville-equinetherapy.org*

When executive director Meg Hill arrived at a horse auction in 2021, she wished it was possible to save all the animals she found there. She couldn't do that, but a blue-eyed, red roan pony caught her eye.

After his young rider had outgrown him, Winston was sold repeatedly, passing through five auctions in two years. At this particular sale, the horses around him were stealing hay right out of Winston's mouth. The pony was so dejected, he didn't try to stop them. Meg purchased Winston that day, convinced she and her team, through love and kindness, could help him heal.

It wasn't easy. Winston's distrust of people meant he was difficult to catch. He bolted away from everyone as if his life depended on it. He flinched at the slightest of movements and was terrified of adults, particularly men.

After a year of patience and kindness, Winston learned to trust again. The pony loved children. One day, seven-year-old Parker, who was completely non-verbal, visited the farm. He pointed repeatedly to Winston, indicating he wanted to work with him rather than his usual equine partner.

Meg handed Parker a halter and stepped back. To her surprise and delight, Winston walked right up to the boy. Parker haltered the pony and said, "Walk on." Winston complied, totally unaware of the miracle that had just happened—Parker had spoken for the first time in his life!

After that day, Winston became a forever member of Asheville's team of equine healers. As for Parker—now, he rarely stops talking.

Besides the PATH and EAGALA certified trainers and facilities, many others use horses to impact the lives of others. The Man O' War Project and Wounded Warriors both find equine therapy to be highly effective in treating the post -

traumatic stress disorder (PTSD) common with veterans, especially those who have served in combat.

And for those who can't make it to a stable, sometimes the horse comes to them. In the case of Shirlene Hvinden of Heritage Horses farm, it's a pint-sized equine named Toby. The four-year-old, brown-and-white miniature horse accompanies Hvinden to nursing homes such as the Good Samaritan Society in Windom, Minnesota.

Fitted with a horsey diaper, Toby struts into the facility. Most of the residents light up at his visits. Toby soaks up the love and attention he receives from the elderly. The pony seems to stir memories in them. Even those suffering from dementia or Alzheimer's perk up and engage with the lovable mini.

65

Carousels

The French word "carousel" is derived from the Italian word "carosella" meaning "little war." One of the competitions for knights was ring jousting. The knight galloped his horse toward a suspended ring and tried to spear it with his lance. A machine was created for practicing, to give the horses a break from the strenuous game. Legless wooden horses were suspended by chains from arms radiating out of a center pole.

These earliest carousels were propelled by a man who walked in circles beneath the platform. Soon, horses and mules served as the power source. The riders of the wooden horses attempted to spear a ring hanging outside the circle, the origin of today's "catching the brass ring." Ring spearing is apparently the reason carousels built in the United States and Europe rotate counterclockwise. Since most people are right-handed, rotating in this direction allows easier access to the ring. However, carousels built in England rotate in the opposite direction.

Spectators of these ring-jousting tournaments began to wonder why the knights should have all the fun. By the 1800s, carousels were being built for entertainment. Thomas Bradshaw invented the first steam-powered carousel in England in 1861. One newspaper described his ride as

… a roundabout of huge proportions, driven by a steam engine which whirled around with such impetuosity, that the wonder is the daring riders are not shot off like cannon-ball, and driven half into the middle of next month.[1]

At the time, carousel horses were suspended from chains, causing them to swing outward as the ride rotated. This was known as a flying-horse carousel. Few of this type remain in operation in the U.S. One of the oldest is The Flying Horse Carousel located in Watch Hill, Rhode Island. It is believed to have been

---

[1] *gracesguide.co.uk/Thomas_Bradshaw*

built around 1876 by the Charles W. F. Dare Company of New York.

A later type had horses mounted on poles in a fixed position on a platform. The oldest operating carousel of this type in the U.S. is the Flying Horses Carousel in Oak Bluffs, Massachusetts, on Martha's Vineyard. Despite its name, the horses on this carousel are not suspended by chains and do not "fly." They do not move at all but are fixed to the platform. This carousel was first located in New York City, then moved to its current location in the 1880s.

In the 1870s, another Englishman, Frederick Savage, invented the mechanism that made the horses move up and down. He called his ride the "Platform Gallopers." Music provided by an organ contributed to the festive atmosphere of the carousel.

It didn't take long for carousels to become popular in the United States as well. Smaller models, which could be easily dismantled and reassembled, traveled to county fairs across the country, while larger ones found more permanent homes at parks, boardwalks, and near the ends of streetcar lines. The Golden Age of Carousels lasted until about 1930. It's estimated that between 2,000 and 3,000 carousels were operating in the U.S. during those years. The men who sparked that golden age were master carvers and woodworkers, primarily European immigrants, each with a distinctive style. Some of the masters carved only the heads, allowing others to carve the rest of the horse. Two world wars and the Great Depression brought the Golden Age to an end.

Carousel horses have one of three stances. Those with three or four legs on the platform are called "standers." They usually do not move up and down. "Prancers" have their two back legs on the platform and the two fronts in the air. Horses with all four legs in the air are called "jumpers."

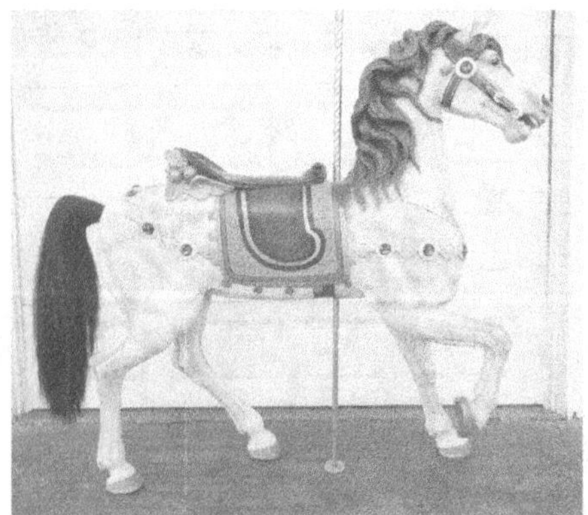

Stander by Looff

Prancer by Dare

Jumper by Herschell

Carousel horse's heads and legs were carved separately and attached to the bodies with dowels and/or glue, never nails. Heads were almost always turned outward, facing slightly toward the public. Manes also were on the outside of the horse. Tails were either horsehair or carved wood. Eyes were often made of glass and placed in carefully carved sockets. Other eyes were carved and painted. Horseshoes might be carved into the hooves. Carousel horses were sometimes named, with the name appearing on the bridle. Most carousel companies did not sign or mark their creations.

Horses in the outside circle are usually more ornate than those in the inner circles. The side of the horse facing the outside of the carousel (right side in the U.S.) is called the "romance" side and is often more decorated than the inside (left). Some claim there is a lead horse on each carousel, the largest, most beautifully decorated one.

There were three basic styles of horses. The **Philadelphia Style** (*below*) is credited to Gustav Dentzel. These horses were elegant, realistic, and graceful with detailed trappings (saddle, bridle, and other decorations).

Coney Island Style horses often had exaggerated poses with windblown manes and intricate trappings. Silver and gold leaf and glass jewels were used. Carvers of this style were M. C. Illions, Charles Looff, Charles Carmel, and Solomon Stein and Harry Goldstein. Loof's horses were jolly with enlarged nostrils and exposed teeth, but as if smiling rather than aggressive. Loof adorned his horses with jewels, silver, gold, and the American flag. They often had secondary carvings such as birds, rabbits, and foxes behind the saddle. The Stein and Goldstein horses tend to be large and more frightening with big heads, large teeth, and no forelocks.

| Charles Carmel | M. C. Illions | Charles Looff | Solomon Stein and Harry Goldstein |

County Fair Style animals were smaller and simpler in appearance for use on the county fair circuit. These carvers included Charles Dare, C.W. Parker, and Allan Herschell. Dare's horses had a martingale on their chest, horsehair tails and manes, and leather saddles and ears.

Charles Dare

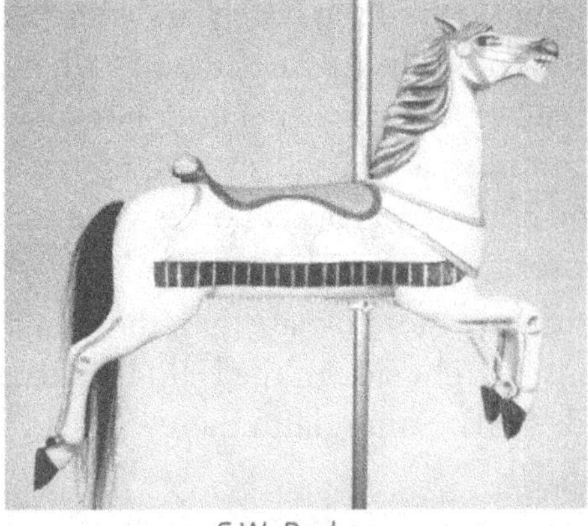

C.W. Parker

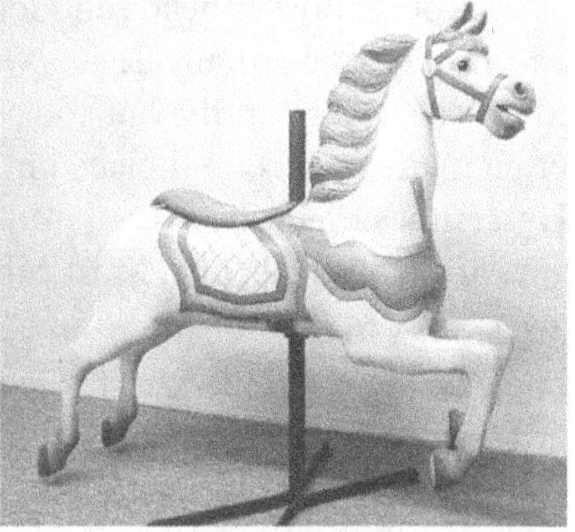

Allan Herschell

A variation of the carousel was called a racing derby. T.W. Prior and F.A. Church were granted a patent for this alternative amusement ride in 1913. In a derby, the horses are positioned side by side in groups of four with each horse in its own slot. In addition to moving up and down, they moved forward and backward, racing each other as the carousel rotated. There were no vertical poles above the horses. They were attached to gears below the platform. Cables under the platform pulled the horses back and forth within its slots. The racing derbies traveled faster than a regular carousel with speeds from fifteen to twenty-five miles per hour. Adults or older children rode the derbies with the younger ones riding the regular carousel.

The first "Great American Racing Derby" opened at Ocean Park, California in 1916. The "race" started with a call from the ride operator, "They're off!" A gong sounded near the end of the race with a call of "Last lap!" Winners in each group of four were given a free ride ticket. Publicity photos were taken of soldiers on the derby horses as if they were training on horseback. The Ocean Park ride had forty horses. Inside the derby racers was a four-row Looff carousel.

From 1916 to 1927, at least seventeen Prior and Church Racing Derbies were built for various amusement parks, the majority in California. Controversy emerged in some areas over the racing derbies when some people began gambling on the outcomes of the races.

One Derby found its way to Ohio and is one of only two racing derbies still in operation in the U.S.

In 1921, the racing derby carousel opened at Euclid Beach Park in Cleveland. The ride had sixty-four, two-seat horses on a ninety-foot platform, carrying a total of 128 riders.

The Euclid derby was sold in 1965 and moved to Cedar Point where it began operation the following year. Cedar Downs is the only fully operational racing derby in the U.S. The other remaining racing derby, built in 1927 with fifty-six horses, is located at Playland Park in Rye, New York. However, the horses at Playland no longer move back and forth.

Horse ride innovations didn't stop with the racing derbies. In 1925, M. C. Illions, a notable carousel carver, invented a self-propelled horse mounted on a wheeled-base. It was called The Stampede and was powered by an electric motor. The Stampede came in single and double-seated version.

In 1928, Illions developed a ride called The Race Track or The Jockey Ride which utilized horses similar to the Stampede. The first was built for a hotel at Coney Island, New York. The mechanical horses raced on a 1,200 foot track with banked curves. Accidents occurred on the ride in 1928 and 1932. Several riders were thrown from their horses and suffered broken bones and lacerations. Lawsuits were filed which certainly diminished the enthusiasm for further sales of the ride.

Even more adventurous were what amounted to a horse roller coaster. Horses were pulled to the top of a hilly, winding track and released. Then, gravity did the rest. Women often rode these horses sidesaddle.

The Steeplechase Ride at Steeplechase Park, Coney Island, New York, opened in 1898 with eight tracks. A fire destroyed the ride in 1907. It was rebuilt in 1909 with two levels of four tracks each. There were virtually no safety measures in place for these rides, not even a seat belt. Riders just had to hang on. Sadly, on August 6, 1935, ten-year-old John Barke fell from his horse and plunged ten feet to the wooden platform below. He died from a head injury.

Another famous horse roller coaster was Peck's Prancing Ponies, patented by Charles F. Peck in 1909. Peck's horses traveled four across on a wooden track, pulled by gravity. His patent stated that the ride "will give the passenger a rocking motion similar to that which is obtained by riding a horse without injuring the person or any undue jarring during the manipulation of the device." Peck's Prancing Ponies was built in Old Orchard Beach, Maine in 1910.

Despite those interesting innovations, it is the traditional carousel that has had lasting appeal. The Richland Carrousel Park in Mansfield, Ohio, opened in 1991 as the first new, hand-carved carousel built in the United States since the 1930s. The fifty-two carousel figures consist of thirty horses, four

Coney Island

Peck's Prancing Ponies

bears, four ostriches, four cats, four rabbits, a goat, giraffe, lion, tiger, zebra, and a mythical hippocampus. All the animals were designed, carved, and painted by the Carrousel Works, also of Mansfield.

There are an estimated 170 antique wooden carousels still operating in the U.S. Today, electricity powers the carousels rather than steam engines, and music is produced electronically rather than by the old organs. Elaborate hand-carved wooden horses have been largely replaced by machine-produced fiberglass, aluminum, or resin ones. However, people young and old continue to experience some of the magic of horses through these enchanting rides.

Richland Carrousel Park in Mansfield, Ohio

References and Credits

Chapter 1 Equine Bookmobiles

appalachianhistory.net/2018/04/first-bookmobile-in-country.
html
bookmobiles.wordpress.com/2013/04/23/the-milk-wagon-library
dspace.kdla.ky.gov

Chapter 2 Gypsy Queen

afinecollection.wordpress.com/2014/05/14/frank-m-heaths-scrapbooks-1920s-30s
Forty Million Hoofbeats, Frank M. Heath, David Turet 1941
full ebook version: babel.hathitrust.org/cgi/pt?id=hvd.hn4udu
loc.gov/resource/npcc.31703

Chapter 3 Frontier Nursing

Wide Neighborhoods: A Story of the Frontier Nursing Service,
Mary Breckinridge, University Press of Kentucky 1981
frontier.edu/about-frontier/history-of-fnu
historynet.com/call-the-midwife-nurses-on-horseback-in-the-appalachian-mountains.htm
americanhistory.si.edu/blog/midwives-horseback-saddlebags-and-science
explorekyhistory.ky.gov/items/show/583
The Forgotten Frontier - youtube.com/watch?v=PtK3QsFpm6M
youtube.com/playlist?list=PLHlbXU986SU_SzDN4PbQfkJP-TauoQKu4k

Chapter 4 Tschiffely's Ride

en.wikipedia.org/wiki/Aim%C3%A9_F%C3%A9lix_Tschiffely
thelongridersguild.com/Heroes.htm
thelongridersguild.com/Beker-story.htm
aimetschiffely.org/tschiffelys-ride.htm
*Tschiffely's Ride: Ten Thousand Miles in the Saddle from Southern
Cross to Pole Star*, Aimé Tschiffely, Century Publishing, 1982
*The Tale of Two Horses: A 10,000 Mile Journey as Told by the
Horses*, Aimé Tschiffely, Long Riders' Guild Press, 2001
upload.wikimedia.org/wikipedia/commons/9/90/Archivo_General_de_la_Naci%C3%B3n_Argentina_1927_cabalgata_en_caballos_criollos.jpg

Chapter 5 Mustang Defenders

nevadawomen.org/research-center/biographies-alphabetical/
velma-bronn-johnston
blm.gov/programs/wild-horse-and-burro/about-the-program/
program-history
en.wikipedia.org/wiki/Velma_Bronn_Johnston
animalwellnessaction.org/abuses-of-wild-horses-continue-with-more-helicopters-barbwire-death-injury
animalwellnessaction.org/equine-groups-call-for-suspension-of-blm-helicopter-roundups-of-wild-horses

Chapter 6 BLM Mustangs

blm.gov/whb
wildhorsesonline.blm.gov
Herd Management Areas Locations/Map
blm.gov/programs/wild-horse-and-burro/herd-management/
herd-management-areas
youtube.com/watch?v=7zPYcHeQIbg
youtube.com/watch?v=yf5cgZguBWs
horse/flag photo - Tara Martinak, Bureau of Land Management/Flickr/CC
en.wikipedia.org/wiki/Wild_Horse_Inmate_Rehabilitation_
Programs

Chapter 7 Woman Bronc Rider

truewestmagazine.com/article/the-last-ride-of-bonnie-mccarroll
cowgirl.net
nationalcowboymuseum.org
pendletonroundup.com
wpra.com
nationalcowboymuseum.org/blog/breaking-trail-bonnie-mccarroll
nationalcowboymuseum.org/explore/mccarroll-rodeo-photographs
images.nationalcowboymuseum.org/islandora/object/
ncm%3A226107?page=1

Chapter 8 Elmer Gantry

time.com/archive/6820365/animals-elmer-gantry/
en.wikipedia.org/wiki/Pride_of_the_Blue_Grass_(1939_film)
tcm.com/tcmdb/title/87100/pride-of-the-blue-grass
moviesofcourse.wordpress.com/2009/08/23/elmer-the-great
imdb.com/title/tt0031823
tcm.com/video/225453/pride-of-the-blue-grass-original-trailer

Chapter 9 Early Equine Movie Stars

* There are many more equine actors, however space prohibits
the description of all of them. This book has more extensive
coverage of the horse and human actors involved in westerns
and other films.
*Hollywood Hoofbeats: The Fascinating Story of Horses in Movies
and Television*, Petrine Day Mitchum and Audrey Pavia,
CompanionHouse Books 2014
b-westerns.com
horseyhooves.com/famous-western-horses/
en.wikipedia.org/wiki/Wonder_horses
en.wikipedia.org/wiki/Trigger_(horse)
royrogers.com
happytrails.org

csmonitor.com/From-the-news-wires/2010/0716/Roy-Rogers-Trigger-along-with-dog-Bullet-sold-to-Nebraska-TV-network-at-auction
farmanddairy.com/top-stories/roy-rogers-dale-evans-items-sold-trigger-goes-for-266500/15388.html
en.wikipedia.org/wiki/Rex_(horse)
b-westerns.com/hoss-rex.htm
humanehollywood.org/production/flicka/
en.wikipedia.org/wiki/Wonder_horses#/media/File:William_Fox_presents_Tom_mix_in_%22The_Great_K&A_Train_Robbery%22_with_Tony_Wonder_Horse.-A_crash_-_a_shriek_-_and_he_plunged_over_the_sandy_precipice..jpg
en.wikipedia.org/wiki/Trigger_(horse)#/media/File:Roy_Rogers_and_Trigger.jpg
en.wikipedia.org/wiki/File:Champion_in_Oh,_Susanna!.png
en.wikipedia.org/wiki/Rex_(horse)#/media/File:The_Devil_Horse_ad_in_Motion_Picture_News,_1926.jpg
en.wikipedia.org/wiki/Rex_(horse)#/media/File:Devil_Horse_lobby_card.jpg

Chapter 10 Phar Lap

trove.nla.gov.au/newspaper/article/30120190
thespectrum.com/story/sports/2018/03/20/dramatic-life-and-times-legendary-australian-race-horse-phar-lap/439831002
nzhistory.govt.nz/media/video/story-phar-laps-skeleton
collections.museumsvictoria.com.au/articles/3074
en.wikipedia.org/wiki/Phar_Lap
youtube.com/watch?v=bOvIxp50WPM
youtube.com/watch?v=bROtR5ivyZw
upload.wikimedia.org/wikipedia/commons/e/e0/Phar_Lap_wins_the_Melbourne_Cup.jpg
en.wikipedia.org/wiki/Phar_Lap#/media/File:Phar_Lap_mount.jpg

Chapter 11 Seabiscuit

seabiscuitheritage.org
pbs.org/wgbh/americanexperience/features/seabiscuit-biography
imdb.com/title/tt0329575
Seabiscuit War Admiral Match Race 1938
youtube.com/watch?v=WVT2MPNCqgM
SportsCentury Documentary
youtube.com/watch?v=8jR6oRHtR7U

Chapter 12 Phantom Ranch

en.wikipedia.org/wiki/Phantom_Ranch
nps.gov/grca/learn/photosmultimedia/grand-canyon-in-depth-03.htm
grandcanyonlodges.com/lodging/phantom-ranch
ps.gov/grca/learn/photosmultimedia/grand-canyon-in-depth-03.htm
upload.wikimedia.org/wikipedia/commons/4/46/Phantom-ranch.jpg

Chapter 13 Pack Horse Librarians

appalachianhistory.net/2018/01/pack-horse-librarians.html
pbs.org/video/the-pack-horse-librarians-of-appalachia-ioouod
en.wikipedia.org/wiki/Pack_Horse_Library_Project

socialwelfare.library.vcu.edu/eras/great-depression/wpa-travelling-libraries
horse-canada.com/horses-and-history/the-pack-horse-librarians-of-eastern-kentucky
youtu.be/zfug2-qXA-0
youtu.be/A6WTdXYHF6o
upload.wikimedia.org/wikipedia/commons/6/6c/Packhorse_librarians_ready_to_start_delivering_books.png
upload.wikimedia.org/wikipedia/commons/e/eb/Packhorse_librarian_on_a_rough_trail.gif
upload.wikimedia.org/wikipedia/commons/f/f6/Pack_horse_librarian_at_a_mountain_school.gif
upload.wikimedia.org/wikipedia/commons/b/ba/Carriers_in_Hindman%2C_KY.gif

Chapter 14 Military Mascots

goarmywestpoint.com/news/2006/8/28/Army_Mules
warhistoryonline.com/featured/us-army-mascot.html
warhistoryonline.com/featured/stolen-west-point-mules.html
roadsideamerica.com/story/42883

Chapter 15 The Quarter Horse

king-ranch.com/about-us/history/quarter-horses
en.wikipedia.org/wiki/Wimpy_P-1
allbreedpedigree.com/wimpy
aqha.com/-/wimpy-p-1
aqha.com/pt/resource-detail-view/-/asset_publisher/D6hvXWsL9zzH/content/wimpy-p-1

Chapter 16 Across Canada

Canada Ride, Mary Bosanquet 1945
archive.org/details/dli.ernet.241626
Another version of her book is titled, *Rare Saddlebags for Suitcases Across Canada on Horseback*
goodreads.com/en/book/show/15986118-canada-ride
leavesandpages.com/2015/03/09/an-extraordinary-solo-journey-saddlebags-for-suitcases-across-canada-on-horseback-by-mary-bosanquet

Chapter 17 The Amish

en.wikipedia.org/wiki/Amish#Migration_to_North_America
ohiosamishcountry.com/articles/the-amish-and-their-horses
organicvalley.coop/blog/a-look-into-why-amish-farm-with-horses
amishfarmandhouse.com/blog/amish-horse-and-buggies-guide
neoamishcountry.com/buggies-horses-and-amish-traditions-a-ride-from-past-to-present
amishamerica.com/years-biggest-amish-horse-festival-is-happening-this-weekend-31st-edition

Chapter 18 Equines in Modern War

quartermasterfoundation.org/horses-and-mules-and-national-defense
January 1942: The Last Charge edwinpriceramsey.com/karber-article0808.pdf
en.wikipedia.org/wiki/Horses_in_World_War_II#/media/File:French_Circassian_Cavalry_in_Damascus,_1941.jpg

upload.wikimedia.org/wikipedia/commons/f/fe/Bundesarchiv_Bild_183-E10457%2C_Polen%2C_Schlagbaum%2C_deutsche_Soldaten.jpg
upload.wikimedia.org/wikipedia/commons/0/04/Bundesarchiv_Bild_101I-217-0473-23A%2C_Russland-S%C3%BCd%2C_Verladen_von_Pferden.jpg
en.wikipedia.org/wiki/Horses_in_World_War_II#/media/File:Soviet_light_infantry_tank_T-26_captured_by_German_Wehrmacht.jpg
upload.wikimedia.org/wikipedia/commons/8/8a/Bundesarchiv_Bild_101III-Adendorff-002-18A%2C_Russland%2C_SS-Kavallerie-Brigade.jpg
upload.wikimedia.org/wikipedia/commons/3/3b/PolishCavalryAttack.jpg

Chapter 19 Sand Pounders

Horses for Coast Guard Beach Patrol. September 1942
youtube.com/watch?v=11U-z-4didM
wrightsvillebeachmagazine.com/the-u-s-coast-guard-mounted-patrol
offbeatoregon.com/1503c.sand-pounders-uscg-ww2-330.html
amazon.com/War-Animals-Unsung-Heroes-World/dp/1621576582
oregonencyclopedia.org/articles/us-coast-guard-sand-pounders-of-world-war-ii/#.ZCCrambMIuU
laptrinhx.com/news/when-fear-of-a-german-attack-was-high-this-coast-guard-unit-guarded-our-beaches-on-horseback-42RKK64
horse-canada.com/horses-and-history/the-sand-pounders-the-u-s-coast-guard-mounted-patrol
horseconnection.com/wp-content/uploads/2014/04/HC_AprMay14_Coastal_spreads.pdf
history.uscg.mil/Our-Collections/Photos/igsearch/horse

Chapter 20 Heroic Mules

leminhkhai.wordpress.com/2014/10/14/the-silenced-mules-of-world-war-ii-burma/
Dr. Moffett's 1983 article on developing the procedure
pmc.ncbi.nlm.nih.gov/articles/PMC1550202
burmastarmemorial.org/archive/stories/1405931-mules-voice-chords-cut-len-reynolds
ww2gp.org/burma/mules.php
chinditslongcloth1943.com/chindits-with-four-legs.html
achillestheheel.com/wp-content/uploads/2016/06/waco2.jpg
chinditslongcloth1943.com/uploads/6/6/9/0/6690962/mule-advert-missiouri-copy-2-2-2-copy-3_orig.jpg

Chapter 21 Chindit Minnie

Silent heroes : the Bravery and Devotion of Animals in War, Evelyn Le Chêne, Souvenir Press 1997
archive.org/details/silentheroesbrav0000lech
lancs-fusiliers.co.uk/feature/Minnie/minnie.htm

Chapter 22 Kellog Ranch

libguides.library.cpp.edu/wkkahl
cpp.edu/news/content/2017/10/when-prized-horses-rescued-from-nazis-came-to-pomona/index.shtml
cpp.edu/wkkelloggarabianhorsecenter/index.shtml

oac.cdlib.org/findaid/ark:/13030/c8pz5gc0/admin
cpplibrary.github.io/postcards-compound
oac.cdlib.org/view?docId=c8pz5gc0;developer=local;style=oac4;doc.view=items
archive.org/details/cpomcp_000096
youtu.be/QIpbNAqiI5w
youtube.com/watch?v=lAIrgBZ3uRE
en.wikipedia.org/wiki/W._K._Kellogg_Arabian_Horse_Center#/media/File:W.K._Kellogg_with_Antez_(1929).PNG

Chapter 23 Operation Cowboy

Ghost Riders: When US and German Soldiers Fought Together to Save the World's Most Beautiful Horses in the Last Days of World War II, Mark Felton, Grand Central Publishing 2018
cnn.com/2016/09/02/sport/perfect-horse-world-war-ii/index.html
militaryhistorynow.com/2018/11/25/operation-cowboy-how-american-gis-german-soldiers-joined-forces-to-save-the-legendary-lipizzaner-horses-in-the-final-hours-of-ww2
historynet.com/patton-saves-austrias-white-horses/
wideopenpets.com/how-the-u-s-army-helped-save-the-lipizzaner-horses-during-wwii
en.wikipedia.org/wiki/Lipizzan
en.wikipedia.org/wiki/Operation_Cowboy
en.wikipedia.org/wiki/Witez_II
And Miles to Go: The Biography of a Great Arabian Horse, Witez II, Linell Smith, Little Brown & Company, 1967
youtube.com/watch?v=Tnw05jI3xGs
upload.wikimedia.org/wikipedia/commons/0/02/Ludwig_Koch_Lipizzaner.jpg
upload.wikimedia.org/wikipedia/en/7/7a/Witez_II.jpg

Chapter 24 Striding Horses

Hitler's Horses, Arthur Brand 2021
faroutmagazine.co.uk/surreal-true-mystery-of-hitlers-missing-bronze-horses
Police find horse statues from Hitler's office
youtube.com/watch?v=gfyg-zheLXA
How stolen Nazi art ends up on the blackmarket
youtube.com/watch?v=UJq7MhvG9-o

Chapter 25 King Ranch Thoroughbreds

Out of the Clouds: The Unlikely Horseman and the Unwanted Colt Who Conquered the Sport of Kings, Linda Carroll, Hachette Books 2018
en.wikipedia.org/wiki/Stymie_(horse)
racingmuseum.org/hall-of-fame/horse/stymie-tx
en.wikipedia.org/wiki/Assault_(horse)
racingmuseum.org/hall-of-fame/horse/assault-tx

Chapter 26 Island Ponies

mistysheaven.com/historyofmisty.html
mistyofchincoteague.org
chincoteague.com/pony-swim
chincoteaguechamber.com/pony-penning
upload.wikimedia.org/wikipedia/commons/d/dc/Chincoteague_Pony_swim_by_Bonnie_Gruenberg.jpg

Chapter 27 Additional Equine Stars

National Velvet
anequestrianlife.com/2020/04/national-velvet-1944/
pedigreequery.com/king+charles19
en.wikipedia.org/wiki/The_Horse_Whisperer_(film)
Mr. Ed
news.amomama.com/177121-mister-ed-20-facts-60s-show-that-fans-mi.html
atlasobscura.com/places/mr-ed-s-birthplace
en.wikipedia.org/wiki/Mister_Ed
en.wikipedia.org/wiki/Bamboo_Harvester
youtube.com/watch?v=STTdvkwppBY
Fun facts about Mr. Ed youtube.com/watch?v=TgRcGqLkA-k
Green Acres, Pumpkin as Mr. Fred youtube.com/watch?v=YS-GKeKwr5VE
Black Stallion
theblackstallion.com/web/cass-ole-is-a-classic-among-stallions
horsenation.com/2013/11/28/friday-flicks-the-real-black-stallion
Dreamer
madeinatlantis.com/movies_central/2005/dreamer.htm
humanehollywood.org/production/flicka
War Horse
Animatronic horse example youtube.com/watch?v=Xre9dos-mgtg
humanehollywood.org/production/war-horse

Chapter 28 Equine High Jumpers

guinnessworldrecords.com/world-records/64351-longest-water-jump-by-a-horse
archive.org/details/sim_harpers-weekly_harpers-weekly_1902-09-13_46_2386/page/n9/mode/2up
amazon.com/Great-Heart-C-W-Anderson/dp/B0007E1QGQ
horsenetwork.com/2021/11/halloffamethursday-high-jumping-legend-fred-wettach-jr
en.wikipedia.org/wiki/Huaso_(horse)#/media/File:Record_salto.jpg
en.wikipedia.org/wiki/Huaso_(horse)#/media/File:Alberto_Larraguibel_y_su_caballo_Huaso_batiendo_el_r%C3%A9cord_mundial_de_salto_alto.png

Chapter 29 The Last Cavalry Horse

history.nebraska.gov/chief-the-last-u-s-cavalry-horse
history.nebraska.gov/collection_section/chief-1932-1968-rg4261-am
artbycrane.com/horse_history_articles_tales/cavalryhorse.html
en.wikipedia.org/wiki/Chief_(horse)
upload.wikimedia.org/wikipedia/commons/3/3d/MountUSArmyCavalrymanYNP.jpg

Chapter 30 Reckless

sgtreckless.com
1stmardiv.marines.mil/Units/5TH-MARINE-REGT/History/SSgt-Reckless
history.com/articles/the-four-legged-marine-who-became-a-korean-war-hero
en.wikipedia.org/wiki/Sergeant_Reckless

Chapter 31 Swaps

Legacies of the Turf: A Century of Great Thoroughbred Breeders, Edward L. Bowen, Eclipse Press 2003
racingmuseum.org/hall-of-fame/horse/swaps-ca
californiahorsehistory.blogspot.com/2024/07/beyond-news-reels-swaps-in-hollywood.html
vault.si.com/vault/1975/02/03/sad-end-of-an-empire
Oral interview with Rex Ellsworth by University of Kentucky
nunncenter.net/ohms-spokedb/render.php?cachefile=2008o-h101_hik061_ohm.xml

Chapter 32 Annie Wilkins

Last of the Saddle Tramps, Mesannie Wilkins, Prentice-Hall 1967
archive.org/details/lastofsaddletram00wilk
The Ride of Her Life: The True Story of a Woman, Her Horse, and Their Last-Chance Journey Across America
amazon.com/Ride-Her-Life-Last-Chance-Journey/dp/B08J-CYZC5Z
ozwisdomsandlessons.com/messanie-wilkins-the-last-of-the-saddle-tramps
Inside the Book: Elizabeth Letts (THE RIDE OF HER LIFE)
youtube.com/watch?v=dR3emAqYaUY
Sea G. Rhyder
freerangerodeo.com/tag/mesannie-wilkins

Chapter 33 Snowman

archive.org/details/snowmanmont00mont
The Eighty-Dollar Champion: Snowman, The Horse That Inspired a Nation, Kindle Edition, Elizabeth Letts, Ballantine Books 2012
My Blue-Ribbon Horse: The True Story of the Eighty-Dollar Champion, Elizabeth Letts, Random House 2022
en.wikipedia.org/wiki/Harry_deLeyer
harryandsnowman.com

Chapter 34 Kennedy Equines

commons.wikimedia.org/wiki/File:Macaroni_(pony).jpg
rarehistoricalphotos.com/macaroni-pony-white-house/
presidentialpetmuseum.com
en.wikipedia.org/wiki/Sardar_(horse)
anequestrianlife.com/2023/12/the-equestrian-life-of-jackie-kennedy-onassis/
upload.wikimedia.org/wikipedia/commons/e/ee/Jackiesardar.JPG

Chapter 35 Black Jack

Black Jack America's Famous Riderless Horse, Robert Knuckle, General Store Publishing House 2002
chronofhorse.com/article/remembering-black-jack
en.wikipedia.org/wiki/Black_Jack_(horse)
horseandman.com/people-and-places/black-jack-the-caparisoned-horse-and-caissons/05/27/2018
arlingtoncemetery.net/blackjack.htm
compassionranch.org
whec.com/national-world/army-to-begin-limited-use-of-horse-drawn-caissons-for-arlington-national-cemetery-funerals
jtfncr.mdw.army.mil/Caisson-Detachment

oldguard.mdw.army.mil/specialty-platoons/caisson
upload.wikimedia.org/wikipedia/commons/b/b9/Riderless_
horse_DF-SD-06-14683.JPEG
arlingtoncemetery.mil/Portals/0/Docs/Fact-Sheets/Tempo-
rary%20Suspension%20of%20Caisson%20Platoon%20Funer-
al%20Operations%20Fact%20Sheet_FINAL.pdf

Chapter 36 RCMP Horses

rcmp.ca/en
horsejournals.com/popular/interviews-profiles/remarkable-
horses-canada-burmese
en.wikipedia.org/wiki/Royal_Canadian_Mounted_Police
upload.wikimedia.org/wikipedia/commons/d/d8/Trooping_
the_Colour_MOD_45155754.jpg
upload.wikimedia.org/wikipedia/commons/8/82/President_
Ronald_Reagan_riding_horses_with_Queen_Elizabeth_II_dur-
ing_visit_to_Windsor_Castle.jpg
upload.wikimedia.org/wikipedia/commons/9/94/Queen_Eliza-
beth_II_and_Burmese_Statue.JPG
upload.wikimedia.org/wikipedia/commons/9/9b/Elizabeth_II_
Ottawa.jpg
upload.wikimedia.org/wikipedia/commons/7/75/RCMP_Musi-
cal_Ride_%282016%29.jpg

Chapter 37 Ride & Tie

rideandtie.org
What is This Madness?, Bud Johns, Synergistic Press 1985
rideandtie.org

Chapter 38 The Great American Horse Race

*The Great American Horse Race of 1976: A Photographic
Documentary,* Curtis L. Lewis and Dennis D. Underwood,
Buckboard Publishing Co. 1993
atlasobscura.com/articles/the-1976-great-american-horse-race-
was-won-by-a-mule-named-lord-fauntleroy
wbur.org/onlyagame/2016/09/09/viri-pierce-norton-horse-
mule-race
horseandman.com/people-and-places/steeplejack-teenager-
mule-won-great-american-horse-race/09/11/2016
theequestrianvagabond.blogspot.com/2011/02/great-american-
horse-race-wild-terror.html

Chapter 39 Man vs. Horse

green-events.co.uk/?mvh_main
facebook.com/greeneventsllanwrtydwells
news.bbc.co.uk/1/hi/wales/mid/6737619.stm
managainsthorse.com
facebook.com/profile.php?id=100094854492711
azcentral.com/story/travel/2015/09/14/dennis-poolheco-ari-
zona-ultra-runner-race-honors/71907336/
prescottdog.com/?p=4122

Chapter 40/41 Secretariat

secretariat.com
racingmuseum.org/hall-of-fame/horse/secretariat-va
americasbestracing.net/the-sport/2019-secretariat-tremendous-
machine

si.com/horse-racing/2015/01/02/pure-heart-william-nack-sec-
retariat
americasbestracing.net/the-sport/2025-meadow-stables-true-
hero-riva-ridge
facebook.com/profile.php?id=100093016316575
patriciamcqueen.com/post/statesman-secretariats-second-son

Chapter 42 Ruffian

*Thoroughbred champions : Top 100 Racehorses of the 20th
Century,* Jacqueline Duke, The Blood-Horse, Inc. 1999
pastthewire.com/all-1s-ruffian-the-real-story
archive.org/details/isbn_9781581500240/page/n119/mode/2up
The Great Match Race (in which she is injured)
youtube.com/watch?v=Nqk41FDWk7s

Chapter 43 Alydar

*Wild Ride: The Rise and Tragic Fall of Calumet Farm Inc.,
America's Premier Racing Dynasty*, Ann Hagedorn Auerbach,
Holt 1995
*Broken: The Suspicious Death of Alydar and the End of Horse
Racing's Golden Age*, Fred M. Kray, Live Oak Press, 2023
fredmkray.com
The Killing of Alydar by Skip Hollandsworth
texasmonthly.com/true-crime/the-killing-of-alydar
bloodhorse.com/horse-racing/features/alydars-final-hours-648
Unbridled Greed documentary by Dominick Dunne
vimeo.com/90352822
en.wikipedia.org/wiki/Alydar
bloodhorse.com/horse-racing/articles/274159/controversial-
calumet-president-j-t-lundy-dies-at-82
calumetfarm.com
Photo: Affirmed, Steve Cauthen up, dueling Alydar, Jorge
Velasquez up, for the win in the 1977 Laurel Futurity (Jerry
Frutkoff/Museum Collection)

Chapter 44 Insurance Fraud

* Lisa Druck, later known as Rielle Hunter was the woman who
had an affair and child with then presidential candidate John
Edwards, which derailed his 2008 presidential campaign.
https://en.wikipedia.org/wiki/Show_jumping_horse_killings
https://vault.si.com/vault/1992/11/16/blood-money-in-the-rich-
clubby-world-of-horsemen-some-greedy-owners-have-hired-
killers-to-murder-their-animals-for-the-insurance-payoffs
https://www.tampabay.com/archive/1996/09/26/horse-killer-is-
given-one-year-term/
https://www.tampabay.com/archive/1994/09/18/the-dirty-little-
secret
https://discover.hubpages.com/politics/The-Horse-Murder-
Scandal
Hot Blood : the money, the Brach heiress, and the horse murders,
Ken Englade, St. Martin's Press 1996
https://archive.org/details/hotbloodmoneybra00engl/page/2/
mode/2up
Horse Hitman Documentary
https://www.imdb.com/title/tt15528096
https://discover.hubpages.com/politics/The-Horse-Murder-
Scandal

https://vault.si.com/vault/1992/11/16/blood-money-in-the-rich-clubby-world-of-horsemen-some-greedy-owners-have-hired-killers-to-murder-their-animals-for-the-insurance-payoffs

Chapter 45 Scamper

charmaynejames.com
en.wikipedia.org/wiki/Scamper_(horse)
cowgirl.net/portfolios/charmayne-james
prorodeohalloffame.com/inductees/livestock/scamper
prorodeohalloffame.com/inductees/barrel-racing/charmayne-james
mysanantonio.com/news/local_news/article/Legendary-horse-once-a-barrel-racing-champ-dies-3697760.php
viagenequine.com/story/clayton-barrel-racing-horse

Chapter 46 Reagan and His Horses

Ronald Reagan's Own Story: Where's the Rest of Me?, Ronald Reagan, Dell Publishing 1981
Riding with Reagan: From the White House to the Ranch, John Barletta, Citadel 2006
reaganlibrary.gov
reaganfoundation.org
presidentialpetmuseum.com/ronald-reagans-ranch-horses
https://animalsinwarandpeace.org/our-heroes
upload.wikimedia.org/wikipedia/commons/8/81/Reagan_Monument_Miami-021.jpg
en.wikipedia.org/wiki/Sergeant_York_(horse)#/media/File:Riderless_horse_DF-SD-06-14683.JPEG
picryl.com/media/president-ronald-reagan-riding-horses-with-queen-elizabeth-ii-during-visit-c51351
nara.getarchive.net/media/president-reagan-and-mrs-reagan-horseback-riding-at-rancho-del-cielo-59fe9a?zoom=true
picryl.com/media/photograph-of-president-reagan-and-mrs-reagan-horseback-riding-at-racho-del-561779
reaganlibrary.gov/public/archives/photographs/large/e13-1.jpg

Chapter 47 Sefton

artbycrane.com/horse_history_articles_tales/sefton_war_horse.html
telegraph.co.uk/culture/culturenews/9685248/Sefton-heroic-horse-who-defied-IRA-immortalised-in-bronze.html
thewarhorsememorial.org/100-hero-horses/100-hero-horses/hero-horse10
horsetrust.org.uk/sefton-passes-onto-greener-pastures-at-the-horse-trust

Chapter 48 Shergar

en.wikipedia.org/wiki/Shergar
https://www.irishcentral.com/roots/history/shergar-irish-horse-kidnap
historicmysteries.com/major-crimes/shergar/26002
allthatsinteresting.com/shergar-kidnapped-horse
upload.wikimedia.org/wikipedia/en/5/56/Shergar_in_1981.jpg

Chapter 49 Harvey Wallbanger

horseandman.com/horse-stories/have-you-heard-of-the-racing-buffalo-harvey-wallbanger/12/05/2021
buffalogrande.com/buffalo-tales-blog-1/harvey-wallbanger-racing-buffalo
cowgirlmagazine.com/harvey-wallbanger-buffalo
youtube.com/watch?v=TbT2txhnJgk

Chapter 50 Sweetwater Oak

paulickreport.com/news/people/this-week-in-history-jockey-grabs-mane-dangles-across-finish-line
globetrotting.com.au/nate-hubbards-wild-ride
youtube.com/watch?v=pARDOnvRNZU
allbreedpedigree.com/sweetwater+oak

Chapter 51 Zippy Chippy

The True Story of Zippy Chippy: The Little Horse That Couldn't, Artie Bennett, NorthSouth Books 2020
thoroughbredracing.com/articles/5420/farewell-racings-loveable-loser-remembering-zippy-chippy-worlds-worst-racehorse
en.wikipedia.org/wiki/Zippy_Chippy
newyorkupstate.com/sports/2018/05/vintage_horse_racing_zippy_chippy_loses_100_straight_races.html
oldfriendsequine.org/horse/zippy-chippy
youtube.com/watch?v=GXaZ5Xn3-AY
en.wikipedia.org/wiki/Haru_Urara

Chapter 52 Black Ruby

muleracing.org
Mississippi Folklife Summer/Fall 1995, pages 20-31
Mule racing in the Mississippi Delta, 1938-1950, Theses Karen Marie Glynn, University of Mississippi 1995 egrove.olemiss.edu/cgi/viewcontent.cgi?article=2964&context=etd
Life on the Mississippi, Mark Twain 1883 gutenberg.org/files/245/245-h/245-h.htm
bloodhorse.com/horse-racing/search?q=black+rubyhorseandman.com/interviews/black-ruby-the-winningest-racing-mule-ever/02/10/2011
idahocountyfreepress.com/farm-and-ranch/mule-racing/article_69ea8bab-faef-5c7a-b266-86f4ed8e6bab.html
horseracingnation.com/blogs/BayAreaBackstretch/Star_Power_of_the_Mule_Variety_123
bloodhorse.com/horse-racing/articles/181309/black-ruby-wins-a-tight-one-finds-new-rival
classic.drf.com/blogs/catching-black-ruby-aka-super-mule

Chapter 53 Zenyatta

zenyatta.com
en.wikipedia.org/wiki/Zenyatta
lanesend.com/zenyatta
dmtc.com/media/news/the-tale-of-zenyatta-is-worth-hearing-again-and-again-644
punters.com.au/news/holy-roller-the-worlds-biggest-racehorse--20190119
en.wikipedia.org/wiki/Zenyatta#/media/File:Zenyatta2009LadySecret.jpg
upload.wikimedia.org/wikipedia/commons/b/b4/Zenyatta_2009_Breeders_Cup_Classic_%284086992195%29.jpg
en.wikipedia.org/wiki/2009_Breeders%27_Cup_Classic#/media/File:Start_of_2009_Breeders_Cup_Classic_at_Santa_Anita_(4087750496).jpg

Chapter 54 Rachel Alexandra

Alexandra the Great The Story of the Record-Breaking Filly Who Ruled the Racetrack, Deb Aronson, Chicago Review Press 2017
en.wikipedia.org/wiki/Rachel_Alexandra
horseracingnation.com/horse/Rachel_Alexandra
stonestreetfarms.com
en.wikipedia.org/wiki/Rachel_Alexandra#/media/File:Kentuck-y_Oaks_2009.jpg
en.wikipedia.org/wiki/Rachel_Alexandra#/media/File:Rachel_Alexandra.jpg
en.wikipedia.org/wiki/Kincsem#/media/File:Emil_Adam_Die_Stute_Kincsem.jpg

Chapter 55 Magna Fortuna

facebook.com/TaxiTheMiracleHorse
ilehc.org
paulickreport.com/features/three-chimneys-presents-good-news-friday/three-chimneys-presents-good-news-friday-the-tale-of-great-fortune/
paulickreport.com/news/ray-s-paddock/court-battle-sullies-feel-good-story-of-rescue-racehorse-magna-fortuna
paulickreport.com/features/lost-and-found/lost-found-pre-sented-horseware-taxi-grown
Gail Vacca, lulu, and Magna youtube.com/watch?v=mV2fO-HCWlsM

Chapter 56 White Bliss

facebook.com/SvanstedtStableUSA
standardbredcanada.ca/news/10-23-15/sjoberg-finds-another-white-horse.html
youtube.com/watch?v=KE7q7qBKzs0
allbreedpedigree.com/white+bliss
stars.ustrotting.com/documents/pedigree/White%20Bliss.pdf

Chapter 57 Recent Triple Crown Winners

American Pharoah Triple Crown Champion, Shelley Fraser Mickle, Aladdin 2017
en.wikipedia.org/wiki/American_Pharoah
upload.wikimedia.org/wikipedia/commons/4/47/American_Pharoah_wins_2015_Belmont_Stakes.jpg
en.wikipedia.org/wiki/Justify_(horse)
twinspires.com/edge/racing/10-interesting-facts-about-triple-crown-winner-justify
upload.wikimedia.org/wikipedia/commons/a/ad/Justify_-_2018_Belmont_Stakes.jpg
https://en.wikipedia.org/wiki/Bob_Baffert

Chapter 58 Almost Triple Crown Winners

bloodhorse.com/horse-racing/triple-crown/triple-crown-near-misses
https://en.wikipedia.org/wiki/Pensive
https://www.champsofthetrack.com/post/three-generations-of-great-starting-something-special
https://kentuckyderbywinners.com/1944-kentucky-derby-win-ner-pensive
https://en.wikipedia.org/wiki/Tim_Tam_(horse)
https://www.horseracingnation.com/horse/Tim_Tam

https://wwwgallopout.blogspot.com/2011/01/courageous-champion-story-about-tim-tam.html
arnotts.com/brands/tim-tam
https://en.wikipedia.org/wiki/Forward_Pass_%28horse%29
https://paulickreport.com/news/bloodstock/forward-pass-life-before-and-after-his-kentucky-derby-promotion-over-dancers-image
https://www.horseracingnation.com/horse/Forward_Pass
https://en.wikipedia.org/wiki/Majestic_Prince
https://www.racingmuseum.org/hall-of-fame/horse/majestic-prince-ky
https://www.americasbestracing.net/the-sport/2024-majestic-prince-racehorse-who-lived-his-name
https://en.wikipedia.org/wiki/Sunday_Silence
https://www.espn.com/horse/news/2002/0818/1419793.html
https://www.racingmuseum.org/hall-of-fame/horse/sunday-si-lence-ky
https://www.americasbestracing.net/the-sport/2025-sunday-si-lence-the-star-no-one-wanted
https://www.racingmuseum.org/hall-of-fame/horse/silver-charm-fl
https://www.horseracingnation.com/horse/Silver_Charm
https://www.bloodhorse.com/horse-racing/thoroughbred/silver-charm/1994
https://oldfriendsequine.org/horse/silver-charm
https://en.wikipedia.org/wiki/Real_Quiet
https://www.americasbestracing.net/the-sport/2023-real-quiet-nose-triple-crown-glory
https://www.thoroughbredracing.com/articles/6120/real-quiet-i-honestly-think-if-we-ran-triple-crown-nine-more-times-wed-never-lose-kent-desormeaux
https://www.horseracingnation.com/horse/Real_Quiet
https://en.wikipedia.org/wiki/Smarty_Jones
https://www.thesmartyjonesstory.com/about/about-smarty
https://www.bloodhorse.com/horse-racing/articles/286124/hall-of-fame-inductee-smarty-jones-still-going-strong
https://www.horseracingnation.com/horse/Smarty_Jones

Chapter 59 Paardenvissers

navigomuseum.be/en/shrimp-fishers-on-horseback
atlasobscura.com/articles/belgium-fishing-shrimp-on-horses
youtu.be/P1c6L-rI8tY?si=MOMY7k_TB9Me7vPl
youtube.com/watch?v=4X_fWy0CrDA
youtube.com/watch?v=Qs_4QtRFGaU
commons.wikimedia.org/wiki/File:Garnaalvissers_te_paard_Oostduinkerke,_Belgi%C3%AB_01.jpg
upload.wikimedia.org/wikipedia/commons/7/7e/Horseback_fishing_Oostduinkerke.jpg

Chapter 60 Wadden Sea

de.wikipedia.org/wiki/Wattwagen
lrgaf.org/articles/neuwerk.htm
inselneuwerk.de/en/experiences/mudflat-walks-off-neuwerk
upload.wikimedia.org/wikipedia/commons/2/28/Bauchtiefe_Pferde.JPG
upload.wikimedia.org/wikipedia/commons/5/55/Wattwagen-Neuwerk.jpg

upload.wikimedia.org/wikipedia/commons/f/f1/Leuchtturm_Neuwerk_2018.jpg

en.wikipedia.org/wiki/File:Karte_Nationalpark_Hamburgisches_Wattenmeer.png

upload.wikimedia.org/wikipedia/commons/0/0d/Wattwagen%2C_Rettungsbake.JPG

https://www.youtube.com/watch?v=FEje4TBZGu4

Chapter 61 Mule Train Mail

facts.usps.com/8-mile-mule-train-delivery

aboutamazon.com/news/transportation/how-amazon-delivers-to-customers-at-the-bottom-of-the-grand-canyon

dailymail.co.uk/travel/travel_news/article-3025731/The-place-America-mail-delivered-mule-Inside-Indian-village-hidden-Grand-Canyon-eight-miles-nearest-road.html

insider.si.edu/2016/08/grand-canyon-u-s-postal-service-still-delivers-mail-mule

havasupaihorses.org

youtube.com/watch?v=HZGtaESzl3w

en.wikipedia.org/wiki/File:SupaiUSMailMules.jpg

Chapter 62 Rich Strike

si.com/horse-racing/2022/05/08/in-result-no-one-saw-coming-rich-strikes-kentucky-derby-win-helps-redeem-racing

kentuckysuccessstory.com/eric-reed-overcoming-the-odds

https://www.horseracingnation.com/news/Rich_Strike_is_sold_to_group_that_includes_trainer_Eric_Reed_123

Chapter 63 Mounted Search and Rescue

mainemountedsar.org/why-horses

highlands-sar.org/equine-air-scent-detection

tylerpaper.com/2017/11/17/east-texas-mounted-search-and-rescue-team-helps-find-missing-grapevine-man-alive

ktul.com/news/local/mayes-county-toddler-found

ktul.com/news/local/teen-hero-speaks-out-on-viral-rescue-of-mayes-county-missing-toddler

jaksstables.com

mountainmulepackers.com

facebook.com/mountainmulepackersranch

missionmules.org

commons.wikimedia.org/wiki/File:MSAR_Training.jpg

upload.wikimedia.org/wikipedia/commons/5/5b/BTSAR%2B-heli.jpg

Chapter 64 Equine Therapy

pathintl.org

pathintl.org/wp-content/uploads/2025/01/PATH-Intl-Facts-2024.pdf

eagala.org

americanhippotherapyassociation.org

mowproject.org

newsroom.woundedwarriorproject.org/Horse-Power-Veterans-Find-Resilience-in-Equine-Experiences

equi-librium.org/our-horses

tnonline.com/20230729/police-horse-george-still-serving-the-community/

facebook.com/BethlehemMountedPolice/posts/it-is-with-equal-degrees-of-sadness-and-appreciation-that-the-bethlehem-police-d/10158698504200275

cincinnatichildrens.org/service/p/psychiatry/programs/residential/therapeutic-recreation

https://upload.wikimedia.org/wikipedia/commons/8/8d/Therapeutic_horseback_riding_2.JPG

https://nara.getarchive.net/media/us-air-force-staff-sgt-cody-wisley-83rd-network-244c57

Chapter 65 Carousels

carousels.org

thecarouselmuseum.org

Watch Hill flying horse chain carousel: merrygoroundbeach.com

oldest platform carousel: en.wikipedia.org/wiki/Flying_Horses_Carousel

vineyardtrust.org/flying_horses_carousel

worthpoint.com/dictionary/p/ethnic-folk-native-american-art/entertainment-/carousel-horses

smithsonianmag.com/smart-news/dizzy-history-carousels-begins-knights-180964100

facebook.com/groups/carousels

carouselhistory.com/racing-derby-revisited

euclidbeach.org/racing-derby-history

cedarpoint.com/rides-experiences/cedar-downs-racing-derby

grunge.com/303835/the-truth-about-everyone-whos-died-at-coney-island

carouselworkshop.com

antiquecarousels.com

ideastream.org/2023-09-29/an-ohio-carousel-carver-is-keeping-mansfields-merry-go-round-history-alive

allaroundcarousels.com

upload.wikimedia.org/wikipedia/commons/3/33/Nunleys_carousel_05.jpg

upload.wikimedia.org/wikipedia/commons/f/f7/Carousel_horse%2C_Herschell_Carousel_Factory_Museum.jpg

SONRISE STABLE

Wholesome and horsey with strong Christian themes, the Sonrise Stable series is unique among modern children's literature.

Read the books alone or use the Companion Guides for additional activities to supplement the series.

sonrisestable.com

Through their bond with humans,
horses shaped our past in ways no machine ever could.
Their contribution has been all but forgotten—
until **Horsestory!**

In **Volume I,** follow horses from the time they arrive with early explorers to the Americas to post Civil War.

The Horsestory series continues with **Volume II,** beginning with the cattle drives in the old West to the 1920s.

sonrisestable.com/horsestory

The colorful **Horseography USA** is an interesting way to study the US states and capitals. Horse information and general facts are provided for each state. Write-in pages allow interaction with the content.

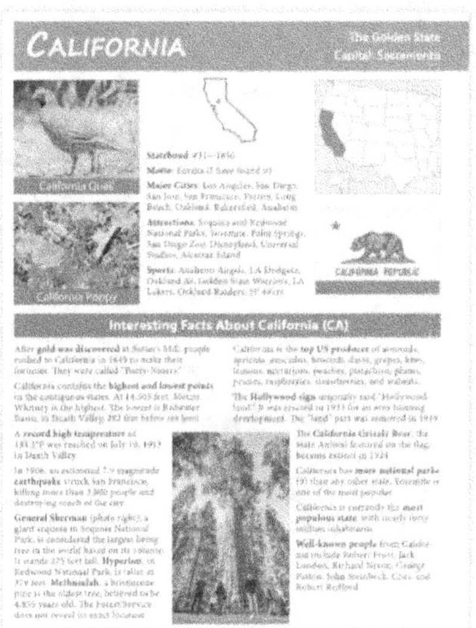

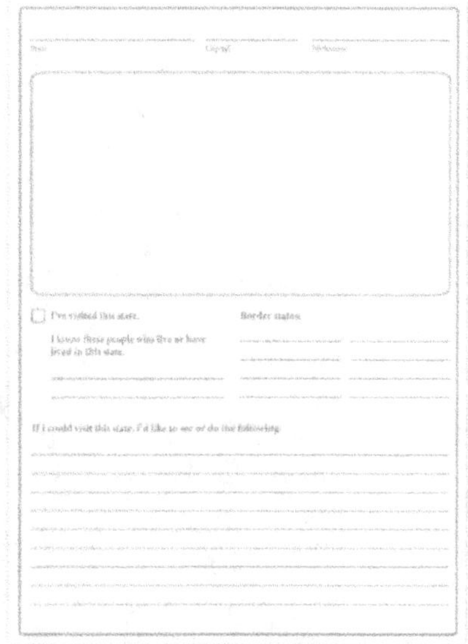

The optional card deck features a horse from each state!

sonrisestable.com/horseography

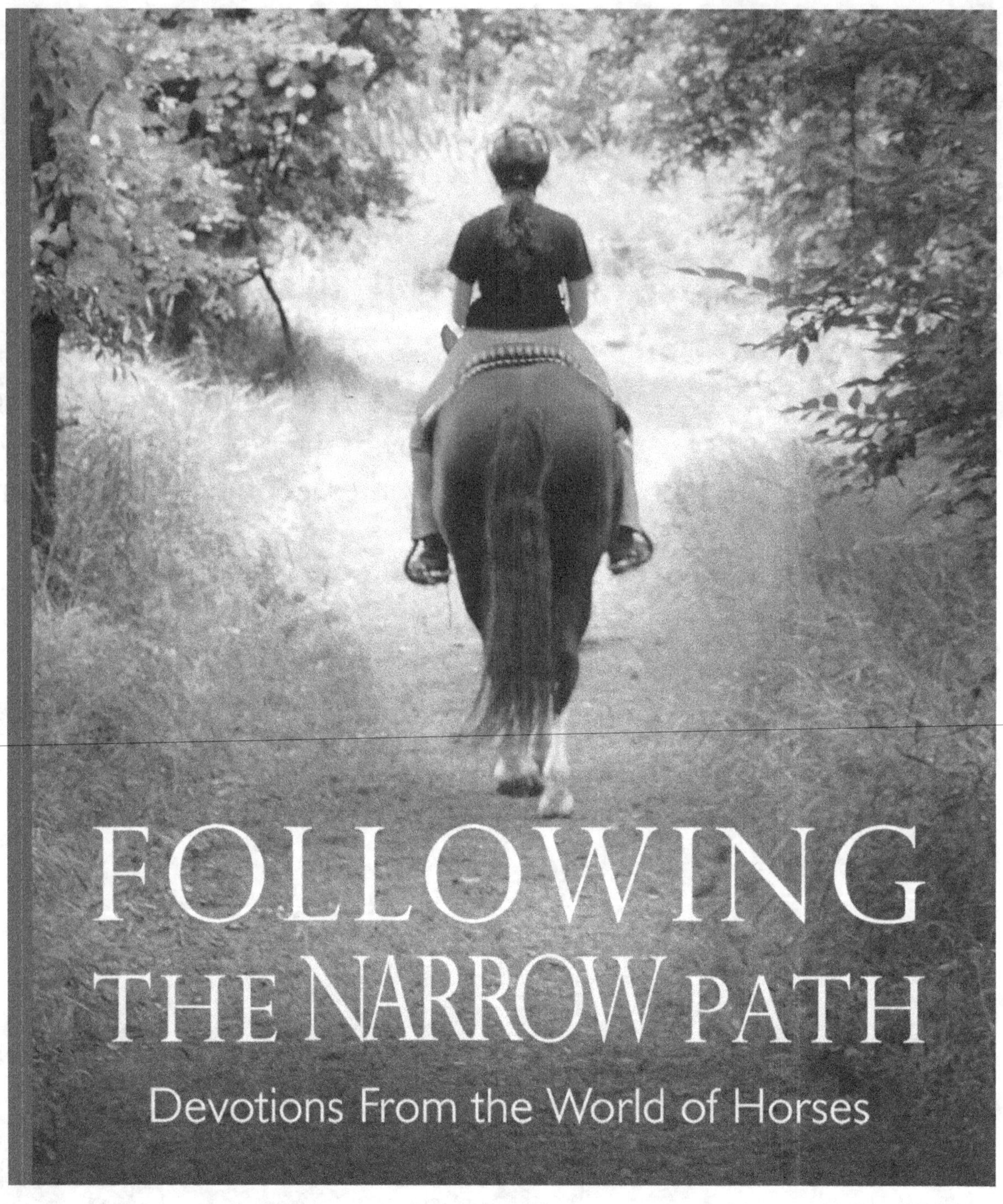

Horses, one of God's most magnificent creations, offer many insights into the nature of our Creator as well as our relationship to Him. This full-color, Christian devotional features a variety of stories, drawn from the author's experiences with her horses and Sassy, a lovable but cantankerous mule. Other famous, and not-so-famous, horses help illustrate Scriptural principles.

Available at sonrisestable.com